LET ME BE ME

SPECIAL POPULATIONS AND THE HELPING PROFESSIONAL

Editors
Nicholas A. Vacc
Joseph P. Wittmer

Contributors

Nell Logan

Joseph P. Wittmer

Joseph L. Norton

Marilyn Jemison Anderson
Robert H. Ellis

Helen B. Wolfe

Roderick J. McDavis

David Sue

Harold C. Riker

Nicholas A. Vacc
Kerry F. Clifford

Donald L. Avila
Antonio L. Avila

Larry C. Loesch

INCORPORATED

Accelerated Development Inc.
2515 West Jackson Street
P.O. Box 667
Muncie, IN 47305

Library of Congress Number: 80-66710

International Standard Book Number: 0-915202-23-9

Editors: Cindy Lyons
         Linda Davis

Printed in the United States of America, June, 1980

For Additional Copies Order From

INCORPORATED

Accelerated Development Inc.
2515 West Jackson Street
P.O. Box 667
Muncie, IN 47305
Tel. (317) 284-7511

PREFACE

Let Me Be Me is comprised of chapters written by members from a variety of America's special population groups. The book is designed to assist counseling psychologists, school counselors, social workers, mental health counselors, counselor educators, and other helping professionals with examining, through the personal perspective of the authors, the unique yet interrelated characteristics of various special population groups. Within each special population group, a wide array of diverse values and/or individual differences exist. Yet, among these groups, the reader will discover an interrelatedness of values emphasizing a focus of "let me be me."

Our view is that much has been written about the subgroups addressed in this book that does not apply to these groups. This irrevalancy may be in part because the respective authors were not, nor never had been, members of the particular population about which they have written. For example, whites have written much more about Blacks than Blacks have written about themselves. In this book, nearly all the contributors either are or have been members of the special population about which they have written.

The book grew from the idea that the wide variation found among America's subgroups and cultural minorities, could be revealed within the context of their genuine virtues, individual potentials, and values without exploiting their uniqueness or picturesqueness. The contributing authors have provided, through an examination of their personal preferences, accurate information, realism, and insight into the special populations they represent, including material which is pragmatically based rather than purely descriptive or picturesque. Recognition is made that helping professionals working with these subgroups constantly are looking for something "that works." Therefore, each chapter has a section on helpful suggestions and effective techniques to use with members of that particular population. Also, each contributor has examined the distinctive historical and cultural roots of his/her respective special population, presented problems the special population has had or is having in school, as well as "fusing"

iii

into the greater American society, and, developed a pretest and post test concerning their particular special population.

Without the support, cooperation, and encouragement from the contributors, the development of this book would have been impossible. The contributors are professionals in their own right, especially concerning the particular group about which they have written. They have all taken time from other scholarly pursuits to prepare their particular manuscript. Each has done an excellent job; we think you will agree as you read their respective works.

In a larger, more therapeutic sense, we hope you will read this book in its entirety regardless of your cultural heritage or where you live. We recognize that you may never meet an Amish child or encounter an Asian-American as a client. Yet only by viewing America's cultural diversity can one hope to gain a true appreciation of the multi-culturalism and different subgroups that exist today which is reflected in the title, **Let Me Be Me.** The intent of this book is to promote that larger consciousness through indepth explorations into each of the different subgroups spotlighted.

Yet, a word of caution is necessary. No author can represent and convey universal cultural values or characteristics of an entire special population group. The reader, however, can look toward this book as a means of self awareness of diverse value structures and the interrelatedness of values among people from special population groups.

Special recognition should be given to our secretaries for their valuable typing assistance. Deep appreciation is extended to our families who through their understanding made invaluable contributions to the final work.

Nicholas Vacc
Joseph Wittmer

April 1980

Accelerated Development Inc.
2515 W. Jackson
P.O. Box 667
Muncie, IN 47305
Tel: (317) 284-7511

CONTENTS

Let

Me

Be

Me

1

Prologue

Special Populations

Nicholas A. Vacc, Ed.D.

Professor, School of Education
University of North Carolina
Greensboro, North Carolina

and

Joseph Wittmer, Ph.D.

Professor and Chairperson
Department of Counselor Education
University of Florida
Gainesville, Florida

PROLOGUE

This book presents an overview of ten special populations. Though the ten groups by no means represent all the special population groups in America, the needs, experiences, and characteristics of the majority of this important and sometimes unaccepted segment of our population are presented.

PURPOSE OF THE BOOK

As stated in the preface, the purpose of this book is to expose practitioners such as counselors, teachers, college professors, mental health workers, social workers, and others to the unique and genuine characteristics of several of America's special subgroups and to effectively assist these same professionals as they work with clients and/or students from these special subgroups. Hopefully, knowledge of special populations and an awareness of those factors which influence the behavior of individuals from these subgroups will assist helpers to be more effective in their work. The fundamental assumption here is that helpers can improve their effectiveness to their own or other groups if appropriate attitudes, knowledge, and self-understanding exist.

This book also was written to partially fill an existing gap of a lack of relevant materials, and a growing consciousness that action needs to be taken to make school and other experiences more meaningful for those individuals whose racial, social, religious, and/or cultural backgrounds, sex, age, or physical and mental abilities may differ from those of the so-called mainstream.

THE EDITORS' PHILOSOPHY

FOR WRITING THE BOOK

Our belief is that helping professionals may hold the key to the process of reducing, if not eliminating, the social and emotional barriers which prevent many of America's subgroup members from becoming secure American citizens. To do this, helping professionals must make a concerted effort to understand cognitively the different subgroup members found among their clientele; an understanding that is over and above affectual understanding. Love and empathy are not enough! We cannot and do not refute the abundance of research findings which indicate that to be effective as a helper one must communicate warmly, empathically, and genuinely with clients. However, if helping professionals are inexperienced in the values and ways of a particular special population, these professionals will be ineffective when encountering members of that particular special population as students and/or clients. Needed is an accurate, cognitive understanding of the total milieu of the individuals who make up these different subgroups or special populations.

Acute disparities are compounded and greatly enlarged when a helper with a lack of cognitive knowledge about a special subgroup interacts with an often confused and bewildered member of that group. The result may be that the helper, functioning in his/her congenial, familiar cultural situation, may be prone to impose his/her idealized values on the client. A lack of cognitive understanding makes one more prone to impose one's own values. In contrast, knowledgeable helping professionals can be catalysts with the process of helping others develop an appreciation of the different subgroups found in America.

Why is a lack of true understanding of the many different subgroups still found in America today? Our feeling is that much of the misunderstanding is because American standards have been determined by college graduates who often feel that everyone is like them or should be. This phenomenon of assumed similarity causes a lack of desire to understand accurately those who are different socially and culturally. Does this mean, for example, that the Amish truly don't want television? As you read Wittmer's chapter concerning them, you will find that they really do not want TV in their homes. Helpers with a sound cognitive knowledge of their clients' cultural background will more easily understand the source and reasons for the behaviors which may appear odd or even peculiar at times.

As you read the different chapters, you will learn that the participants of most of the special groups included in the book do not want to be mainstreamed, to develop middle-class values, or be robbed of their individuality and dignity. They want their difficulties and differences to be understood rather than interpreted and evaluated. They desire to be understood for what they are—members of a particular subgroup who have a right to exist in America as long as they are productive, non-harmful, and tax-paying citizens. Many of the special population groups addressed in this book are still sadly misunderstood and the experiences many members of the subgroups are having in today's schools and in society, in general, are a long way from being positive and/or growth producing.

Since you are presently reading this material, you probably recognize that most things are relevant to the group in which one was reared. You also may realize that what is considered peculiar behavior by a culturally distinct client or student, actually may be viewed as proper and necessary behavior for existence and adjustment in that individual's own cultural setting. You should realize also that clients or students who are members of a special population, may never be completely at ease with you. However, these clients or students will communicate with you if you accept them on the affective level as fellow human beings and reveal a cognitive understanding within the context of their own unique cultural setting. We further urge that you work hard to preserve your own self-respect as well as the self-respect of the special population client or student. In conclusion, your job is not to stamp out mistakes nor to institutionalize, but rather to help each client or student become a productive and worthwhile individual within a society regardless of race, social beliefs, sex, age, religion, or cultural background.

HISTORICAL INFLUENCES

Special population groups frequently have been politicized and historically influenced by the social mood of the times. The dominant thought until the 1960's was that America was a melting pot of cultural differences with its social institutions, schools, and industries reflecting the democratic ideal of providing opportunity to all and mobility to the deserving. An assumption basic to this thought was that cultural homogeneity or assimilation was success and that cultural heterogeneity was failure. Assimilation denoted that the minority populations' culture, language, and folkways were not acceptable in America. At this time a new interpretation relative to special populations is being viewed with increasing favor, that the democratic ideal serves to stamp out diversity and that it has been imposed by the majority on individuals through education. Ravitch (1976) stated:

For a variety of reasons, the despair which followed the political assasinations of the Kennedy brothers and Martin Luther King, the anger which flowed from urban riots and the Vietnam War, and the cynicism which followed the Watergate disclosures—the failure theory of the radical revisionists is strongly in the ascendancy. (p. 214)

The discernable interest by American minorities for recognition and preservation of their uniqueness, for whatever reasons, has added impetus for greater understanding of America's special populations.

America unfortunately, has a long history of oppression of minority groups. With no group can we point to a longer history that was so purposeful as in the case of the American Indian. Both missionaries and government officials attempted to assimilate or Americanize the Indians; a process that was funded by Congress in the early 1800's to "promote civilization among the aborigines" (Ravitch, 1976). Not until the 1930's did the government's Bureau of Indian Affairs relax its efforts for assimilation and then it was only for a brief period of time.

8

Assimilation was basic to the American system, particularly during and after World War I. Many an immigrant's children were made to feel ashamed of their family's speech, customs, and cultural values (Ravitch, 1976). During World War II, heightened patriotism and fear of subversion caused the relocation of thousands of Japanese Americans and served to ingrain to all minority groups the assumption of the negative value of being different.

Whether oppression to minority populations can be characterized as super patriotism or coercive assimilation to an American ideal, it was not until the late 1940's, after World War II, that some significant events took place providing evidence of accepting differences. In 1947, President Truman created the President's Committee on Employment of the Handicapped to promote, on a voluntary basis, more jobs for handicapped people. In 1954, the landmark Supreme Court decision for the case of Oliver Brown brought an end to existing patterns of segregated schools. Starting with the Kennedy years in the early 1960's and more decisively during President Johnson's term of office, policies were formulated and political forces initiated that gave impetus to rights of individual differences. The Economic Opportunity Act and the Civil Rights Act of 1964, as well as the Elementary and Secondary Education Act of 1965, helped foster the rights of individuals. No one act or legislation granted all "rights" but each served as a ripple effect for minority or special populations. Legislation affecting blacks or Indians also affected the handicapped; each provided national attention. Pathways were established for all special groups. Coalitions among members of special populations became evident and quiet organizations became more active lobbying at all levels of government, demonstrating for their "rights" or for "Why not us?"

Historical influences relative to special populations can be easily oversimplified and explained by simplistic slogans or by topographical historical accounts. But, to do so would be to mock what is explicitly being sought by these groups— individuality and recognition of uniqueness.

This brief attempt at synthesizing some of the influences affecting special populations has been included to assist you in gaining a sense of the complexity of the situation and the political factors which bring us to this point. As stated by Ravitch (1976):

> Until late in the nineteenth century, this nation was considered by its majority to be a white Protestant country; at some time near the turn of the century, it became a white Christian country; after World War II, it was a white man's country. During the past several years it has become a multi-ethnic, multi-racial country intensely aware of differences of every kind . . . (p. 228)

The emerging sense of worth of members of special populations and knowledge of their different values, attitudes, desires, aspirations and beliefs, will have an effect on everyone's life.

USERS OF THE BOOK

We urge teachers, counselors, and others, as they work with members of special populations to seek out the natural existing characteristics that will aid the "different" students or clients as they learn. In other words, rather than bending the student from a special population to match the curriculum, we suggest cultivating the talents and unique cultural characteristics that already exist within that student.

The writers of the subsequent chapters in this book are of course writing from a particular perspective. In most cases, they either have been members of the respective subgroup or are members of that group today. We caution you not to stereotype each individual within a special population strictly on the characteristics outlined within the respective chapter. For example, after reading the chapter concerning the American Indian, one might react that all American Indians are reserved and shy relative to receiving assistance. However, this is not necessarily the case. You may even encounter an American Indian client or student who is highly extroverted and wishes to shed any vestiges of the Indian culture. Thus, we urge you to avoid stereotypic generalizations of particular groups as you work with their members.

Basic to working with individuals in a special population group, are a number of assumptions which are woven into the succeeding chapters:

1. Individuals rather than mass methods of working with individuals are important.

2. The total individual is the unit of consideration rather than the individual as a black, Mexican-American, single parent, or member of another special population.

3. The social aspects of an individual's life to include the home and relationships at work and school, are equally as important as his/her body and mind.

4. Authentic information needs to be gained by helpers as a foundation for providing services for the individual.

5. Staffing of services for special populations needs to be provided by adequately trained professionals via pre-service and inservice programs of preparation and skill development.

The process of helping each person to understand and be aware of others and the variations among individuals is a basic goal of a helping professional's instruction or training. In our opinion counselor educators, sociology and psychology professors, and teacher educators will find this book very useful as a text for many of the courses that are now being developed at the college level concerning minority groups and the training of individuals to work with America's unique sub-groups. We also feel the book will be useful in inservice consultation activities with school counselors, teachers, para-professionals, social workers, and others. Although the book basically is aimed at helping professionals, we are convinced it also will be a worthwhile reference and text for high school teachers preparing units on America's subgroups. The informative nature and authenticity of the book, we think, will greatly enhance the interest level of high school students and others. Helping children to understand the diversity of America's population is basic to fostering a healthy American society and developing a greater understanding and appreciation of the societies of the world.

We suggest that you read each chapter, responding to the awareness index and post test of each, and then thoroughly read Loesch's chapter, the epilogue. Loesch gives many helpful suggestions concerning the importance of preservice and inservice education of helping professionals relative to special populations.

Reference List

Ravitch, D. On the history of minority group education in the United States. *Teachers College Record*, 1976, *78*, 213-228.

2

The Single Parent

Nell Logan, Ph.D.

Director, Child Psychiatry Clinic
Abraham Lincoln School of Medicine
and Institute for Juvenile Research
Chicago, Illinois

Nell Logan, Ph.D.

Nell Logan is Director of the Child Psychiatry Clinic, Department of Psychiatry, Abraham Lincoln School of Medicine, University of Illinois Medical Center, Chicago, Illinois, and clinical psychologist with the Child Psychiatry Clinic and the Institute for Juvenile Research. She also is currently involved in a Divorce Project, a clinical and research project focused on the effects of divorce on children. She earned the Ph.D. in clinical psychology from Washington University, St. Louis, Missouri, in 1973 and worked in the Counseling Center, State University of New York, Fredonia, New York, before moving to Chicago.

THE SINGLE PARENT

Nell Logan

AWARENESS INDEX

Directions: Mark each item true or false.
Compute your score from the scoring guide at the end of this awareness index.
A post test is provided at the end of the chapter.

T   F   1. Most single parents in our society today find that they have more freedom and fun than most married parents.

T   F   2. Approximately 80% of all American children today live with a mother and a father.

T   F   3. Single parents today rarely experience discrimination in obtaining housing.

T   F   4. Those families with a married male head and unemployed wife present have higher median incomes than those families with a single male head.

T   F   5. Growing up in a two-parent family is not necessarily an advantage for a child.

T   F   6. Most very young children show increased anxiety, fearfulness, irritability, and expressions of insecurity after parental separation, divorce, or death.

T   F   7. Most older children experience parental death, divorce, and separation as painful experiences.

15

T F   8. Many children adjust satisfactorily to living in a single-parent family.

T F   9. Most children adjust more satisfactorily to living in a single-parent family if the noncustodial parent does not keep in touch with them.

T F   10. Gender identity arises primarily from identification with the parent of the same sex.

T F   11. Approximately 2,000,000 single parents are in the United States today.

T F   12. Other people in the United States today generally are quite tolerant toward single parents.

T F   13. Little systematic research exists on the attitudes toward and treatment of single parents and single-parent families.

T F   14. Few single parents experience conflicts over how to cope with their sexuality.

T F   15. Single parents usually find that they do not need to develop new support networks.

Scoring Guide for Awareness Index

1. F	5. T	9. T	13. T
2. T	6. T	10. F	14. F
3. F	7. T	11. F	15. F
4. T	8. T	12. F	

A CASE EXAMPLE

Sue is a 35-year-old divorced woman with two children, Greg and Amy, 13 and 10 years of age. She feels fortunate that her husband sends child-support money once a month, remains interested in the children, and sees them occasionally. He lives in another city, however, and Sue worries that her son and daughter may have some difficulty obtaining a solid understanding of loving relationships between men and women and of an integrated family life without their father's active presence. These values are important to her, and she would like to pass them on to her children.

Sue also thinks about specific ways in which fathers con-tribute to the welfare of their children. Greg was active in Cub Scouts, but decided not to join Boy Scouts. He said that fathers usually attend the monthly outings with the boys. His father will not be able to attend the outings, so Greg does not want to go either. Sue finds herself in frequent conflict with Amy. A father might act as a buffer or help to resolve the conflict.

Sue has a hectic schedule. She works to help support herself and the children and takes two evening courses which are requirements toward the college degree she has not obtained. Balancing these activities, her relationship with her two children, and her own personal and social needs is not easy.

SINGLE PARENTS,

A SPECIFIC CATEGORY

Delineation of the Category

The category of "single parents" comprises those individuals who are not married and who are parents of one or more children. These individuals may be separated, divorced, widowed, or never married. They may be custodial or non-custodial parents and biological, adoptive, or foster parents. The category of single parents is being used formally and informally because of the recognition that single parents face common concerns.

This category encompasses people with varied issues. A widowed parent, for example, will face problems different from the single person who becomes a foster parent. This chapter will focus on important commonalities, however, with some emphasis on divorced and separated single parents.

Problems exist in the delineation of any category. The def-inition of single parents in terms of both marital status and parenthood is somewhat awkward, especially when one

17

realizes that the logical accompaniments, "married parents," "married nonparents," and "single nonparents" are rarely used. This category of "single parents" indeed is not used in some formal settings. The United States Bureau of the Census (1977), for example, does not use the phrase "single parents" in presentations of census information.

Single parents also are not as distinct from married parents as the label may imply. Some single parents live upstairs, down the street, or in the same apartment building as the former spouse and children spend almost as much time with them as before the separation or divorce. Other single parents receive help from friends or relatives who live in or out of the home. Married parents, on the other hand, frequently divide responsibilities such that one parent, usually the mother, assumes primary responsibility for the children. In some families the father or the mother spends considerable time away from home because of job or other responsibilities. Some parents, such as those in military service, remain away from their homes for extended periods of time; the parent at home feels in many ways like a single parent. All parents, regardless of their specific life arrangements, face similar issues. Despite the similarities, however, the concerns of single parents differ in important ways from the concerns of married parents.

Population

Data on the toal number of single parents in the United States currently are not available. The U.S. Bureau of the Census (1977) has presented information from which very rough estimates can be made. Census data indicate, for example, that in 1975 there were 7,384,000 black and white women in the United States who were heads of households containing their own children under 18 years of age (U.S. Bureau of the Census, 1977, p. 45). This figure does not include single female parents without children in their households, single male parents, single parents of other racial backgrounds, or single female parents living in households of which they are not the head. If one assumes that the number of single parents is approximately equal to twice the total number of black and white female heads of households, a

18

rough estimate of the total number of single parents in the United States in 1975 was 14,500,000 individuals. Census figures also indicate that the total number of female family heads is increasing in the United States, thus suggesting that the total number of single parents is increasing. An estimate of the number of single parents is an estimate for a specified year only. An even larger number of people have been or will be single parents at some time during their lifetimes.

PROBLEMS IN SOCIETY

FOR SINGLE PARENTS

A perusal of census information, popular books, magazines, and books on child development suggests that a dominant value in American society is marriage and family life, and a basic belief is that child-rearing can be accomplished best within a family which includes both a mother and a father. These attitudes are expressed in many ways. Elementary school textbooks frequently picture and describe activities of a mother, father, and their children. Popular television shows such as "The Brady Bunch" portray two parents and their children enjoying family activities or a mother and a father successfully helping their children meet a variety of crises. Organizations such as the Boy Scouts and Girl Scouts of America plan activities for a child and specified parent, including father-son camping trips and father-daughter banquets. Furthermore, the beneficial effects which life in a nuclear family (mother, father, and children) has on parents and children, have been discussed in the psychological and sociological literature. Examples abound in the literature of parents who remain together in unhappy marriages for their own or their children's welfare.

Census information suggests that these attitudes are reflected in behavior. Most primary families, that is, families consisting of two or more persons related to the head and living together in a household, for example, are husband-wife families. In 1976, of all families in the United States 47,297 out of 56,056 families or 84% of all were husband-wife families

(U.S. Bureau of the Census, 1977, p. 45). Census information, furthermore, showed in 1976 that 80% of all children in the United States were living with two parents (U.S. Bureau of the Census, 1977, p. 45).

Attitudes seem to be changing somewhat as people experiment with alternative life styles and find them satisfactory (Scanzoni & Scanzoni, 1976; Smart & Smart, 1976). Within the past ten years a significant number of single men and women in the United States have been keeping their own children born outside of marriage, adopting children, or becoming foster parents to children of their own or other racial and cultural backgrounds. These single parents as well as widowed, divorced, and separated parents are finding value in their status as single parent with new opportunities for personal growth. Some change in attitudes in the general public is reflected in the acceptance of such television shows as "The Courtship of Eddie's Father" and more recently, "Miss Winslow and Son."

Little systematic research exists on the actual attitudes toward and treatment of single parents and single-parent families. Interviews with single parents, however, indicate that many such parents have faced negative attitudes and unfair treatment, including anger from relatives, withdrawal of friends, and difficulty in obtaining an apartment, credit card, or insurance (Finer, 1974; Klein, 1973; Schlesinger, 1975). Despite the existence of such problems, some single parents also are encountering admiration and support for their position (Bowerman, Irish, & Pope, 1966; Hunt & Hunt, 1977; Stuart & Abt, 1972).

PERSONAL ISSUES
OF SINGLE PARENTS

Single parents face several major personal issues as listed by various authors (Gardner, 1976; Hunt & Hunt, 1977; Klein, 1973; McFadden, 1974; Schlesinger, 1975; Stuart & Abt, 1972; Tessman, 1978):

1. maintaining an adequate standard of living,
2. fulfilling personal needs, and
3. providing adequate caregiving and parenting for children.

These issues also confront other adults in our society. When an individual first becomes a single parent, however, these problems must be handled in new ways. Even after adapting to the new circumstances, single parents continue to grapple with these problems.

Maintaining an Adequate Standard of Living

All single parents experience financial changes, including increased expenses, when they first become single parents. Many single parents also experience financial problems.

No figures are available on the average income of single parents compared with other parents or change in income level with change in marital or parental status. Census information, however, shows that the median income of families with a married male head and employed or unemployed wife present is higher than the median income of families with a single male or single female head (U.S. Bureau of the Census, 1977, p. 443). This information suggests that single parents have lower incomes than married parents and thus are more likely to experience financial difficulties. Figures on median incomes of families indicate, furthermore, that the median income of families with a female head is lower than the median income of families with a male head, thus suggesting that single female parents are more likely to experience financial difficulties than single male parents (U.S. Bureau of the Census, 1977, p. 443).

Specific financial changes experienced by single parents vary widely. When a parent dies, the family may be deprived of the income of one person. Insurance and other benefits typically do not provide as much income. In the event of separation or divorce, the family also may have one less source of income. Many departing parents make no alimony or child support payments. Even where such payments are made, the amount in most cases does not match the previous financial support. Not only is income frequently less after a

21

separation or divorce, but also maintenance of two households is more expensive than the maintenance of one. A single person who assumes the new responsibility of caring for a child incurs added financial responsibilities. Any single parent usually incurs additional expenses around the time at which the change in marital or parental status occurs, including expenses for funerals, health care, resettlement, legal arrangements, and child care.

Many single parents experience some problems with financial arrangements including paying bills, budgeting, and planning. Some have difficulty in making necessary expenses fit limited budgets. Some had let a spouse handle the financial affairs previously and thus lack experience. Others have more general difficulties with planning and organization. Still others find that financial changes necessitate a change in life style and have difficulty accepting and planning this change.

Many single mothers in particular are forced to meet all or most of their own financial needs for the first time ever or in many years. Some of these women have poor educational backgrounds, little or no specific skill development, and little work experience. Choices frequently exist between accepting a low paying job, attending high school or college, or entering a job training program. New opportunities may enhance a woman's personal and professional development but often will not ease financial burdens for some time.

Some single parents find themselves with a low socio-economic status, frequently with difficulties providing necessities for themselves and the children or the need to forgo previous luxuries such as a private home, trips, and recreational activities. A change in income level also may necessitate a move to a new neighborhood with less expensive residences. Some single parents feel guilty that they are not able to provide for their children in the way they had planned. Some, on the other hand, find new opportunities for the family members to work together.

Fulfilling Personal Needs

Change of Status. A task of all single parents is to face and cope personally with the event which led to their change in status: death, divorce, separation, or new parenthood. Single parents also must meet their own continuing social and emotional needs.

A parent who assumes responsibility for a child for the first time may feel happy, unhappy, or ambivalent about the new status. The parent who decides to rear his or her own child born outside a marital relationship faces the attitudes of parents, friends, and other members of society as well as personal feelings about the circumstances of the child's conception and birth. The person who assumes the care of a friend's or relative's child or an adoptive or foster child must cope with personal feelings about this new child and the circumstances leading to parenthood. If the child is from another cultural background, the parent must learn about and cope with cultural differences. If the child exhibits physical or psychological deficiencies or has experienced abuse or neglect, the parent must adjust to the effects on the child of these experiences. Some children, on the other hand, fulfill the parent's idealized wishes to a very high degree, resulting at times in parental overidentifications and unrealistic expectations. Any new parent must integrate the requirements of the new child into the parent's personal characteristics.

Other single parents must cope with the experience of death, divorce, or separation. The period preceding and following this event typically involves painful feelings, including anger, disappointment, guilt, anxiety, fear, and sadness. The individual may feel rejected or abandoned with an accompanying sense of worthlessness. Not all ensuing feelings are unpleasant, however. Some individuals feel a sense of relief after the event has occurred. Some feel buoyant with a sense of freedom and eagerness for new experiences. Some show mixed feelings, occasionally with extreme mood swings.

People cope with a major event in their lives in widely varying ways. They typically use psychological defense

23

mechanisms, such as denial, rationalization, and repression for tempering affect and protecting self-esteem. Some withdraw into themselves. Others become busy with people and activities. Some continue to have difficulty adjusting to the major changes in their lives. Others move into new experiences and relationships. Some find that their new status provides them with an opportunity to experiment with new relationships and to change patterns of behavior. Changes may lead to increased personal maturity.

Many initial reactions to the major event diminish as the person copes with day-to-day life and develops new patterns of thought and behavior relevant to the new status. Modes of coping with the major event, however, sometimes become more deeply incorporated into personality, noted in characteristics such as increased cynicism or bitterness on the one hand, or flexibility and tolerance on the other.

As they move into new areas of interest, single parents frequently experience difficulties in fulfilling personal needs for affection, approval, sexual response, relaxation, and fun. Some single parents feel tied down to children and work, suffer anxiety over personal worth, and feel drained of energy after an intense emotional experience. These parents sometimes experience difficulties in investing themselves in relationships with other people. Other single parents are ready for social interactions but find themselves left out in a society that is oriented toward couples. When included in activities, they frequently feel pressures to find a mate and become attached.

Sexuality. An important issue for many single parents is coping with sexuality. Some encounter difficulties in finding an appropriate person, while some feel inexperienced with contemporary dating norms and sexual pressures. Many had a monogamous relationship for a number of years and enjoyed sexual expression within that relationship. They wish to continue this type of satisfaction but no longer have the same outlets. Many grew up with traditional sexual standards but face for the first time more liberal sexual attitudes along with their own and their partner's desires for continued gratification. The resultant ambivalence may be difficult to

24

resolve. Many parents become concerned about how their behavior will affect their children. If parents decide to continue with sexual activity, they raise questions about whether or not to have someone sleep over, who, how often, and what effects this behavior will have on the children.

Very little research exists on the sexual attitudes and behavior of single parents and effects on children. A recent study of divorced men and women provides some initial exploration into this topic (Hunt & Hunt, 1977). This study indicated that a very large number of divorced men and women go through three stages in their post-divorce sexual expression. The first stage is a stage of "ego repair" in which the person uses sexuality in order to feel desirable and worthwhile to a person of the opposite sex. Then comes a second period of more active exploration of sexuality with a desire to experiment. In the third stage at some later point, many people recognize the limitations of these heterosexual relationships and begin looking for a relationship in which to combine sex with caring and love for the other person. Not all divorced men and women go through this sequence of stages however. This study did not focus on the effects on children.

Loneliness. Loneliness is a feeling with which most single parents contend. They are alone in coping with the major event which led to their status as a single parent. They also are alone in coping with the status of single parent in a society in which most adults are married and bring children into a family with a mother and a father. Many single parents have made a conscious choice to become or to remain single or to become a parent while single. Such a choice is made at least to some extent alone. Regardless of how much choice is exerted, many single parents feel they are a part of a minority group in our society. They feel different from the dominant part of society and experience disapproval and rejection from other people. Some feel a sense of failure over their inability to find or to keep an appropriate marital partner. Single parents also are alone in coping with daily events, handling financial responsibilities, meeting their own personal needs, and parenting their children.

Despite the existence of problems, many single parents seek opportunities for continued personal development and express renewed hopes. They find they have an opportunity to set new goals and to work toward these goals. Some find they become more aware of themselves, other people, and the outside world. Some tap and develop unused resources inside themselves.

Providing Adequate Parenting for Children

Child Development Theory. Events of death, separation, divorce, and living in a one-parent family are major occurrences in a child's life. Two important questions are how parental death, separation, and divorce affect children and whether children develop important capacities in single-parent families. Many single parents seek answers to these questions and wonder how they might parent their children adequately.

Children attempt to make sense out of their experiences at the same time that they are coping with intense feelings associated with the experiences. They feel the pain of a loss or an absence and try to understand these feelings. As they see other children engaged in activities with two parents, they feel the lack in their own lives and long for the absent parent.

Child development theory specifies that a child must gradually acquire a variety of internal capacities in order to function later as a reasonably mature adult (Freud, 1965; Jersild, Telford, & Sawrey, 1975; Murphy & Moriarity, 1976). These include capacities of basic trust in people, sense of security, tolerance of frustration, independence, personal identity, interpersonal competence, standards and ideals, problem-solving skills, and capacity for love and intimacy. A common-sense understanding of children suggests that these basic capacities develop through interactions with one or two parents as well as through experiences outside the family. These capacities can develop very likely in children growing up in single-parent families.

Psychological theory also suggests, however, potential value for a child in living with a mother and a father who have a stable, loving relationship. Two parents contribute in comple-

26

mentary and supplementary ways to a child's well-being. The parents' relationship to each other can provide a model for and experience with intimacy, love, and mutuality, facilitating a child's internalization of these capacities. Parents, furthermore, can become identification figures for a child of the same sex and a model for heterosexual relationships for a child of the opposite sex, again facilitating a child's development of sexual identification and capacity for heterosexual relationships.

A common-sense understanding of children again suggests that these important characteristics can develop in a single-parent family. The capacity for love, intimacy, and mutuality, for example, emerge from a loving relationship with one or two parents and ripen in relationships with other people. People outside the immediate family frequently serve as identification figures and provide experience with heterosexual relationships. Psychological theory, furthermore, stresses children's capacities for flexible adaptation to circumstances.

Despite some possible potential value for the child to live in a two-parent family, this experience is not always an advantage. Children sometimes experience difficulties if one or both parents show disturbed personalities or if much conflict and turmoil exist in the home.

Research concerning the effects on children of major deviations in life circumstances is limited. Studies on the effects of parental separation, divorce, and death and the effects of father absence on children, however, provide initial data on some aspects of the broader topic of parenting.

Effects of Parental Separation, Divorce, and Death on Children. Recent clinical research describes effects of parental separation, divorce, and death on children (Furman, 1974; Gardner, 1970, 1976, 1977; Kelly & Wallerstein, 1976; Miller, 1971; Nagera, 1970; Stuart & Abt, 1972; Tessman, 1978; Wallerstein, 1977; Wallerstein & Kelly, 1974, 1975, 1976). These authors agree that parental death, divorce, and separation are painful experiences for most if not all children. In the period immediately following this experience, most very young children show increased anxiety, fearfulness, irritability,

27

moodiness, and expressions of insecurity and vulnerability. Some of these children show regressions in toilet training, specific phobic ideation, temper tantrums, withdrawal into fantasy, possessiveness, and clinging behaviors. Many older children express sadness and feelings of deprivation, vulnerability, and helplessness. Some older children also show intense anger, fears for the future, loss of self-esteem, wishes for reconciliation, feelings of rejection and abandonment, fantasies of personal responsibility and guilt, shame, humiliation, loyalty conflicts, somatic complaints, concern over money, disturbed sense of personal identity, and anxiety over personal capacity as a marital partner. Some older children also show poor peer relationships, problems in academic work, withdrawal into fantasy, aggressive behavior, and delinquent behavior. Even though most children experience parental death, divorce, and separation as difficult experiences in certain ways, some feel a sense of relief and look forward to more peace and organization at home and to movement ahead in their own personal development.

Adjustments a year or so later to parental death, separation, or divorce vary widely between children. A large number of children regain a sense of security, confidence, and enthusiasm and proceed with their development. Other children continue to experience difficulties. Problem behavior patterns become consolidated and internalized in some of these children.

Children are more likely to adjust in a satisfactory way to the changes in their lives if the parents make a satisfactory adjustment and maintain adequate relationships with their children. Children also are more likely to adjust in a beneficial way to the change in their lives if they are older, were previously doing well in various areas of personal development, have personal interests outside the home, have support from friends and relatives, continue an organized home life, and have the capacity and opportunity to talk or play out feelings and thoughts. Improvements in the home atmosphere and parent-child relationship sometimes occur with the change, enhancing the possibility for the child's adjustment. Decreases in tension and conflict may occur. Parents frequently have more time, interest, and energy once the emotional upheaval is reduced and feel freer to interact with a child. Parents who see their children only occasionally may attempt to enhance the quality of the relationship when with the child.

Effect of Father Absence on Children. Many single parents express concern over the development of gender identity in their children. They fear that those children who are living only with the parent of the opposite sex will not have an adequate identification figure. Several recent reviews indicate that gender identity is a very complex characteristic which is influenced by many variables, including physiological, environmental, and personal variables (Lee, 1976; Maccoby, 1976; Maccoby & Jacklin, 1974). Parents and other people teach sex roles through their expectations, support, reinforcement, modeling, and discussion. A mother, for example, may buy her son trucks, support aggressive behaviors, and discourage dependent behaviors. Children learn from many sources through observation, interaction, expectation of reinforcement, and identification. The development of gender identity is a complex process in which the child learns that he/she is a boy or girl and then acquires ideas about boys and girls. These ideas are modified and integrated in a kind of self-socialization process as new experiences occur. That children learn sex role identity in ways other than identification with a parent of the same sex is obvious in numerous examples. Boys play with guns, join athletic teams, and become physicians even when their fathers are not involved in these activities. Research on gender identity, therefore, suggests that this identity can develop in a one-parent family.

A few systematic investigations have focused on the effects of father presence and absence on children (Biller, 1976; Herzog & Sudia, 1973; Hetherington, 1972; Lamb, 1976; Lynn, 1974). Results have suggested that warm, competent, available fathers have positive influences on sons and daughters. Effects of the father, however, depend upon characteristics of the child, the mother-child relationship, the father-mother relationship, and the sociocultural background. Girls who have experienced absence or low availability of the father seem somewhat more likely than do girls with fathers in the home to show conflicts over their sex role identity, discomfort and difficulty in relationships with males (peers and adults), anger at males, and dependence on mother. Boys in fatherless homes seem somewhat more likely than boys

29

with fathers in the home to show difficulties with sex role identity. Exceptions exist to these general trends, however. These trends also are more evident when the absence of a father begins early in the child's life and continues until the child is an adolescent. Although some initial information exists on the effects of father absence, studies are limited and need further replication and expanded study. Very little research exists thus far on mother absence.

Parenting. Primary issues for single parents are changing their relationships with their children to keep pace with the change in the family structure, establishing continuity between the old and new relationships, consolidating a new family structure, helping children cope with the major changes in their lives, and providing optimal opportunities for children's continued development. These tasks are major ones, enhanced by the necessity for parents to match their own personalities to the personalities and developmental levels of their children. Fathers in particular who become the custodial parent sometimes are confronted for the first time with primary responsibility for child care. Both mothers and fathers, however, face these issues.

Such tasks are difficult even for two parents working together in a relatively comfortable way. Two parents, however, frequently share various aspects of the responsibility. A single parent has primary responsibility for caring for an ill or handicapped child, setting limits, determining privileges, answering difficult questions, and coordinating family activities.

Old and new conflicts with a former spouse frequently compound child-rearing issues. These include conflicts over how often and when a child will visit a noncustodial parent. Some parents use children as pawns in a continuing conflict with a spouse. Some parents denounce the other parent to a child, threaten the loss of love if the child acts in certain ways with the other parent, or limit a child's freedom in order to retaliate against a former mate.

Noncustodial parents must work out new patterns of behavior with their children. Those noncustodial parents who see their children infrequently sometimes view the child

30

somewhat as a stranger and find it difficult to establish a meaningful relationship. Parents who see their children more frequently are still not involved in many events which are important to the child. Children's favorite possessions and friends frequently are at the more permanent home. A non-custodial parent, therefore, may not feel a part of the child's personal world and may have difficulty coping with this issue.

Many single parents find that balancing needs, interests, and goals becomes a greater problem after they become single parents than before. The custodial parent in particular transports children for appointments and activities, helps with school work or special interests such as Scouts, tries to keep in touch with the child's personal world, and plans other leisure activities with a child. The parent must mesh these activities with a job, extra courses or training, a personal and social life, and other interests.

The potential for problems exists in any parent-child relationship. Several hazards concern single parents in particular. Some parents overindulge their children as a way of trying to make up for the loss. Noncustodial parents may be tempted to overcompensate for the less permanent home life by planning extravagant occasions, allowing extra freedom, or handling their own and their children's discomfort with the changes by becoming busy with activities and unavailable to the children. Some parents compensate for their own weaknesses by developing contrasting characteristics. They become punitive rather than indulgent or distant rather than dependent. Single parents frequently fear that they are being too permissive, controlling, possessive, or distant.

A number of books on death and divorce have been written in recent years for parents and children to help them understand and cope more effectively with these experiences (Gardner, 1970, 1977; Grollman, 1969, 1970; Richards & Willis, 1976; Tessman, 1978). These books primarily describe the reactions which are triggered by death and divorce. They encourage children not to blame themselves, to face and accept the change in their lives, and to work at coping with the situation, for example, by talking to someone and seeking new friends and activities. Parents are encouraged to answer children's questions in a simple, honest, straightforward manner in the way a particular child understands; to maintain an active interest in the child; and to establish some organization at home.

Although single parents and their children face difficult-ties, they may develop important strengths as they cope with their personal situations. They may learn to help support each other and to communicate more effectively, leading to closeness and strong personal ties. They sometimes gain a more realistic view of human inadequacies and become more tolerant of each other. Other adaptive capacities also may develop, including courage, perseverance, independence, and capacity to cope with stress.

SERVICES

FOR SINGLE PARENTS

Very few services are designed specifically for single parents. Important services available to single parents, however, include:

1. psychosocial therapy and counseling services,
2. other social agencies,
3. formal organizations, and
4. informal support systems.

A few services are designed for single parents as a whole or subgroups such as widows. Other services are available for a broader population but provide services also needed by some single parents. Mental health professionals have to be aware of needs and concerns of single parents and their children, to provide relevant help where it seems indicated, and to guide people to appropriate services.

Psychosocial Therapy and Counseling Services

Psychosocial therapy and counseling services exist for people with concerns ranging from severe emotional problems to temporary disruptions in their personal lives. Some single parents have found that short-term or long-term individual, family, or group therapy or counseling is helpful for them and their children.

Therapy or counseling can help people cope with painful feelings, look at alternative goals or ways of achieving goals, gain new perspectives on themselves and their situations, and reorganize themselves or their families. Therapists and counselors provide some additional support in times of crisis as well as help for people in looking more specifically at personal concerns. In group therapy other individuals provide support and ideas as well as help in realizing that other people face personal crises, too.

Other Social Agencies

A variety of other social agencies provide services that are useful to some single parents. State public aid offices have programs which provide financial aid and job training for those parents with limited financial resources and job skills. Public and private employment offices provide information on specific job opportunities and job training programs. Some employment offices help applicants to assess job interests, aptitudes, and skills. Legal aid offices give advice and aid on legal issues related to adoption, divorce, separation, child custody, child protection, and women's rights. These agencies might benefit from a deeper understanding of concerns of single parents and their children.

Formal Organizations

A number of formal organizations exist throughout the United States and other countries for single parents. Probably the largest and most well-known of these groups is Parents Without Partners, Inc., commonly known as PWP. This organization began in 1957 and has grown rapidly, so that most cities and many small towns now have one or more chapters. PWP was formed because of the common concerns and difficulties faced by single parents. Most chapters provide lectures, formal and informal workshops, discussion groups, and social activities. Some activities are for parents only, some for children only, and some for parents and children together. Some chapters provide additional services such as information centers, crisis intervention centers, telephone hotlines, and social service projects.

National and local groups and programs also exist in the United States for subgroups of single parents such as widows and widowers, children of single parents, and young single parents. Some communities for example, have organized programs using widows as volunteers to visit new widows (Silverman, MacKenzie, Pettipas, & Wilson, 1974).

Informal Support Systems

Most single parents are able to continue some previous relationships. Many, however, experience ruptures in relationships with relatives and friends. Many feel the need for new support systems. These support systems may include relatives, friends, neighborhood groups, and church, temple, or other religious affiliation. Involvement in formal organizations often leads to the development of small, congenial groups within the larger organization.

Additional Service Needs

A major need at present is for more educational and therapeutic programs focused specifically on concerns of single parents and their children. More professionals must take this area as a major topic of concern, become knowledgeable on the topic, and design educational programs for mental health professionals, paraprofessionals, teachers, physicians, single parents, children of single parents, and others. Educational programs should focus on the potential effects of divorce, separation, death, and living in a single-parent family on adults and children. Such programs also should focus on specific concerns and problems of single parents and their children.

New therapeutic programs should be designed for single parents and their children to focus with them on their own unique issues as well as those concerns faced by many other single parents and their children. Therapy, rap, or social groups for single parents or children of single parents may meet some needs. Family therapy or counseling might focus more specifically on helping families to restructure themselves after a divorce, death, separation, or introduction of a new member, new child, or new parent. Family therapy also might focus on those personal or group problems triggered by changes in the family system.

Much more systematic research is needed. This research then can guide professionals in planning new programs. Professionals with a thorough understanding of the many issues faced by single parents and their children must plan and carry out new programs, serve as consultants to groups of people interested in discussing the concerns of single parents and their children, and consult on problems of specific individuals.

CONCLUSIONS

Single parents constitute a large group of people increasing in size in the United States. Even with the growing recognition of the many common concerns of single parents, little research or literature exists for enhancing an understanding of these concerns. In a society which highly values the nuclear family, single parents and their children face many evidences of their deviation from this value, including rejection and isolation. These attitudes in society compound the many personal issues confronting single parents, which include the necessity to cope with financial changes; emotional demands from a death, separation, or divorce; aloneness in a society oriented toward couples; and adequate parenting of children. Despite the complexity of these tasks, few resources exist for helping single parents. Many agencies and groups which might provide resources have been only somewhat aware of specific issues. Much more study and education on the topic of single parents and their children is needed.

This chapter has deemphasized the diversity among single parents in order to highlight the commonality. The category of single parents however, includes widowed, separated, divorced, and never married parents, and biological, foster, and adoptive parents. The literature on widowed, separated, and divorced parents is growing. A dearth of information exists on single men and women who keep their own children born out of wedlock or adopt or serve as foster parents to children, including disadvantaged children from other racial, cultural, or socioeconomic groups or with physical or psychological handicaps. Vast differences exist between an elderly and a young single parent, a widowed and a never-married parent, a parent who has borne a child and a foster parent, and a parent with a young child in the home and a parent with grown children away from home.

Despite diversity within the category of single parents, the value of this category lies in its focus on a large group of people with important common issues. As people begin thinking more fully about the common issues, the distinctive issues for each subcategory should emerge more fully. An awareness of the diverse issues in turn will generate more knowledge of the broader category. A deeper understanding of these issues should enhance the capacity of various people and agencies for working with single parents.

POST TEST

Directions: After reading the chapter, mark each item true or false.

T F 1. The category of "single parents" is a relatively homogeneous category consisting of those adults who have borne children out of wedlock.

T F 2. A basic belief in American society today is that child-rearing can be accomplished best within a family which includes both a mother and a father.

T F 3. Single parents in general have little difficulty in maintaining an adequate standard of living.

T F 4. Most single parents move quickly into new relationships and activities.

T F 5. Children react intensely to parental separation, divorce, and death.

T F   6. Coping with divorce, separation, or death in a family leads to increased personal maturity.

T F   7. Many single parents find themselves left out in a society that is oriented toward couples.

T F   8. Sexual experimentation by parents has no effects on children.

T F   9. Loneliness is a feeling with which most single parents contend.

T F 10. Absence or low availability of the father has very little effect on girls.

T F 11. Attitudes in the United States towards single parents seem to be changing somewhat.

T F 12. One major personal issue for single parents is fulfilling personal needs.

T F 13. Those single parents who have gone through a separation or a divorce usually feel at least some anger, disappointment, and anxiety.

T F 14. An important issue for many single parents is coping with sexuality.

T F 15. Children growing up in single-parent families have serious difficulties in developing adequately.

Scoring Guide for Post Test

1. F	5. T	9. T	13. T
2. T	6. F	10. T	14. T
3. F	7. T	11. T	15. T
4. F	8. F	12. T	

Reference List

Biller, H.B. The father and personality development: Paternal deprivation and sex-role development. In M.E. Lamb (Ed.), *The role of the father in child development*. New York: John Wiley, 1976.

Bowerman, C.E., Irish, D.P., & Pope, H. *Unwed motherhood: Personal and social consequences*. Chapel Hill, N.C.: Institute for Research in Social Science, University of North Carolina, 1966.

Finer, M. *Report of the committee on one-parent families.* London: Her Majesty's Stationery Office, 1974.

Freud, A. *Normality and pathology in childhood, assessment of development.* New York: International Universities Press, 1965.

Furman, E. *A child's parent dies, studies in childhood bereavement.* New Haven: Yale University Press, 1974.

Gardner, R.A. *The boys' and girls' book about divorce.* New York: Jason Aronson, 1970.

Gardner, R.A. *Psychotherapy with children of divorce.* New York: Jason Aronson, 1976.

Gardner, R.A. *The parents' book about divorce.* Garden City, N.Y.: Doubleday, 1977.

Grollman, E.A. *Explaining divorce to children.* Boston: Beacon Press, 1969.

Grollman, E.A. *Talking about death, a dialogue between parent and child.* Boston: Beacon Press, 1970.

Herzog, E., & Sudia, C. Children in fatherless homes. In B.M. Caldwell and H.N. Ricciuti (Eds.), *Review of child development research*, Vol. 3. Chicago: University of Chicago Press, 1973.

Hetherington, E.M. Effects of father absence on personality development in adolescent daughters. *Developmental Psychology*, 1972, 7, 313-326.

Hunt, M., & Hunt, B. *The divorce experience.* New York: McGraw-Hill, 1977.

Jersild, A.T., Telford, C.W., & Sawrey, J.M. *Child psychology* (7th ed.). Englewood Cliffs, N.J.: Prentice-Hall, 1975.

Kelly, J.B., & Wallerstein, J.S. The effects of parental divorce: Experiences of the child in early latency. *American Journal of Orthopsychiatry*, 1976, *46*, 20-32.

Klein, C. *The single parent experience.* New York: Walker & Co., 1973.

Lamb, M.E. (Ed.). *The role of the father in child development.* New York: John Wiley, 1976.

Lee, P.C., & Stewart, R.S. (Eds.). *Sex differences.* New York: Urizen Books, 1976.

Lynn, D.B. *The father, his role in child development.* Monterey, Ca.: Brooks/Cole, 1974.

Maccoby, E.E. Possible causal factors of sex differences in intellectual abilities. In P.C. Lee & R.S. Stewart (Eds.), *Sex differences.* New York: Urizen Books, 1976.

Maccoby, E.E., & Jacklin, C.N. *The psychology of sex differences.* Stanford, Ca.: Stanford University Press, 1974.

McFadden, M. *Bachelor fatherhood, how to raise and enjoy your children as a single parent.* New York: Walker & Co., 1974.

Miller, J.B.M. Children's reactions to the death of a parent: A review of the psychoanalytic literature. *Journal of the American Psychoanalytic Association*, 1971, *19*, 697-719.

Murphy, L.B., & Moriarity, A.E. *Vulnerability, coping and growth from infancy to adolescence.* New Haven, Ct.: Yale University Press, 1976.

Nagera, H. Children's reactions to the death of important objects, a developmental approach. *Psychoanalytic Study of the Child*, 1970, *25*, 360-400.

Richards, A.K., & Willis, I. *How to get it together when your parents are coming apart.* New York: David McKay Co., 1976.

Scanzoni, L., & Scanzoni, J. *Men, women, and change, a sociology of marriage and the family.* New York: McGraw-Hill, 1976.

Schlesinger, B. *The one-parent family, perspectives and annotated bibliography* (3rd ed.). Toronto: University of Toronto Press, 1975.

Silverman, P.R., MacKenzie, D., Pettipas, M., & Wilson, E. (Eds.). *Helping each other in widowhood.* New York: Health Sciences Publishing Co., 1974.

Smart, M.S., & Smart, L.S. *Families, developing relationships.* New York: Macmillan, 1976.

Stuart, I.R., & Abt, L.E. (Eds.). *Children of separation and divorce.* New York: Grossman Publishers, 1972.

Tessman, L.H. *Children of parting parents.* New York: Jason Aronson, 1978.

U.S. Bureau of the Census. *Statistical Abstract of the United States: 1977* (98th ed.). Washington D.C.: U.S. Government Printing Office, 1977.

Wallerstein, J.S. *Responses of the preschool child in divorce: Those who cope.* In M.F. McMillan & S. Henao (Eds.), *Child psychiatry: Treatment and research.* New York: Brunner/Mazel, 1977.

Wallerstein, J.S., & Kelly, J.B. The effects of parental divorce: The adolescent experience. In J. Anthony & C. Koupernick (Eds.), *The child and his family: Children at psychiatric risk.* New York: Wiley, 1974.

Wallerstein, J.S., & Kelly, J.B. The effects of parental divorce: Experiences of the preschool child. *Journal of the American Academy of Child Psychiatry*, 1975, *14*, 600-616.

Wallerstein, J.S., & Kelly, J.B. The effects of parental divorce: Experience of the child in later latency. *American Journal of Orthopsychiatry*, 1976, *46*, 256-269.

3

Culturally Different By Religion

The Old Order Amish

Joseph P. Wittmer, Ph.D.

Professor and Chairperson,
Department of Counselor Education
University of Florida
Gainesville, Florida

Because photography is forbidden by the Amish, no pictures are available of Joe Wittmer as a child. This drawing of him as a youth is as imagined by his 17 year old son, Scott Wittmer.

Joseph P. Wittmer, Ph.D.

Joe Wittmer, reared in the Old Order horse-and-buggy Amish faith in Indiana until age 16, holds a Ph.D. from Indiana State University in Psychological Services. Prior to earning the Ph.D. in 1968, he was a teacher-counselor and guidance director in Fort Wayne, Indiana, schools. Dr. Wittmer also worked in the National Teacher Corps Program in the slums of Gary, Indiana, for two years. He is currently Professor and Chairperson, in the Department of Counselor Education at the University of Florida.

Dr. Wittmer's professional interests include writing and consultation in interpersonal communication. He has co-authored three books and has published more than eighty-five articles in refereed journals.

Dr. Wittmer has been vice-chairperson of the National Committee for Amish Religious Freedom since 1970 and has been actively involved in litigation activities concerning their religious freedom.

CULTURALLY DIFFERENT BY RELIGION

THE OLDER ORDER AMISH

Joseph P. Wittmer

AWARENESS INDEX

Directions: Please test your knowledge by responding to the following questions before proceeding to the text in this chapter.
Compute your score from the scoring guide at the end of this Awareness Index.
A post test is provided at the end of this chapter.
Select the best response for each item.

1. Approximately how many Old Order horse-and-buggy Amish are in America today?
_____a. 10,000
_____b. 20,000
_____c. 40,000
_____d. 60,000

2. When Amish parents have a marriage-age daughter they do which of the following:
_____a. paint the barnyard gate blue.
_____b. move the hex signs off the barn onto the house.
_____c. put an ad in the Amish newspaper.
_____d. behave similarly to most American parents.

3. Today, the Amish are located:
_____a. basically in Pennsylvania.
_____b. throughout 20 states, Canada, and several South American countries.
_____c. a and b above, plus Europe.
_____d. none of the above.

4. Another common name for the Amish is:
_____a. the Amana.
_____b. the Mennonites.
_____c. the Plain People.
_____d. all of the above.

5. The Amish left Europe for America:
_____a. to escape religious persecution.
_____b. at the invitation of William Penn.
_____c. in search of religious freedom.
_____d. all of the above.

6. Amish parents forbid their children to:
_____a. salute the flag.
_____b. pledge allegiance to the flag.
_____c. attend educational movies at school.
_____d. all of the above.

For each item mark true or false.

T F   7. The Old Order Amish are growing in numbers.

T F   8. The Amish family organization is strictly patriarchal.

T F   9. Divorce is non-existant among the Amish.

T F   10. The first language of all Amish is German.

T F   11. The Amish are offshoots of the Mennonites.

T F   12. The problems with high school education caused several thousand Amish to migrate to South America during the late sixties and early seventies.

T F   13. Hex signs on barns are popular among the Amish.

T F   14. Amish farmers are exempt from social security payments.

T F   15. Tourism offers no monetary benefits to the Amish by their own choice.

T F 16. A 1972 Supreme Court decision exempted the Amish from compulsory high school education.

T F 17. The Amish produce and market a popular, brand-name refrigerator.

T F 18. In the absence of any type of indoor plumbing, it is common for the Amish to have BO.

T F 19. Upon marriage, Amish men grow a full-beard.

Scoring Guide for Awareness Index.

1. d	5. d	9. T	13. F	17. F
2. d	6. d	10. T	14. T	18. F
3. b	7. T	11. T	15. T	19. F
4. c	8. T	12. T	16. T	

INTRODUCTION

I think they are beautiful people. They are so sober.
The way they think, the way they feel, the way they
dress—it is all one unit. They mind their own
business and live their own life and I think this is
beautiful.

These words are from Mauricio Lasansky, the artist of the famous intaglio portrait, "Amish Boy," in his description of the more than 60,000 Old Order Amish people scattered throughout twenty states, Canada, and more recently, Central and South America. Americans often confuse the Old Order Amish with the Mennonites, Amana, House of David, Hutterites, Beachy's and other such religious sects in America that are culturally different because of religion and dress. As an illustrative example of these special populations, this section concerns the Old Order, German speaking, no electricity, horse-and-buggy-driving Amish often referred to as the "Plain People."

The writer was born and reared as an Amish youth until the age of sixteen.

ABOUT THE WRITER[1]

I am often asked what being Amish is like. Most Americans know them only by newspaper reports as a simple, virtuous people who live on farms, use no electricity, automobiles, trucks, tractors, radios, television, or other such "necessities" of modern life. Their broad-brimmed black hats, black buggies, and past tussles with educational authorities all have further stereotyped the Amish as anachronisms in the space age.

Religion on our Indiana farm was a seven-day-a-week affair. The way we dressed, the way we farmed, the German we spoke—our whole lifestyle was a daily reminder of our religion, as it is for all Amish.

The fourth of six children, I learned the Amish way by a gradual process of kindly indoctrination. At five I was given a corner of the garden to plant and care for as my own and a small pig and calf to raise. Amishmen are either farmers or in related occupations such as blacksmithing and buggy-making. My father had no doubt that I would someday be a God-fearing farmer like himself, and my mother often added in her German dialect, "and a nice black beard like your father's, you will have yet."

Because Amish parochial schools were not yet in existence, I entered the strange world of public schools at age eight. My parents deliberately planned this late entry into school so that I would be sixteen, minimum age for quitting, in the eighth grade. High school to the Amish is a "contaminating" influence that challenges the Biblical admonition to be a "peculiar people." Old Order Amish children are not permitted more than eight years of formal education. The Amish also resist education below the eighth grade if it originates in modern consolidated schools. America was at war with Germany when I entered the first grade. Without radios and

[1]From "Good Guys Wear White Hats" by J. Wittmer, *Liberty*, 1972, 67, (2), 12-17. Reprinted by permission.

newspapers or relatives fighting (all Amish are conscientious objectors), I had little opportunity at home to keep up with its progress. School was another matter.

Boys played war games and talked constantly about the war and the branch of service they someday would join. Often I was asked where I would serve. I knew that as a conscientious objector I would never go to war.

I often wished that I could help the non-Amish children gather sacks of milkweed pods, used to make parachutes for American flyers. However, I was taught to engage in activities that would further the war effort was sinful. Because I did not participate, I was often the object of derision.

The ordeal of Amish students reached its cruel peak during the daily pledge to the flag, which for religious reasons, our parents taught us not to salute or to pledge allegiance. The jibes of the students and the disappointed looks of the teacher as we remained seated cut me deeply. How could I explain that the Amish believe in praying for all governments, which, they hold, are ordained by God? How could I explain that hate is not in the Amish vocabulary? Explain it, moreover, in a German accent, for German was the first language of all Amish youth, the church requiring it to be spoken at home.

In retrospect, I can understand all too well the feelings of the non-Amish students. I can understand also why the Amish have established their own schools. What was at stake was not the feelings of Amish youth, but a way of life.

The average person often has difficulty understanding the pressures on a nonconformist in the public school system. Many activities are strictly off limits to the Amish youth; not only dancing and other "worldly entertainments," but also class pictures and educational movies. When such activities were scheduled, we Amish children were herded into another room usually to the chiding and laughter of our classmates.

My most vivid memories of boyhood days concern hostility and harassment endured by my parents and others in the Amish community because of our non-resistance stanze to the war. Often "outsiders" attacked us when we rode in our buggies. They threw firecrackers, eggs, tomatoes, even rocks. Soldiers home on leave burned our fodder shocks, overturned our outdoor toilets, broke windows, and stole buggies. A favorite tactic was to sit in a car trunk and hold onto a buggy while the car sped down the road. The buggy was turned loose to smash into bits against a road bank. After witnessing many such acts of vandalism I became terrified of non-Amishmen. Because the Bible admonished them to be "defenseless Christians," my father and the other elders of the community refused to summon law officials to their defense. By Scripture they lived and by Scripture they would die if necessary. They turned the other cheek.

Although turmoil and conflict occurred outside the Amish community, peace was the watchword within its borders. We worked hard and we played hard, though without the competition of the outside world. Thrashing days, barn raisings, and public auctions were a more than adequate substitute for radios, comic books, and organized sports.

Amish families are close-knit. We worked as a unit for ourselves and for the Amish community. We played together. We ate together—no meal was started until all members were present, and dinner was never interrupted by Walter Cronkite. Security and love abounds within the Amish way of life.

Why, then, did I, at sixteen, make the decision to continue in school—the first step away from my Amish origins? The answer is not simple. It includes (1) a passion for knowledge and (2) a growing resentment toward my Amish heritage, sparked by the years of derision and scorn in public schools. Somewhere on my way to a Ph.D. I fulfilled the one and outgrew the other, leaving still some unanswered questions with which the psychiatrists wrestle.

Perhaps my Amish kinsmen community claimed me. And, indeed, the campus on which I teach is a far cry from my father's farm. And "a nice black beard like your father's" I do not have. But there is no animosity, no shame, among the Amish that I have left. And though I live within mainstream society, I am also vice-chairman of the *National Committee for Amish Religious Freedom*, the organization which defended the Amish right not to attend high school all the way to the Supreme Court and won (May 15, 1972) a unanimous decision.

ABOUT THE AMISH

The Amish are unique, picturesque, and strive to follow the biblical dictate to be a "peculiar people." They want no part of the values and ways that exist in the modern world about them; they wish to be left alone to live their life away from the mainstream of the secular society.

The Old Order Amish strive continually to remain different from the "other people," the "outsider" or the "English" as non-Amish are called. They shun the use of television, radio, telephone, most other modern technological luxuries, and travel via horse-drawn carriages. Their homes are extremely plain and lack running water, electricity, refrigerators, and most other conveniences that are found in the modern American home. Their within-group conversation is in a German dialect and they wear home sewn garb reminiscent of the 18th century.

> . . . I know why we don't have TV like the outsiders do. We are different like God wants. The outsiders can have their TV because it's not good for you. Mom and me were in Sears one day and I saw TV a bit. Mom said they use bad words and dance on TV. We didn't watch any more. I don't want TV ever in our house . . . Amos, 4th grade[2]

Values of peace, total nonviolence, and humility are in evidence in any Amish community. They do not teach the skills of violence and technology. An Amishman realizes early in life that he is totally non-resistant and that he will never go to war. These values, lived by the Amish adults, gain the allegiance of the Amish youth, as less than five percent leave the sect. Further, no indigence, divorce, or unemployment exists. There is very little delinquency and no record of an Old Order Amishman ever being arrested for a felony and none

---

[2]These excerpts as well as others which follow, were taken from essays written by Amish elementary school children in response to an assignment: *What It's Like to be Amish.* Appreciation is extended to the Amish school teacher for sending me the essays. She wishes to remain anonymous.

has appeared on a welfare roll. The Amish also value calmness and tranquility—it is difficult to be in a hurry while driving a horse and buggy!

> . . . Our horse is almost red. He is a nice horse and he takes us where we want to go. Some horses kick, but ole Jamie doesn't. I sit in the back of the buggy and I get scared when the cars come. They get close and make dust. Once Uncle John's got hit and the driver died. I was sad. Uncle John was hurt . . .
> Rebecca, 3rd grade

Mainstream society's emphasis on high-powered cars, computers, and contraceptive devices is conspicuously absent from the horse-and-buggy Amish world. The Amish constantly live by the scriptural admonitions to "Come out from among them, and be ye separate," and "Be ye a peculiar people." They live in isolated communities attempting to stay apart from the secular influences of the "outsider's" world. However, the Amish feel the pressing-in of America's emphasis on technology, violence, and twentieth century progress.

All Amishmen are oriented toward one goal—that of eternal life and they equate their personal pursuance of this ultimate goal with present methods of attaining it. Industry, careful stewardship, the sweat of the brow, and beards on married men, are all means to an end—eternal life.

Uniforms of any type are taboo among the Amish and dress is uniform. Youngsters are attired as miniature adults. No change in style is to be concerned about and status is not attributed to type of clothing worn. This alleviates coveting and self-pride while building group cohesion. Thus, a deviate is highly conspicuous and the similarity serves as a boundary-maintaining device.

> . . . We wear plain clothes because the Bible says we should. Sometimes the outsiders stare at you but they never have said anything to me about my clothes. We can be a witness for others by being plain . . . But, just wearing plain clothes doesn't make you a Christian. I think sometimes we forget that . . .
> Elizabeth, 7th grade

An Amish man begins growing a chin beard the preceding week of his marriage, but the upper lip and neck are kept clean shaven. This custom is in keeping with their non-conformity to "worldly" values and ways; an "outsider" with a moustache is often in evidence. A straight line is shaved across the back of his neck and his hair is bobbed in a "crock-line" appearance. An Amishman doesn't part his hair and it is never "tapered" on the sides. The men wear large broad-brimmed black hats, suspenders, homesewn shirts without buttons or pockets, homesewn pants without hip pockets or zippers, and homesewn underwear without stripes. All shirts are sewn in such a manner so as to necessitate being put on and removed by slipping over the head.

> . . . My dad said when he was little one time he was with my grandpa and some outsider boys called them "bushhogs." Then the boys said baa-baa like a goat. I think that is funny. Dad has whiskers but nobody went baa-baa yet . . . Noah, 4th grade

Amish women do not wear make-up of any sort, nor shave any part of their body. They wear dresses that are full-blown and not adorned with buttons, hooks and eyes, press buttons, or zippers. The only means of keeping their dresses intact is with straight pins. They do not wear lacy under clothing and bras are prohibited. The female's hair is never cut and is always parted in the middle.

To an Amishman the "world" begins at the last Amish farmhouse. He has not acquired the "worldly" need for a tractor with which to farm. He may rely on a tractor for belt power, but it will be mounted on a steel-wheeled wagon and pulled from job to job by horses. He also uses horses to plow his fields and to pull his black buggy. Work is a moral directive. Labor saving devices are mere temptations and "something new." Something new or different is of the Devil while tradition is sacred. Although these customs may seem stern from the outside looking in, the Amish are healthy and happy. They have not acquired the methods of the "world" to attain their happiness or to fulfill their needs.

As a former Amishman, it is difficult to explain the feeling of being truly different from the dominant, surrounding society. Amish youngsters are reared very carefully and various methods are employed to protect them from the contaminating influences of the "outsider." The fact that one is different and peculiar is a continuous indoctrinating process for the young. They develop a strong conscience. Once indoctrinated, a person indeed finds difficulty in altering oneself to accept the values and ways of others without experiencing extreme psychic pain.

> . . . Being Amish means not doing what the world
> does. It means living a plain life for God on earth.
> It means being happy without the things outsiders
> have . . . Elam, 5th grade

ABOUT THE FAMILY

The family system is the primary unit which organizes the dominant patterns of value orientation in the Old Order Amish culture. Older members of the family funnel the cultural heritage to the younger offspring. Within the Amish family setting the child first learns to respond to authority, to play roles in the cooperative structure, and to obey the norms of the sect.

Rank differences are not extreme within the Amish sect nor within the family structure. However, father commands the highest rank with mother being second. Sibling rank is based according to age. The older siblings' roles include disciplining the younger children.

Amish married couples do not reveal overt affection for one another in public. An Amish husband refers to his wife as "her" and she makes reference to "him." However, there is mutual respect and seldom does arguing occur in presence of the children.

The Amish family organization is strictly patriarchal. The father rears his son in the exact same manner he was reared by his father. The father-son relationship is excellent and the generation gap seldom exists.

Women of the family take a back seat to the men in most endeavors and the Amish male rarely does the tasks of a female, although women are expected to help with most all male tasks. Only on special occasions such as butchering, cooking apple butter, and weddings, does the husband participate in household tasks. However, women and adolescent girls frequently help with the harvest of crops, especially during cornhusking.

Although varying degrees of cooperation are present between the husband and wife in the fulfillment of their roles, the Amish generally adhere to the biblical tradition in which the husband is in direct charge over both his wife and children. Male and female roles clearly are differentiated and the woman's place is perhaps best typified by the biblical admonition: "The head of the woman is the man."

Divorce is non-existent and no written or unwritten provisions exist for securing either divorce or a separation. Marriage is supported by kinship and religious sanction. As mentioned previously, Amish couples do not reveal any overt signs of affection for one another. And, although procreation may be upper-most in their minds, it is the opinion of the writer that Amish couples permit themselves to enjoy sex.

Most Amish couples have several children and realize that as they grow older the children will care for them. The older one becomes, the wiser one becomes. The Amish never use nursing homes; it's nice to grow old. The youngest son brings his bride to his parents farm upon his marriage. At this time, a second residence is built for the parents, often adjacent— grossdawdy haus. The old folks get the new homes in the Amish community! The management of the farm is then turned over to the son and the parents retire. Relationships between the two families are cordial, and even the mother-in-law/daughter-in-law relationship, which is so troublesome for other cultures with patriarchal family customs, appears amicable.

ABOUT CHILDREN AND GROWING UP

Amish couples do not practice birth control of any type and pray for children. It is indeed a happy occasion when a child is born to Amish parents. A new baby is showered with love and neighbors come from miles around for sees koffee— "sweet coffee." "Sweet coffee" is the custom of visiting and eating at the home of the proud Amish parents. Neighbors provide the food. There are no Godfather ceremonies nor gifts.

The birth of a child is a welcomed event in the Amish community. A baby means another corn husker, another cow-milker, but, most of all, another God-fearing Amishman. The birth is always seen as a blessing of the Lord. Thus, Amish parents feel that their children really don't belong to them; they belong to God.

Few Amish couples are without offspring. Families usually range from eight to ten children; two Amish families in my former community had sixteen children. My Old Order sister has fifteen. Couples without children almost always adopt, often from outsiders.

People marvel at the attention, the love, and the affection given to the newborn Amish infant. Even when asleep the baby will be in someone's arms. For the first several months of life he/she will be held constantly by some member of the family. The baby goes where the parents go, even to the fields to work and also will attend the long and tiresome church services when just a few weeks old.

The Amish baby is a pleasure, a gift from God and is too precious to be left in a nursery or with a baby sitter. A baby is an integral part of the family from the moment of birth.

They may spoil babies, but Amish parents seldom refer to an infant as being spoiled. Infants can do no wrong; they remain blameless. If they have adjustment problems, the parents and community erred.

As previously mentioned, an Amish baby receives much attention and affection. For example, an Amish baby is always

56

diapered on someone's lap, usually the mother's or an older sister's. Amish parents do not read books on child rearing and do not stick to strict time schedules; if babies cry, something is wrong and if hungry, they are fed regardless of the hour.

Food from the table is shared with the baby at a very early age. It is not unusual to see a four month old baby being fed mashed potatoes directly from the table while sitting in the mother's lap. Eating time is an important time and activity for an Amish family. They feel that one always eats better in a group. Eating is a family affair which includes the new baby.

To others the Amish mother may appear to be hiding her infant from the eyes of the world when in public as the baby is entirely covered with a blanket. An Amish woman always wears a black shawl over her shoulders, and a mother carefully tucks the baby away under her shawl, often making the child unnoticeable to the public. The Amish child is to be protected, even at an early age, from the "world."

Every Amish baby, if physically possible, is breast fed. No turmoil ever occurs concerning whether to breast feed or not. It is simply the only thing to do. Breasts are not viewed as sex symbols and nursing may occur whenever Amish are gathered socially, in church, and so forth. Breast feeding is done without any apparent shame, but never in the presence of an outsider.

The new baby sleeps with the parents for the first few months of life. Along with the security this practice affords, it also is convenient for breast feeding and provides warmth in the poorly heated homes. Psychologically, this practice may contribute more to the Amish youths' apparent security than any other factor. It is difficult to pinpoint the age at which weaning occurs, but usually around age two.

Toilet training usually begins around age two with no apparent harshness or anxiety attached to the endeavor. As previously stated, Amish babies are held constantly, and of course, in the absence of rubber pants (which are considered "worldly") they often leave their "mark" on the holder's lap. Although this may draw a snicker from an "outside" observer, the wet spot warrants no attention or concern from the Amish people present. In the absence of modern, closed-in bathrooms, waste containers for human elimination are evident in all Amish bedrooms. To the Amish, human elimination is simply a natural activity and thus toilet training is facilitated by the process of imitation and observation. This activity should not be construed to mean that there is no privacy; however, much less concern over privacy is associated with toilet activity than in the "outsider" culture. Bedroom doors are not fitted with locks.

Amish parents believe that one of their basic duties is to transmit the Amish cultural heritage to their children. They are not alone in this high priority activity as the total Amish community is highly involved in the rearing of all its participants.

ABOUT AMISH ORIGIN

The Amish sect was born out of the religious turmoil of the Anabaptist movement in 16th Century Europe. To say the least, the sect's emergence was turbulent.

The Anabaptist refused to baptize their offspring before the age of reason and also refused to bear arms. They were a unique group during that time in history. They were not directly involved in the fierce fighting (in the name of religion) that surrounded them and were in total disagreement and disfavor with the Catholics, Martin Luther, and the whole Reformed movement. The Anabaptists yearned to return to a primitive, earlier brand of Christianity. To bring back this primitive Christianity, the Anabaptists literally accepted the Bible as their dictate. They made it clear to both Church and State that they would stop taking oaths, would not baptize their offspring before the age of reason, would not drink, and would never again pick up a sword. Further, this return to primitive religion brought the wrath of the Reformers, the Catholics, and several Protestant groups upon the Anabaptists. The Anabaptists were denounced as being heretics and were subjected to the death penalty when caught.

Despite much suffering and death, the Anabaptists prevailed. They migrated throughout Europe in their attempts to avoid persecution. Mennonites were in Holland and North Germany, the Hutterian Brethren in Moravia, and the Swiss Brethren in Switzerland.

In the early 1600's a division occurred among the above mentioned Mennonite Anabaptists in Holland. In 1632 Mennonite ministers from several different areas in Europe met in Holland in an attempt to heal this breach within their church. Menno Simon, a former Catholic priest, was the leader of the Anabaptists in Holland and his followers became known as "Mennists." The name "Mennonite" was later applied to them. The rift came about regarding the practice of shunning, or *Meidung*; total avoidance, both physically and spiritually of the excommunicated member. The ruling bishop of the Mennonite group did not enforce shunning. A deep split developed within the Church and the leader of the emerging group which enforced the *Meidung* was an aggressive young man named Jacob Amman. Amman, a Swiss Brethern bishop who lived in Canton of Bern, Switzerland, took it upon himself to excommunicate all those Mennonite bishops and ministers not enforcing the *Meidung*. Amman's followers became known as "Amish."

History records that thousands of Amish and members of other Anabaptist sects were martyred for their religious convictions during the 15th and 16th centuries throughout Europe. As mentioned previously, the Anabaptist were especially persecuted for their rejection of infant baptism. Also, their refusal to bear arms was considered treason. *The Martyrs Mirror*, a 1,582-page book found in most Amish homes today, contains a careful account of hundreds of Amish martyrs with details of how they met their deaths. Accounts are recorded of the severing of hands, tongues, ears, and feet plus many eyewitness accounts of drowings, crucifixions, live burial, stake-burnings, and suffocations. These accounts are related over and over again to Amish children by their parents and elders. This past persecution has been an important element in Amish historical memories, has helped to keep alive their present sense of distinctiveness, and has definitely contributed to their group cohesiveness.

One historical event alone, saved the Amish from extinction—William Penn's tour of Europe offering Pennsylvania as a haven from religious persecution. The Amish accepted the invitation to take part in Penn's religious experiment and came to America in the early 1720's and settled in Pennsylvania. No Amish are left in Europe today.

ABOUT THE AMISH AND PROGRESS

. . . Sometimes I wonder what the world is coming to. Everybody in the outsider community seems to be in a hurry when you meet them. I read in the Budget that this is why they have so many heart attacks. They are no longer satisfied with cars and airplanes as they are building rockets to ride in. Will they ever be satisfied? For me the buggy is quick enough . . .
Esther, 7th grade

How long will civilization go along with the Amish? How long can the Amish with their closed society housed within a highly progressive secular society survive? My opinion is that the Amish will survive and maintain their distinctiveness so long as they can keep the figurative wall between themselves and the secular society. Although the Amish are growing in numbers, failure to maintain this wall brought about their disappearance in Europe which could occur in America.

Urbanization is threatening the Amish way of life. This fact is especially so as farming becomes more mechanized and real estate developments increase the price of land. Economic problems of a people committed to a primitive technology, but embedded in a highly technological society with which it must make exchanges across system lines are immeasurable. For example, one of the Amish farmers' largest economic supplements is the selling of fluid milk to the local dairies. However, the new laws and demands of milk inspectors have made it almost impossible for an Amishman to continue to sell milk to these dairies. Indiana recently passed a law drastically lowering the required temperature of milk which would have eliminated the 3000 non-mechanized

Amish milk producers had an interested group not intervened on their behalf. The law was changed to the Amish milker's benefit during 1978.

Many Old Order Amish members have gone along with the new type milk parlors and gasoline engine operated cooling systems, but the notion of milking machines is not compatable with the Amishman's belief in non-conformity. However, the milk buyers no longer wish to buy milk that has been produced by hand. Further, the Amish continually have refused to allow their milk to be picked up on Sunday and dairies require the Amishmen milk seven days a week or not at all. Many more such examples could be cited.

The Amish settlements most threatened by urbanization are those located near metropolitan areas. In central Ohio (Madison County) an Amish community is faced with the spread of urban life from the state capital of Columbus. Many Amish farms are selling for as much as $3,000 per acre. And, if they are close to large metropolitan areas, they often bring up to $5,000 per acre. Amish farmers have always supported one another financially and used to outbid their non-Amish neighbors for land within the settlement. However, the going prices are more than they can afford to pay. Also, more and more farm auctions are being held on Sunday to eliminate the sabbath-keeping Amish bidder. Thus, many Amish people have found themselves dividing their acreage into much smaller plots and taking jobs in industry on the side. Others are moving to Central and South America in search of "new lands." As a matter of fact, several Central and South American countries are successfully recruiting the Amish today, offering them inexpensive land, no military inscription, and total religious freedom.

Almost half of the Amish people in Starke County, Ohio, one of the larger Amish settlements in America, have given up farming during the past ten years. Some have maintained a small farm for cattle and pasture to graze their driving horses while turning to traditionally approved occupations of masonry and carpentry. However, many are now pursuing work in church-approved factories, which in the past were strictly taboo, while many other families are moving to other states and/or to Central or South America.

I'm confident that factory work, in time, will erode many of the values the Amish have so long treasured. Industrial work is a departure from tradition made necessary by the changing economy. Factory hours are shorter and pay checks are higher but factory work is especially detrimental to the Amish farm family organization. Also, joining the Union is strictly forbidden by the Amish church. Recently a group of Amishmen lost their factory jobs in Ohio because of the closed-shop situation in that state. Some Amish churches that recently permitted factory work have now reversed that decision. And, many outsider factory owners are perplexed when, because of a new rule made on Sunday, not one of their hard-working Amishmen shows up for work the following Monday morning.

In the past the Amish farmer has had a lower overhead than his non-Amish neighbor simply because he used horses and had more "hands" around to help. The horse drawn equipment used to cost much less than the mechanical type. However, with inflation and scarcity, this type of equipment is increasing in price everyday. Also, an Amish farmer never accepts a subsidy of any type from the government. And, observing his outsider neighbor accepting government subsidy for not growing a particular crop, for example, is personally stressful and difficult to understand.

Not only has urbanization and progress brought about a change for many Amishmen, but also it is changing the lifestyles of many Amish females. A few young men always have been leaving the Amish church for the more liberal Mennonite way of life or even to "join" an outsider church, but now some young women are following suit. In the past, a woman leaving the Amish church was unheard of. Why this sudden shift? Most Amish elders blame it on "working out" in modern outsiders' homes. When young women work as maids for another Amish family they earn between $15 to $20 per week. However, they learn quickly that they can earn the same amount in one day by doing housework in town for outsiders. Also, some young Amish women, much to the disdain of the elders, are taking jobs in factories. However, many Amish women are still keeping with tradition—my mother recently, at age 80, gave up her job as maid among the outsiders.

America's emphasis on education threatens the Old Order Amish sect's way of life. They teach their young that formal education is worthwhile up to a point, but that too much is unchristian and only for the foolish. If a fear is among Amish parents, it is that of losing their children through too much formal education. The parents yearn for complete jurisdiction over their children's activity and have it everywhere except in the public school classroom.

Against formal education beyond the eighth grade (and sometimes below that level if it requires attending a modern consolidated school), they are especially opposed to the "godless" science, the competitve atmosphere, and the alien teachers found in the modern school. They prefer the old-fashioned one-room school with its limited facilities, since this type is more in keeping with their simple domestic life. The Amish want to train their youth at home in the care and operation of farms and, to them, this requires no more than eight years of reading, writing, and arithmetic. This view has caused tremendous conflict for them because most states require that a child attend school until he/she is at least 16 years of age. To meet this requirement, the Amish initiated a vocational plan of their own for all students beyond the eighth grade not of legal quitting age. The vocational plan came under repeated legal attack by state and local school authorities across the country.

These school battles were fought in communities in Michigan, Ohio, Iowa, Pennsylvania, Kansas, and several other states. In Iowa, in 1966, deputy sheriffs chased Amish children through cornfields in an attempt to bus them to a public school after school officials had demanded that the Amish comply with the state's attendance laws. The jailing of many Amish parents with fines totaling nearly $10,000 had failed to alter their beliefs.

Literally dozens of documented legal encounters could be cited. One of the most publicized took place in Kansas in a 1967 test case. An Amish farmer, convicted for sending his fifteen year old daughter to the sect's vocational school instead of to the local high school, disregarded a centuries-old stricture against litigation and permitted the then recently formed National Committee of Amish Religious Freedom to take his case to the State Supreme Court. By a four to three vote, the Court refused to hear the case. This ruling created a precedent as many subsequent cases were lost as lower courts continuously ruled against the Amish. However, the troublesome predicament ended on May 15, 1972 when the previously mentioned committee won a unanimous U.S. Supreme Court decision exempting the Amish from state laws compelling their children to continue schooling beyond the eighth grade. In essence, the Court indicated that compulsory, formal education beyond the eighth grade would greatly endanger, if not destroy, free exercise of the Amish religious beliefs. The ruling affirmed a 1971 judgment by the Wisconsin Supreme Court. Legal scholars indicate that this case is the first time in the history of America that compulsory education laws have been challenged successfully. In simple terms, the ruling means that the Amish cannot be forced by any state authorities to continue the schooling of their offspring beyond the eighth grade.

Although the school controversy, as summarized previously, was the basic reason for the emigration of several thousand Amish to Central and South America in the late 60's and early 70's, there are currently more eminent ones. Impingement, persecution, and harrassment come from several different sources. Local, state, and national legislators often pass new laws without the consent, knowledge, or consideration of different minority groups. A case in point was a law passed in Indiana requiring a triangular shaped reflectorized emblem to be affixed to the back of all slow-moving vehicles. The Amish viewed this three-cornered emblem as a hex symbol, or "the mark of the beast" as described in the Bible and refused to affix it to their buggies (contrary to popular belief the Amish do not affix HEX signs to their barns!). They further felt that the gaudy emblem would glorify man rather than God. The Amish offered to use neutral color reflector tape in an attempt to compromise but failed and several served 20 days in jail. Finally a compromise was reached. The Indiana Amish farmers placed in local jails for following their religious scruples never raised their voices and served their jail sentences without any apparent feelings of animosity.

In general, Americans seem to feel that social security is a good idea. However, it has caused immeasurable problems

64

for the Amish who view it as a form of insurance which is religiously taboo. Many an Amish farmer lost good cattle and horses confiscated by the Internal Revenue men during the middle sixties for failure to pay social security even though they would never collect one cent. Many documented stories are told about this problem. When the IRS men came to an Amish farm to confiscate livestock, the non-aggressive Amish would unselfishly assist them in choosing the livestock they felt would best make up for their lack of paying social security. They were extremely kind to the IRS men and local newspapers carried stories about them being taken to the house, given coffee, fed, and in one case they loaded the livestock and went fishing with the Amishman in the farm pond. Other news accounts reveal how the government men left (with the confiscated livestock) with tears in their eyes. However, unlike many other controversies involving the Amish, this one has a happy ending—President Johnson attached a rider to the Medicare Bill exempting all Amish farmers from paying social security.

One of the Amish counties being most threatened by urbanization and progress today is Lancaster County, Pennsylvania, the county first offered as a sanctuary to the Amish by William Penn. Civilization is refusing to go along with the Amish in this county and many are leaving it. Lancaster County is the Amish heartland. The more than 12,000 Amish in this beautiful area of Pennsylvania are the target of more than 3,000,000 tourists per year. The tourists go through the county's back roads in tour buses or sometimes rent buggies and are a nuisance to the Amish. Several Amish have written me about this problem telling of the tourists' rudeness. Recently a scribe wrote to the *Budget*, the weekly Amish newspaper, describing how a busload of tourists trampled his garden in pursuit of a glimpse of him and his family as they worked in the garden.

Traveling through Lancaster County, Pennsylvania, one finds an endless string of supposedly Amish motels, Amish food, Amish restaurants, Amish gift shops, Amish museums, Amish amusement parks, and so forth. This exploitation of the Amish is growing at an alarming pace. A Lancaster County newspaper indicated recently that the director of the tourist bureau stated that tourism in this one Amish community was now a 100 million dollar a year business!

In the winter time, one can travel through Lancaster County, going through such tiny Amish villages as Paradise and Intercourse, which have been left undisturbed for a 100 years. One sees the horse and buggy driving Amish, water wheels, windmills, and other sights reminiscent of 100 years ago. But, in the summer time the mood changes to a carnival atmosphere as bumper to bumper traffic and billboards indicate that "it's real—it's genuine, you're here. Visit the house and farm occupied by the German-speaking Amish, stop and talk to these genuine Amish people." Their inquisitiveness has become a nuisance to Amish who strive to avoid publicity as well as photographs which are strictly forbidden by the church.

> . . . the tourists often bother us. They have camera's
> and we don't want pictures. The other night dad was
> milking and the man kept trying to take dad's picture.
> He kept hiding his face . . . Esther, 5th grade.

Tourism in Lancaster began only some 14 years ago, but is now a bonanza for the owners. They succeeded well beyond their wildest dreams and today Pennsylvania Dutch county is the seventh largest tourist attraction in the United States. As many as 10,000 visitors a day in season swarm down over the Amish back roads. Tourists seldom ask permission to take pictures. They snap pictures from their car windows and burst uninvited into the easily accessible, quaint, inviting Old Order school houses.

> . . . I don't know what the tourists want at school.
> They just want to look at us maybe. I wish they would
> leave us alone . . . Esther, 5th grade.

Tourism offers no monetary benefits to the Amish by their own choice. They are not in the selling business, nor the hotel and motel business. One of the most damaging aspects of tourism is that Lancaster County has now been "discovered" and recently married Amish farmers cannot find land to purchase. People who are benefiting the most from the Amish leaving the farms are the local industry owners. Amish men have been groomed to awake at 4:00 AM and work is a moral directive whether on the farm or in a factory. They make excellent factory workers, but, as previously mentioned, usually unhappy ones.

Most material written about the Amish, although often filled with myths, is favorable. But, frequently an unfavorable article is written. In July, 1979, the *TV Guide* contained an editorial type article titled "The Amish Hadn't Changed Much Since 1693—And Then Came TV" in which the author wrote some damaging untruths, that is, that volumptuous Amish maidens flirt with the young men of the city while at the market, that Amish men relish TV shows with half-clothed girls, are girl-crazy, and have low morals. He also further exploited the myth that Amish fathers paint their barnyard gate blue when a daughter reaches marriageable age. A cartoon, accompanying the article, depicted an Old Order Amish man admonishing the cow he was milking to be quiet as he secretly watched a TV hidden under a blanket in the corner of his barn.

The total effects that America's progress has on a people such as the Amish who are committed to a primitive technology in the midst of a modern world bent on secularization are difficult to measure. However, the Amish are a tenacious people and are intent on maintaining their way of life since the family and closeness to one another is everything to the peaceful Amish. With such ties they have survived for over 300 years. Now, the land offered them as a haven from religious persecution is causing them difficulty with refraining from becoming "modern man."

ABOUT COUNSELING THE OLD ORDER AMISH CHILD[3]

What role does public education play in the threat to the Amish way of life? In the past, most Amish communities were content to send their children to the local public elementary schools and approximately 10,000 still attend today. However, the emphasis on science and evolution, the apparent increase of violence and drug usage, and educational TV have contributed to a sudden increase in the number of Amish parochial elementary schools.

---

[3] Parts of this section are from "Counseling the Old Order Amish Child" by J. Wittmer and A. Moser, *Elementary School Guidance and Counseling*, 1974, *8* (4), 263-271. Reprinted by permission.

Public school personnel who come into daily contact with Amish children can lessen the Amish people's perceived threat. This lessening of threat is especially so with elementary school counselors, since many varied methods or approaches can be used effectively when working with these "peculiar" children. Some common counselor functions, however, might be ineffective with Amish children.

Rebecca is a young child who attends a public elementary school. In her broken English, she says, "It makes me wonder why outsider kids make fun when a movie is on by the teacher and we make quick to leave the room."

Amos, a young boy attending the same school and who, like Rebecca, speaks German as a first language, also wonders about his relationships at school. "The Englisher boys are mad with me for not pledging the flag. Dad says a graven image it is. Why do they hit me, already?"

And Elam, another child in the same school, says, "The coach he says that shorts I must wear next PE class. What should I tell him, yet?"

How would you respond to these children? Would you tell little Rebecca that she might enjoy the movie if she stayed in the room? Would you suggest that Amos should be patriotic and join in the pledge of allegiance? And Elam? Would you tell him that he should put on the PE shorts because physical education is good for his health? Would you respond differently if you knew that these children are Amish and that pledging allegiance to the flag, attending any type of movie, and wearing shorts are contrary to their religious beliefs?

Are Amish children different from other non-Amish children? Because the Amish are suspicious of "outsider" investigations, very few studies have been completed concerning their personalities, but of the few available studies, all but one have Amish children. The research indicates that Amish youth are significantly more introverted and submissive than non-Amish youth (Engle, 1945; Engle & Engle, 1943; Hostetler & Huntington, 1972; Lembright & Yamamota, 1965; Loomis & Jantzen, 1962; Smith, 1958; Stuffle, 1955). These studies also describe the Amish personality as being quiet, responsible, and conscientious. The first and only research concerning the personality of Amish adults (Wittmer, 1970) suggested that the adult Amish personality parallels that of Amish elementary school children.

An uniqueness exists about the Amish personality which is unlike any other American group. Its elements are common to all members of the sect. This model personality or psychic unity among the Amish people is largely due to common childhood experiences and child-rearing practices.

Hostetler and Huntington (1972) administered the Myers-Briggs Type Indicator (Myers, 1962) to 251 Amish elementary children. Further evidence of homogeneity was found when more than 60 percent of the total Amish population fell within two personality types: (ISFJ) Introversion, sensing, feeling, judgement, and (ESFJ) extraversion, sensing, feeling, judgment. One of the most interesting findings in the Hostetler—Huntington (1972) study dealt with the "happy time drawings" of Amish children. Amish and non-Amish children exhibited striking differences in their happy time drawings. The Amish drawings always included work-related activities, whereas non-Amish drawings frequently showed competitive activity and some hostility; neither of these factors was found in any of the Amish drawings. Further, the drawings revealed that regulation and conformity, rather than spontaneity, were dominant Amish characteristics. One important finding for teachers and counselors was the de-emphasis of the self and the person and the importance of the group. The family, the church, and the community are seen as having more significance than the individual.

About the Effective Counselor

The counselor who is effective with Amish children will be genuine and empathic, but also will follow the guidelines presented.

De-emphasize the concept of self. The Amish child is taught to be cooperative rather than competitive, innovative, or aggressive. To the Amish, a child is not a unique individual. He/she is simply one member of a God-fearing group and should be treated as such. Individual resolution is undesirable. Humility is a virtue, and pride, especially self-pride, is a cardinal sin. Amish children do not show pride in dress or appearance (no mirrors are in the home) or self-accomplishments (e.g., they never recite memorized prayers aloud as this would show pride in one's ability to memorize). Yet, Amish children, like other children, have basic psychological and developmental needs. They desire to be wanted, to be needed, and to gain acceptance from peers and authority figures. If Rebecca however seems aloof to your praise for a task well done, don't confuse her reactions with indifference. Her reactions most likely coincide with her culture's sanctioned behavior.

Amish youth seek academic achievement and most teachers report that Amish children are good students. This fact may appear contrary to denial of self-accomplishment. However, work is a moral directive within the culture. The Amish child works hard in school and achieves, but he/she does not talk about these accomplishments and does not expect praise for doing those things expected of him/her. For example, when an Amish boy does an excellent job of cleaning the barn, his father simply states, "The barn is now clean."

Any attempt on the part of educators to introduce competitive activities in order to achieve educational goals could only mean, in Amish terms, the loss of humility, simple living, and God's love!

Recognize the limitations of tests. Can you imagine the frustration of taking a test that requires you to identify a gas tank correctly being removed from a car, a well-known cartoon character, or a particular control dial on an electrical appliance when you've never seen them before? Amos, for example, sees school as a bewildering environment, and most of his experiences there are new. The Amish child will most likely never have heard of the Jackson Five, Sesame Street, or the Miami Dolphins. When using the school's restroom for the first time, he/she will not understand how a commode functions. For Amos, it is likely to be a perplexing experience.

Speed is rarely stressed in the Amish culture and children are admonished by their elders to do careful, accurate work. Amish children are told to work steadily and to do well what one does, rather than do a great deal and make careless mistakes. Children are taught never to skip anything that they do not understand. They are to ponder it, to work at it, until they have mastered it. Thus, a teacher or counselor who administers a speed test to an Amish child could increase unnecessary psychological stress and fail to gain a true picture of the child's skill.

Amish children are at a disadvantage when taking any standardized test, especially if they are being compared to non-Amish children. The Amish see no purpose in formal schooling beyond the elementary grades. Performing well on a standarized test in order to gain a better job or enter high school or college has no special meaning and is useless as a motivational scheme. In addition, testing is often taboo within an Amish community, and educators should seek the consent of Amish parents before administering any test. Educators also will find that Amish parents are not interested in knowing their children's achievement test scores or a comparison of their child's scores with those of other children in the United States, or for that matter, even in the classroom.

Understand culturally different groups varied "worlds of work." The world of work of Amish children is rather limited. Both children and parents are uninterested in career exploration. The vocational preferences of Amish children, for example, tend toward service occupations and manual work. These children emulate the work roles of Amish adults and want to be farmers or farmers' wives. Studies reveal (Hostetler & Huntington, 1972) that Amish boys prefer farming or farm related work, whereas girls prefer housekeeping, gardening, cooking, cleaning, and caring for children. These vocational aspirations and dreams are realistic and attainable within the limits of Amish culture. One should note that the feminist movement has not brought about any changes in the Amish life style. The Amish interpret the King James Bible literally, especially those sections concerning the submissive role of women.

71

Respect the need for social distance that Amish children have with non-Amish children. A very real concern among Amish parents today is the possibility that their child will form close, personal friendships with non-Amish children and become too comfortable with the ways of the "outside world" before they totally understand their own Amishness. Any attempt on the counselor's part to have Amish children form friendships (such as mixed group counseling) with non-Amish children will be contrary to the wishes of Amish parents.

Avoid probing into home or Amish community problems. Because institutions such as the home and the church are held in high esteem, Amish children enjoy participation within these institutions. The possibility of bringing shame on their family will inhibit talking about family or cultural problems. For example, even though an Amish child may be overwrought concerning an excommunicated family member, it would be even more shameful to discuss it with a non-Amish person.

Realize that a caring relationship is not enough. Affective understanding alone is not sufficient when counseling Amish children. The effective counselor also will be knowledgeable of the customs, traditions, and the values existing in the Amish child's unique environment. The acute disparities in culture will most certainly be compounded if a counselor lacks knowledge and then interacts with a confused and bewildered Amish student.

Accept the fact that an Amish child's parents may have asked him/her to avoid counselors. Amish parents are responsible for training their children and are morally accountable to God for doing it correctly. Thus, your counseling or talking with them concerning values or morals may appear disrespectful and even belittling to an Amish parent. If the home is responsible and obligated for moral and religious training, then you may appear as a meddler.

In summary, to be an effective counselor with an Amish child in a public school setting you will need to learn about the values and ways of the Amish culture. It often will be necessary to keep your own cultural biases in check. Be

72

genuine and empathic. Don't bend the child to match the curriculum. Let the curriculum meet the Amish child's needs.

The Amish are only one distinct religious minority group found in public schools. They are easily recognized, but other such groups are not. Mennonites, Hutterites, Christian Scientists, and many other groups may, in appearance, blend into a school's population. But their values, beliefs, and attitudes, like those of the Amish, play a significant part in attitudes toward school and the way in which they learn.

POST TEST

Directions: After reading the chapter, complete the following items.

1. According to recent research, Amish children are:
____a. more introverted and submissive than non-Amish.
____b. similar in personality to Amish adults.
____c. quiet, responsible, and conscientious.
____d. all of the above.

2. Research reveals the Amish personality to be:
____a. very individualistic.
____b. homogeneous.
____c. feeling oriented.
____d. similar to the general population.

3. Research has revealed:
____a. a de-emphasis of self among the Amish.
____b. the importance of the group.
____c. a de-emphasis in the person as an individual.
____d. all of the above.

4. Praise, among the Amish, is:
____a. not a sanctioned behavior.
____b. sanctioned for individuals only.
____c. sanctioned for the group only.
____d. never sanctioned.

5. When using standardized tests with Amish children, school personnel should recognize that:
____a. performing well on a standardized test is very important to the Amish student.
____b. Amish parents are not highly interested in the test's results.
____c. Speed is important to them.
____d. Amish are not disadvantaged when taking standardized tests.

6. Amish parents tend to view school counseling as:
_____a. meddling.
_____b. disrespectful to them as parents.
_____c. unimportant.
_____d. all of the above.

T F 7. Research reveals that Amish children's happy time drawings always include work-related activities.

T F 8. Spontaneity is a common Amish characteristic.

T F 9. The Amish child is taught cooperation at the expense of competition.

T F 10. Individual resolution is highly desirable among the Amish.

T F 11. Amish children, in general, are good students.

T F 12. Amish children readily enter into competitive activities in school settings.

T F 13. The vocational preferences of Amish children tend toward service occupations and manual work.

T F 14. Amish parents encourage the children to strike up friendships with non-Amish.

T F 15. Amish children readily discuss community problems with non-Amish adults.

T F 16. Among the Amish, humility is a virtue while self-pride is viewed as sin.

T F 17. Amish parents are not opposed to their offspring "dressing" for physical education activities.

Scoring Guide for Post Test

1. d	5. d	9. T	13. T	17. F
2. b	6. d	10. F	14. F	
3. d	7. T	11. T	15. F	
4. c	8. F	12. F	16. T	

Reference List

Bracht, J.V. *Martyr's mirror*. Scottdale, Pa: Mennonite Publishing House, 1938.

Engle, T.L. Personality adjustments of children belonging to two minority groups. *Journal of Educational Psychology*, 1945, *36*, 543-560.

Engle, T.L., & Engle, E. Attitude differences between Amish and non-Amish children attending the same schools. *Journal of Educational Psychology*, 1943, *34*, 206-214.

Hostetler, J., & Huntington, G. *Children in Amish society*. New York: Holt, Rinehart & Winston, 1972.

Lembright, M.L., & Yamamoto, K. Subcultures and creative thinking: An exploratory comparison between Amish and urban American school children. *Merrill-Palmer Quarterly of Behavior Development*, 1965, *2*, 49-64.

Loomis, C., & Jantzen, C. Boundary maintenance vs. systematic linkage in school integration: The case of the Amish in the United States. *Journal of Pakistan Academy of Rural Development*, 1962, 59-83.

Myers, I. *The Myers Briggs type indicator*. Princeton, N.J.: Educational Testing Service, 1962.

Smith, E.L. Personality differences between Amish and non-Amish children. *Rural Sociology*, 1958, *23*, 371-376.

Stuffle, C.R. A comparison of the adjustment of Amish and non-Amish children in Van Buren Township Schools. Unpublished master's thesis, Indiana State Teachers College, Terre Haute, 1955.

Wittmer, J. Homogeneity of personality characteristics: A comparison between Old Order Amish and non-Amish. *American Anthropologist*, 1970, *72*, 1063-1068.

Wittmer, J. Good guys wear white hats. *Liberty*, 1972, *67*, 12-17.

Wittmer, J., & Moser, A. Counseling the Old Order Amish child. *Elementary School Guidance & Counseling*, 1974, *8*, 263-271.

4

Same Sex Preference

Joseph L. Norton, Ph.D.

Professor of Education
State University of New York
Albany, New York

Joseph L. Norton, Ph.D.

Joseph L. Norton, a Professor of Education at the State University of New York at Albany, has been a counselor and counselor educator since 1949. He has been active in the New York State Personnel and Guidance Association, serving as President 1970-71, and has served in governance of the American Personnel and Guidance Association and the SUNY State-wide Faculty Senate. He founded the National Caucus of Gay and Lesbian Counselors, and has served on the steering committee of the Association of Gay Psychologists. Co-founder of the Gay, Lesbian, and Bisexual Interest Group of the American Association of Sex Educators, Counselors, and Therapists, he has transferred much of his efforts in sex education and work with professional groups to the support of gay counseling and gay liberation.

SAME SEX PREFERENCE

Joseph L. Norton

AWARENESS INDEX

Directions: Mark each item true or false. Compute your score from the scoring guide at the end of this awareness index. A post test is provided at the end of this chapter.

T F   1. Most male homosexuals want to be females.

T F   2. Most male homosexuals get sexual excitation from wearing women's clothes.

T F   3. Lesbians have not been studied with real research efforts.

T F   4. Lesbians are a lower proportion of the population than are male homosexuals.

T F   5. The gay male is to be found in all male occupations, not just hairdressing, theater, and interior decorating.

T F   6. Homosexuals engage in child molestation more (proportionately) than heterosexuals.

T F   7. Homosexuals have seldom been subjected to blackmail.

T F   8. The gay militant is highly susceptible to blackmail.

T F   9. Those with homosexual and lesbian behaviors are easily changed by therapy to heterosexual behaviors.

T F   10. Male hormones make homosexual men more active homosexually.

Scoring Guide for Awareness Index

1. F	4. T	7. F	10. T
2. F	5. T	8. F	
3. T	6. F	9. F	

FOUR CASES

Three young men came to this counselor's office last month. John was a tall, "All American boy," who had decided he was gay. He had told his mother, who accepted it openly, but John had little notion of how to go about meeting other gays. He felt he was gay because he fantasized about males while having sex with his girlfriend. He also had talked with her some about his inclinations toward males, but had never had the "typical adolescent homosexual experiences," and had never had gay sex. He sought ways to get to know other gays.

Joe was less attractive physically, a bit overweight, and, like John, a college student. He had been having sex with males for three years, had a lover with whom he was having some hassles, and also was bothered about how to tell his parents if at all, and still have their support through his last year of college and graduate school. Unlike John, Joe had *told* no one he had homosexual feelings (except those with whom he had sex), but had found his way into the gay scene through overhearing gossip of his (presumed) non-gay acquaintances who mentioned a gay bar.

Jim's was another situation. Somewhat older, late 20's, Jim was married and had a two-year old son. His work as a salesman took him on the road a lot, and through a chance out-of-town acquaintance he discovered that he enjoyed sex with men as much, maybe more, than with his wife. But he did not want to lose his son, whom he loves dearly. He did not want to lose his wife, nor hurt her, but he found himself increasingly seeking out gay locales on his travels. He had found a gay guide book which contained information so Jim could find gays easily in a new city. Jim wondered if he is likely to bring VD, now called STD (sexually transmitted diseases), home to his wife, and whether he can or should continue to keep his gay leanings from his wife.

A fourth young man did *not* come to the counselor. Knowing he was gay from the earliest teens, he fought the feelings and married early to prove he was "straight." Three children later, he found himself increasingly turned off sexually by his wife, and finally turned again to clandestine, impersonal homosexual contacts in the local bus station and so forth. Caught by the police, he was unable to face the public humiliation he felt and took his own life. The latter is a true report. However, there *have* been happy endings even for this exact situation wherein there is divorce followed by continued happy contacts with children.

These cases are, as in using any illustrative cases, only four of hundreds who brought, or should have brought, problems to the counselor. For every John, Jim, and Joe, there are myriad variations, some of whose stories have ended up in print and will help the counselor get a broader picture of the needs of lesbians and gay men. Lesbians are noticeably missing from these cases, reinforcing the finding that they are often not even thought of when the words "homosexual" and "gay" are used. Actually, Jane did come for counseling: 46, having trouble both with her lover and her small private business, she sought both vocational and relationship counseling. Her lesbianism was not the problem, but she needed to see someone who would not make it the problem.

One of these problems is, in a sense, insoluble: Jim can hardly avoid hurting *someone* sooner or later, either himself or someone else. So decisions can sometimes only be about how to lessen the hurt, or how long to postpone it, or how best to balance counselee's needs with others' needs.

Different counselors will find these people varying in difficulty, dependent on their own attitude and knowledge. Is the counselor's first reaction "Certainly John is the best off, the easiest to help," or "I wonder if I can help John enjoy women more?" Is the first inclination to refer John and Joe and Jim *all* to the local psychiatrist to see if they can be "cured"? Such a response flies in the face of current research. It would be easier to find out about the local gay scene to help John find his way than it would be to resolve whether Joe's dad really is homophobic enough to cut off his son's support, or to facilitate a decision in Jim's stand off of "hide unhappiness in the closet" versus "come out in the open so as to be free to be my true self." And Jane's problem is a long-term one of improving relationships as well as resolving financial problems.

DEFINITIONS

Varying definitions of homosexuality are presented (Kennedy, 1977; West, 1977). The simplest is "one who has an affectional and sexual preference for a person of the same sex." This definition seems simple but, is an individual with *no* same-sex experiences but regular fantasies, homosexual to all counselors? Or do some opt for the requirement that two people of the same sex set as a mutual goal getting each other to climax? Enough males respond sexually to pressure on the genitals, or to other external stimulation that it almost seems as if *intent* should be part of the definition. And evidence clearly shows that a single or a few homosexual acts do not necessarily make one a homosexual. In fact, it has been noted that persons with similar sexual histories may label themselves heterosexual, homosexual, or bisexual depending on environmental factors (Blumenstein & Schwartz, 1977).

As Father Paul Shanley states, a homosexual act neither defines nor causes a person's sexual orientation. Many youth have same-sex experiences and grow to be adult heterosexuals; yet for many this experience is not "just a phase," and the orientation persists for life. Although for some, extensive behavior leaves no doubt as to the label, for others it seems to have to be a matter of self-definition. Yet, that very self-labeling has been devastating to hordes of youth

82

in the past. In this chapter, homosexuality means having a strong affectional or erotic attraction to members of the same sex.

One can question if a label, noun or adjective, should be used at all, as one's sexuality is not the only aspect of life. Perhaps it is best only to talk of homosexual behavior, including imagery as behavior. Perhaps some day society can acknowledge simply that humans are sexual beings who can develop a wide range of related behaviors, depending on a myriad of complex factors. But whatever the terminology, the homosexual person generally does develop a homosexual identity. Many males who have identified themselves as homosexuals use the term "gay" as a self-chosen, non-clinical term; most homosexual females prefer to be called "lesbians" rather than the other labels which, as used, tend to ignore the female. The term "gay," not involving "a feigned happiness in spite of it all," came out of the theatre; the gays say it in preference to the outsiders' terms: homo, faggot, dyke, queer, pansy.

Use of the term "same-sex orientation," might be best because the word "preference" used previously implies to some a *choice*. The vast majority of lesbians and gay males simply "found themselves" or "discovered" they were wishing for love and affection from members of their own gender. They did not choose to be gay or lesbian; the only choice was whether to act in accord with their own feelings.

Another problem in definition stems from the fact of in-creasingly visible bisexuals, who respond sexually and affectionally to both genders. Although some gay males have never been able to respond to women, the majority have had successful heterosexual experiences, thus dispelling the myth that all gay males hate women and have a revulsion toward the female genitals. Many lesbians are mothers, and many gays are fathers.

DIFFERENCES

Identifying differences between homosexuals and the population in general, is helpful as these differences are not usually visible. One ironic difference is that members of the gay and lesbian population can be members of any of the other populations discussed in this book. For example, gays also can be disabled, black, hispanic or handicapped, all of whom are doubly special since counselors must not think of heterosexuality alone as the norm for their clientele, although one can note that sexuality itself has been pretty much ignored for the retarded and the disabled in general until just recently.

The most crucial difference, which really defines the population, is that gays and lesbians feel a strong affection and/or sexual attraction toward people of the same gender. As indicated, most *discover* their feelings. Some counselees are distressed at the discovery, while some find the problem is not the homosexuality but, as with Jane, other matters. For others, the problem is the hassles society imposes on one with this orientation.

Another often crucial difference, is that a lesbian or gay male does not have or at least fears the lack of the family support. While most blacks have the "black is beautiful" atmosphere, many gays and lesbians are very fearful. If your counselee watched parents chortling with glee when Anita Bryant won in Dade County, that counselee is unlikely to turn to those parents for support.

One more difference is that the homosexual *can* hide. This population is an invisible minority, and many have fought their societally labeled "affliction" all alone for years with some even taking it to the grave.

NUMBERS

With such amorphous definitions and with a condition readily kept invisible, one finds difficulty in giving precise figures on the gay and lesbian population. Kinsey's old figures of 37 percent of males and 33 percent of females having had a climax with another of the same sex after the age of 18, and 8 percent having a primarily homosexual life for a period of three years stand unchallenged. These data show fewer homosexual females than males. Estimates of 4 to 10 percent of the U.S. population, i.e., 20,000,000 Americans, have general support. Considering that each gay male and lesbian has 1 or 2 parents, often siblings, and frequently children, some 50,000,000 Americans or more have intimate contact with homosexuality. Yet this topic has been virtually ignored in all of the counselor education programs of the country.

FURTHER DESCRIPTION OF THE POPULATION

Altogether generalizing about the gay and lesbian population is difficult. Lesbians have been virtually invisible in the research as well as fewer in actual numbers, and studies of gay men are spotty. However, these studies have been sometimes surprising. One study by Saghir and Robins (1973) showed that gay men had heterosexual experiences earlier than a comparison group of heterosexual men. No actual research shows gays to be more creative, but they have been shown to be more intelligent (Bonnell, 1976). More recently, Riddle and Morin (1977) reported the average ages when selected events occurred in the lives of 63 lesbian and 138 gay male psychologists. These selected events and the average ages for the lesbians and gay males, respectively, were as follows: aware of homosexual feelings—14, 13; first same-sex sexual experience—20, 15; understood the term "homosexual" —16, 17; first homosexual relationships—23, 22; considered self homosexual—23, 21; disclosed identity to parent—30, 28; and disclosed identity professionally—32, 31. Interesting to note is that in the area of awareness of homosexual feelings, males were a year ahead of females, although women usually mature two years ahead of men. Males were active sexually five years ahead of females. Either gay males mature earlier than men in general, as suggested by Tripp (1975), or there simply is more of a gap for the women between puberty and awareness of lesbian feelings.

Except for their sexuality and how this may affect them in a hostile society, the gay and lesbian populations seem to differ little from the heterosexual world.

85

CURRENT PROBLEMS

The question of how lesbians and gays are being treated in schools has one main answer: they are being ignored. Yet, if they are open or happen to be part of the visible, so-called "effeminate" or "butch" groups, they are reviled. One gay was forced to take classes with females only (because he wanted to be one? (the myth) or because he was no threat to them?), and to eat lunch alone for a year. "Faggot" is still the favorite put-down word from fifth grade up. If one is non-gay, such peer put-down can be handled as is any other, but for the gay it is likely to arouse the fearful unspoken response, "Does he really know?" Clearly the school's sex education of youth is not being very helpful in overcoming hostility if local young men scream "faggot" out of the school bus window at the writer, as has happened. Coaches brag of heterosexual success but malign the same-sex successes of others. And counselors can still be heard telling and laughing at "faggot jokes." Not as many counselors refuse to put up with the anti-gay jokes as reject the anti-semitic ones.

Probably the best generalization is that counselors are mostly uncomfortable with the topic since the school population is rather hostile. One can hope that the first response to a youngster who comes in to talk about sexual orientation is not, "Well, I'll have to call your father so he can take you to a psychiatrist." While some counselors are "pretty cool" about homosexuality, many are still misled by the myths and truly believe the following falsehoods:

1. gays want to be of the opposite gender

2. gay men are primarily hair dressers, antique dealers, and interior decorators

3. all gays are promiscuous

4. homosexual males are weak, introspective, and inactive physically

5. removing laws against homosexuality will increase its frequency

6. gays hate those of the opposite sex

7. gays are a menace to children

8. just give a gay male some male hormones and he will want women.

Special counseling may be needed to dispel the myths that tend to limit the lesbian or gay male. For instance, the stereotype is that gay men are effeminate. Brown (1976), Kopay and Young (1977), and many others say they "knew" they could not be homosexual, despite their strong affectional and sexual attraction to other males, because they did not swish, flip their wrists and cross dress like the few visible gays they saw. Actually, most transvestites (cross dressers) are heterosexual. Only 10 to 20 percent of gay males are "drag queens," and considerably fewer lesbians dress like men to an extent that would distinguish them from heterosexual women. Also, the fact is that many lesbians are very dainty and feminine, quite unlike the "bull dyke" stereotype.

Another misconception is that gays and lesbians want to be of the opposite sex. It is ironic that another myth listed previously is just the opposite, that gays and lesbians *hate* the opposite sex; how can we have such contradictory generalizations? People who wish to be of the opposite sex are properly called transsexuals. Lesbians and gay men are delighted to be the gender they are, but just love others of the same gender and prefer them as sex partners.

Anita Bryant's "Save the Children" campaign has finally and clearly brought out the facts, much to her consternation: gay men do not molest children even in proportion to their numbers. Child molestation is primarily a heterosexual phenomenon with a couple of notorious mass murderers notwithstanding; one of them may have been homophobic since it involved killing young men who would sell themselves to men for money. Gay teachers do not molest their students; the *New York Times* estimated there are 120,000 to 240,000 gay teachers in the U.S. (Macroff, 1977). Although the New York City school system has numerous records of heterosexual child molestation, no recorded incident exists of homosexual child molestation despite a membership of over 200 in the Gay

Teachers Association. Further research on role modeling does not support Bryant's fear that gays and lesbians, either as parent or other role models, would create gay and lesbian children (Kirkpatrick, Roy, & Smith, 1976; Riddle, 1978). And an up-front role model would have made life much easier for Brown (1976), Kopay (1977), and others.

Another falsehood is that lesbian and gay couples take on "husband and wife" roles. While this arrangement may have occurred in the past, present day couples "just don't do those things" (Jay & Young, 1979; Oberstone & Sukoneck, 1976).

Besides being faced with these stereotypes and myths, gay males and lesbians bring other orientation-related problems to the counselor. For instance, the fear of a lonesome old age is a specter held up before gay males, who also are indoctrinated that the gay male subculture is totally youth oriented. In fact, many older gays have lovers or a circle of friends for companionship or sex. While some older homosexual males have accepted this much-repeated stereotype, others find it inappropriate (Kelly, 1977). Some research reports that the gay male who is already isolated from his family is *better* able to cope with the isolation of old age (Francher & Henkin, 1973).

As pointed out in John's case, some gays need help in finding others of like mind, which is where the counselor can help. Inquiring of the local gay liberation group will provide the counselor with a person or two to contact to introduce the counselee to "the gay scene." Unfortunately, for too many years the gay or lesbian bar was the only meeting place, but now gay alliances are on many college campuses, in community groups and community centers, and in several church groups: Dignity (Catholic), Integrity (Episcopalian), and the Metropolitan Community Church, a primarily gay and lesbian church which has grown in just a few years to over 100 congregations and 30 affiliated groups. The Unitarian Universalist Association has an Office of Gay Concerns in denominational headquarters in Boston. Counselors can acquire or help their counselees acquire published guides to gay and lesbian groups and meeting places. John incidentally has made such contacts and is moving along through college.

Some newly self-recognizing gays need help in realizing that not all gays fall in love the instant they meet another gay of the same sex. There is discrimination, pickiness, and selectivity in the homosexual as well as the heterosexual world. Neither gay life nor gay sex is necessarily more idyllic than heterosexual life or sex; it is just that for gay men and lesbians, gay lifestyles are better, more satisfying, and more fulfilling.

While fewer come to counseling these days with "I'm afraid I'm homosexual," that still is a question for some. How does one know he or she is gay or lesbian? A good counselor query is "What makes you think you might be?" As indicated in the discussion of definitions, being gay or lesbian is mostly a matter of feeling; a few homosexual acts do not make one a gay or lesbian although apparently for the lesbians, many do not act until they are sure of the feeling or identity. It is the fantasy, the affection as *well* as the sexual attraction. If the person masturbates, any fantasy at that time can give clues. A review of the person's whole developing sexuality may still not give a clear answer, in which case keeping all options open seems advisable.

How did I get this way? Most of the research into this question seems to have been done with an eye to preventing this "sickness" in others. For someone presently same-sex oriented the question seems superfluous. Yet many still ask and the answer has to be that no one knows. All the experts currently agree that it is impossible to tell: hormonal influences; family influences, environmental, or genetic; childhood sexual experiences. Any or all of these influences may be involved. Some know from earliest memories that they are different from their peers while others do not recognize their orientation until after years of heterosexual marriage.

Can I get over it? This question has no absolute answer, although most generally the answer is "no." Most counselors concede the easiest help is to make a person content with the same-sex orientation, but some psychoanalysts, behavior therapists, and Aesthetic Realists claim "cures." Much criticism from militant gays indicates that these "cures" make clients asexual, not heterosexual. Some behavior therapists now question if it is proper to try to cure, even if asked to do so (Davison, 1976), but others forge ahead with their aversion therapy (Adams & Sturgis, 1977). *Most* lesbians and gay males are happy with themselves and their lives, and do not want to change, even though some at first had wanted to change. Some therapists report 20 to 50 percent success in changing those with a strong motivation *to* change (Marmor, 1976; Masters & Johnson, 1979). Yet counselors should remember that such motivation is the result of an oppressive society, which formerly resulted in cliterectomies for women who thought it bad to feel sexual. Male hormones make gay men more active with men; it does not turn them to women.

One point counselors should make very clear to anyone who seems to have a same-sex orientation is that a heterosexual marriage does *not* create a "cure." It is dishonest to enter into a heterosexual relationship expecting it will "cure," although this is another myth held by many non-gays. Unfortunately, what is often heard is "All you need is a good—the right—man (or woman, for the male) and you'll get over your lesbian feelings." Jim is a case in point; what heterosexual responsiveness he had died out before long. Actually, some wives are relieved to learn a husband is gay, as it relieves them of guilt—they had thought themselves to blame for a poor sex life and marriage (Gochros, 1978). But the notion that gays and lesbians do not marry heterosexually is wrong; one estimate is that 50 percent of gays and lesbians are heterosexually married. Although many couples are monogamous, in no state in the United States may two same-sexed people be legally married to each other.

Should I "come out" to others? Researchers say "Yes," but counselors need to counsel about, rather than give answer to this question. That is, the open gay or lesbian has been found to be better adjusted than the "closeted" one, and even better adjusted than some non-gays (Freedman, 1975). Understandably so, because the open gay has overcome the avoidance of changing pronouns when talking about the weekend, of having no picture of one's lover on the desk, and of other dissimulations. The open gay can be her/his true self.

Yet circumstances vary. Joe's father might refuse to pay his tuition. Both sides of the question of "coming out" to family and other non-gays need to be explored. How likely is it

90

to slip out accidentally, or to be discovered from some other source? If Joe decides it is unwise to tell, and has managed his double life without pain, what counselor wants to override his decision? Many parents *must* actually know but appear to want not to bring it out in the open. Yet resources are available for one to use with one's parents such as Silverstein (1977), Hutchinson (1977), Clark (1977), and Fairchild and Hayward (1979). Many an upset, disappointed, fearful, or hostile parent has been won over with patience, by reading relevant materials, or by a loved one's lover. And, too, there are the *not* apocryphal stories of the parents who respond, "How nice, so am I." But some gay fathers feel guilty that they "caused" a son's orientation, although research does not support such an anxiety.

Sometimes openness leads to hassles from a hostile society: a swishy gay beat up at a local shopping center, "fag" painted on a garage door, urine poured under a dorm room door. More often, openness is met with a shrug: "I couldn't care less;" sometimes with "I'm glad you shared this with me, it makes us closer." With such a range of responses, it is difficult to know what to do. But counselors can be somewhat supportive and reassuring that more gays and lesbians than not, say "They really were more understanding and accepting than I expected."

Will I be blackmailed? In the past this happened more often than one would like. This benefit is one of gay liberation, for the openly gay or lesbian individual is not subject to such threats. But the left-over idea that all homosexuals have to hide from society does still let some disreputable people prey on others more readily than might happen in the non-gay world, e.g., theft after sex. Although this problem is a minor part of the gay world and almost unheard of in the lesbian, it is one thing in the gay world about which the gay males might benefit from some warning.

Pair bonding or no? Since most gay males and lesbians have been brought up at first with heterosexual expectations, most also have absorbed society's dictate of pair-bonding in monogamous relationships. But without the strictures of a legal marriage, many gays find it easy to stray from monogamy. Whether to stick with heterosexual patterns or venture into freer patterns of relationships and sex is a problem often facing this population. Research shows this decision is less of a problem for lesbians. Most of them are at least serially monogamous (Peplau, Cochran, Rook, & Padesky, 1978; Peplau, Rubin, & Hill, 1977). Obviously, no one has to be promiscuous, but there is no denying the opportunity is easier for gay males than for the rest of society. Some gay male couples are monogamous for thirty years or more, but the higher incidence of STD's in the gay male population attests to a fairly extensive exchanging of partners for many.

How to combat societally dictated sex roles is an issue for some of this population especially for the women. Lesbians defy society by asserting they will not be dependent on a male for life and some of them by opting out of motherhood. Such defiance of sex role stereotypes creates some hazards for women. Gay males who are "macho" fit externally in to the expected sex role, but internally their affectional and sexual needs are met quite differently from those of most men. Because most hostility seems to come from those with very narrow stereotypes of what it is to be a man or a woman and from those with rigid attitudes about sex, some counselees may need help in sticking with their own feelings instead of letting the world dictate to them.

All of these current problems confronting the gay and lesbian population are related to the counseling needs of this group, and for some of these problems counseling approaches have been suggested. The next section discusses some further counseling needs.

FURTHER PERSONAL COUNSELING NEEDS

As indicated, one relatively unique problem faced by this group is the possibility of remaining invisible. One can "suffer in silence," as was pointed out, and "carry this burden," never fully expressing one's self, always hiding, always having to lie to cover up. Many have lived their entire lives hating themselves. As discussed previously, the counselor cannot tell the counselee what to do, but can discuss the pros and cons of coming out, helping the client weigh the alternatives. Three helpful pamphlets are by DeBaugh (1978), National Gay Task Force (1978), and Mombello (1977), all with the same phrase in the title: *Coming Out.*

Another somewhat unique problem faced by this group in contrast to other special populations is lack of security, even in the family. As mentioned previously, black children are not rejected by parents because they are black, although some disabled children *are* rejected for their status, but then the parents feel guilty. More parents who reject gay or lesbian children appear to be self-righteous than to be feeling guilty.

Most personal problems concerned with relationships, loneliness, bashfulness, and so forth are much the same as those of heterosexuals. Unrequited love is unrequited love; yet, falling in love with a straight roommate does pose special problems as most heterosexuals are not as closely exposed to their non-responding loved-one.

Because of the hostility of some of society, special counseling on the legal aspects of living may be needed. Bernstein (1977) points out the need for clear and undisputable contracts on joint ownership, wills, and so forth, that will stand up to hostile family reaction should one of a couple die.

CAREER NEEDS

As a group, homosexuals are as disparate as hetero-sexuals. Unlike the myth, gays and lesbians are in all occupations and all walks of life although proportionately they number greater among the college educated. The gay caucuses in many professions attest to this variety: the American Psychiatric Association, American Psychological Association, American Personnel and Guidance Association, American Nurses Association, Modern Language Association, National Council of Teachers of English, American Association of Sex Educators, Counselors and Therapists, American Public Health Association, Social Workers, Lawyers, and New York City's Gay Teachers Association. Thus, career counseling needs should not differ much from those of the heterosexual client.

Important factors to consider when making career choices, some of which have been pointed out by Canon (1973) and Norton (1976) are the following:

1. Probably a large city is the best location for most.

2. Students should not put school or college gay alliance activity on a vita (although failure to do this was the final reason the court accepted for the removal of one teacher from his post).

3. Be reasonably discreet.

4. Make use of the National Gay Task Force's list of industries which state they do not discriminate against gays (National Gay Task Force, 1977). It may still be wise to use this as reassurance to the lesbian or gay male, not to encourage the counselee to ask for affirmative action!

5. While in the past a gay personnel manager has sometimes been harder on open gays than a non-gay since it threatened his own exposure, nowadays some business gays are looking for like-minded personnel. A recent issue of a gay bi-weekly listed 26 openings (*The Advocate*, 1979).

SOCIETY'S UNDERSTANDING

The youth who reported that friends and family "really are more understanding than I expected" may well reflect the state of American society today. Yet, one cannot forget the high school students in Tucson who went downtown to "beat up a queer" and killed a visitor from out of state, but were back on the Student Council within six months. Over half of the population, when polled, say they are for civil rights of homosexuals, although only in Seattle has a majority voted to retain such civil rights. Lesbians are still pretty much ignored —an invisible group, except when their child custody rights are challenged. And decisions are beginning to come in favor of the lesbian mother. Support for civil rights comes from many church groups, including the National Council of

Bishops of the Roman Catholic Church and the Central Conference of the American Rabbis of the Reform Movement in Judaism. But not many groups actually condone same-sex behavior and orientation. While the majority seem to favor a "live and let live" policy, seemingly the majority do not understand and accept same-sex orientation (Leo, 1979). And a vocal minority actively oppose it.

HOMOPHOBIA

A term used by George Weinberg (1972), Homophobia, is the state of excessive fear of contact with homosexuals. Since most people with Homophobia do not view it as a disease, counselors usually will not counsel such counselees. Occasionally, a gay or lesbian counselee will get her/his Homophobic parent(s) to come in for counseling. Should the latter happen, hopefully the counselor will respond as did one psychiatrist who asked the parents in after talking with their gay son and said, "You have the problem, not him." But counselors should know that negative attitudes toward homosexuals are functional in the dynamics of maintaining traditional sex roles, and fear of being labeled homosexual keeps both men and women within the confines of what society has traditionally defined as sex-role appropriate behavior (Morin & Garfinkle, 1978).

HISTORY OF SERVICES TO GAYS

The history of services to gays and lesbians has been one of oppression: at first just punishment, then of treatment to "cure" the "illness." Such treatment has included isolation, incarceration, psychoanalysis, aversive therapy, electric shock, lobotomies, and even castration. Many a youth was forced into an insane asylum by parents hostile to same-sex orientation. Not until 1974 did the American Psychiatric Association remove homosexuality from its list of illnesses, leaving in "sexual orientation dysphoria" for those unhappy with being lesbian or gay.

95

Laws have forbidden homosexual acts throughout the United States, although since 1971 some 22 states have decriminalized sex between consenting adults. But in 28 states the law still invades the bedroom and labels 10 percent of the population as criminal. The history of court decisions until recently has been one of either direct punishment or at least of depriving gay males and lesbians of their children, often depriving them of visiting rights—at least if the gay or lesbian had a partner in the home. A reversal has begun, and the American Psychological Association has taken the position that affectional and sexual orientation should not be the primary consideration in determining child custody. Despite this stand, four years later Garfinkle and Morin (1978) found that therapists rate the "same" hypothetical client differently when the client is homosexual rather than heterosexual, the former being rated less healthy.

Change in some of the 22 states and in some public and professional attitudes has followed a surge of gay liberation sparked by the drag queens who refused to be docile any longer during a routine raid in 1969 of a bar, the Stonewall, on Christopher Street in New York City. Quiet efforts at reform have been progressing since the 1850's (Lauritsen & Thorstad, 1974), and quiet acceptance exists in some areas such as San Francisco, a comfortable home for many. But after 1969 the Gay Liberation Front, the Gay Activists Alliance, Street Transvestites Action Revolutionaries (STAR), and then gay and lesbian campus groups rapidly got started. Annual parades to celebrate the Stonewall riot have in nine years spread to major cities throughout America. Some 40 communities passed gay civil rights ordinances and, as mentioned previously, professional associations developed caucuses which pressed education about gay and lesbian issues on their colleagues.

Opposition to gay groups has been most associated with Anita Bryant and her conservative forces, who brought about the rescinding of civil rights for gays in Dade County, Florida; Topeka, St. Paul, and Eugene, Oregon, then followed. Boulder, Colorado already had voted to rescind its civil rights for gays without help from Bryant. These events were followed by a proposal from Senator Briggs in California that any teacher supporting homosexuality be immediately subject to a hearing and dismissal; the proposition got on the California ballot.

However, many varied groups, working together in Coalitions Against The Briggs Initiative (CABI's) waged a successful campaign against this frightening invasion of privacy. Even Governor Reagan came out in opposition to the proposition.

The same day as the balloting in California a well organized campaign *against* a referendum to repeal the gay civil rights statute in Seattle defeated a poorly organized campaign for the referendum. Thus the "steam roller" towards gay rights repeal was halted finally. Such votes however do not reflect for many a real approval of homosexuality, but only an affirmation of the civil rights regardless of sexual orientation and the affirmation of the right to privacy (Leo, 1979). Sodomy repeal is still lacking in 28 states, so that the organizations of lesbians and gays in coalition with many other groups have much to do.

At local, state, and national levels, organizations are at work on the reeducation needed to continue the improved state of lesbians and gay males. The National Gay Task Force (NGTF), in addition to pushing tremendously for the 1974 action of the American Psychiatric Association, has moved the Civil Service Commission, the Peace Corps, the Bureau of Prisons, the IRS, and other governmental agencies to life restrictions on homosexuals. This Task Force also publishes support packets for gay parents, sodomy repeal, and gay teachers, and has published a book, *Our Right to Love*, to help end lesbian invisibility. The Task Force has worked to promote gender parity in all of its activities. The Gay Rights National Lobby is seeking civil rights legislation through Congress.

Interesting to note is that some cultures have not *needed* gay liberation. In those countries, homosexuality did not lead to the decline of the civilization nor to the decline in world population. The Biblical injunctions are now seen as inveighing against idolatry and selfishness, against religious practices of other sects (McNeill, 1976). An interesting speculation is why homosexuality was ignored so much in America, apparently with the hope it would go away. Because of the public militancy, there can be some decrease in the many attestations to the loneliness, the feeling "I am the only person in the world who feels this way." How could ten percent of the population be so invisible?

Counselors should be aware however that just because progress has been made does not mean that all professionals have been won over by the education of their gay militant members. Noteworthy is that the American Psychiatric Association decision to declassify homosexuality as a disease was opposed by some members; enough signatures were collected to require a vote, and one third of the members voting still felt that homosexuality should be retained on the list. This thinking is not surprising when one realizes that most of the early writing on the subject was based on homosexuals who came into treatment and that a very gloomy picture of the condition was the only one available. Not until Hooker's 1957 study did the first data on well-adjusted homosexuals appear, and only in 1969 did her National Institute for Mental Health study committee recommend nomenclature changes and legalizing consensual homosexuality. Counselors who feel they must make a referral should recall that one third of the APA voted against "curing by referendum," and should make sure they know of the orientation of anyone to whom counselees are referred. The number of castrations, lobotomies, and incarcerations in mental hospitals is decreasing with the efforts of gay militants and others. Some aversive therapy still is used, although as indicated previously, a former head of the Association of Behavior Therapists has raised the question if such therapy should be used even for those who ask to be "cured" (Davison, 1976). Would we still perform cliterectomies on request of a woman taught by her parents that it is improper for a female to have sexual feelings, as was done in the past century?

THE HELPING PROFESSIONAL'S ROLE

Because most counselors were reared in our heterosexually oriented society, the vast majority have absorbed the misinformation and myths about, and some even the hostility towards, lesbians and gay men. The first responsibility is for counselors to reeducate themselves. The quickest way is by meeting and talking with same-sex oriented people, to discover that they are people, not devils. Reading can take the place of personal meetings where such meetings cannot be arranged and can supplement such meetings as do occur. *Our Right to Love* (Vida, 1978), *The Homosexual Matrix*

(Tripp, 1975) and *Loving Someone Gay* (Clark, 1977) would be a good beginning. Three books written for parents of gays could help (Fairchild, & Hayward, 1979; Hutchinson, 1977; Silverstein, 1977), as well as three pamphlets on coming out written for young people (DeBaugh, 1978; Mombello, 1977; NGTF, 1978). Once counselors have confronted any personal hostility, doubts, or uncertainties about homosexuality so as to be better able to keep personal values out of counseling as much as possible, they can go ahead and counsel with the gay male or lesbian just as they would with anyone else. Gays and lesbians have relationship problems, financial problems, motivational problems; not all go to a counselor because they are gay. They go because they are gays or lesbians with a problem. Actually, many avoid personal problem counseling just because they are afraid of the reaction they will get. Many have gone to counselors with another problem, but the counselor had made being gay or lesbian the problem.

Counselors have the responsibility to let it be known that they will listen to gays and lesbians as well as to non-gays. They can reject anti-gay jokes; they can put articles about Gay Civil Rights or gay leaders on bulletin boards or in school papers; they can make clear that they have discarded, if they ever had, the stereotypes about gay males being "effeminate" and lesbians, "butch."

Once the gay or lesbian is in the office, library, or wherever counselors counsel, the responsibility is to counsel as well as possible, keeping in mind the myths and the hostilities the counselee may have incorporated into her or his self-concept or met in the world outside. As with any counseling situation, generating a feeling of acceptance and understanding is crucial, and can be genuine if the counselor has rid her/himself of the myths. Correcting misperceptions, giving appropriate reassurance, evaluating pros and cons of coming out—all regular counseling activities will come into play with working with lesbians and gay males.

Specific suggestions have been scattered throughout the discussion of special problems of this population. Yet the counselor cannot expect to have answers to all problems. Jim's dilemma has a variety of possibilities. Some wives are relieved to find that the absences do not mean another

99

woman, and accommodate to give some free time for their husband. More are horrified at the disclosure (Gochros, 1978), and insist on divorce, often fighting even visitation rights with the children. Some heterosexual husbands are happy to be rid of both the lesbian wife and the children, and go off to seek greener pastures. Others can accept a wife's outside interests with equanimity. Some gay husbands feel they *have* to lead a double life (Miller, 1978) and continue to have "illicit sex on the side." Some handle this well, others with great guilt. As mentioned, some wives feel so relieved that they are not the cause of the marital problem that, although upset, they can move quickly to making rational decisions about the future. But knowledge of others' behavior does not solve Jim's problem, and only he alone can decide. Exploration of all his needs is crucial, as is true of all counseling. And this can be done only in a warm, permissive, non-judgmental situation. A well-informed, self-aware counselor is what all lesbians and gay males need.

POST TEST

Directions: After reading the chapter, mark each item true or false.

T F 1. You can be sure a person is not a lesbian or gay male if the person is legally married.

T F 2. Lesbians may be married to each other legally in at least 5 states in the U.S.

T F 3. Evidence shows that open lesbians and male homosexuals are as well-adjusted as non-gays.

T F 4. Job discrimination against lesbians and gay males is a thing of the past.

T F 5. The civil rights of gays have never been taken away by law or by popular vote.

T F 6. Most homosexuals have a choice of being "straight" or gay.

T F 7. Most transsexuals *and* transvestites are heterosexual.

100

T F   8. Venereal disease is less of a problem for gay males than heterosexuals.

T F   9. Indicating on job applications work with a local gay alliance is a good way to show you are a productive person.

T F 10. Gays and lesbians moving to a new city can easily find "the gay scene" by buying a guide to gay bars, baths, and groups.

Scoring Guide for Post Test

1. F	4. F	7. T	10. T
2. F	5. F	8. F	
3. T	6. F	9. F	

Reference List

The Advocate, 1979, March 22 Issue, 1730 South Amphlett, Suite 225, San Mateo, CA 94402.

Adams, E., & Sturgis, T. Status of behavioral reorientation techniques in the modification of homosexuality: A review. *Psychological Bulletin,* 1977 *84* (6), 1121-1188.

Bernstein, B.E. Legal and social interface in counseling homosexual clients. *Social Casework,* 1977, *58* (1), 36-40.

Blumenstein, F.W., & Schwartz, P. Bisexuality: Some social psychological issues. *Journal of Social Issues,* 1977, *33* (2), 30-45.

Bonnel, C. Heterosexuality, an enlightened view. *Christopher Street,* 1976, *1,* 26-27.

Brown, H. *Familiar faces, hidden lives: The story of homosexual men in America today.* New York: Harcourt, Brace, Jovanovitch, 1976.

Canon, H.J. Gay students. *Vocational Guidance Quarterly,* 1973.

Clark, D. *Loving someone gay.* Millbrae, CA: Celestial Arts, 1977.

Davison, G.C. Homosexuality: The ethical challenge. *Journal of Consulting Clinical Psychology,* 1976, *44,* 157-162.

De Baugh, A. *Coming out!* Washington, D.C.: Universal Fellowship of Metropolitan Community Churches, 1978.

Fairchild, B., & Hayward, N. *Now that you know.* New York: Harcourt, Brace, Jovanovitch, 1979.

Francher, S., & Henkin, J. The menopausal queen: Adjustment to aging and the male homosexual. *American Journal of Orthopsychiatry,* 1973, *43* (4), 670-4.

Freedman, M. Homosexuals may be healthier than straights. *Psychology Today,* 1975, *8* (10), 28-32.

101

Garfinkle, E.M., & Morin, S.F. Psychotherapists' attitudes toward homosexual psychotherapy clients. *Journal of Social Issues*, 1978, *34* (3), 101-112.

Gochros, H.L. Counseling gay husbands. *Journal of Sex Education and Therapy*, 1978, *3* (2), 6-10.

Hooker, E. The adjustment of the male overt homosexual. *Journal of Projective Techniques*, 1957, *21*, 18-31.

Hutchinson, B. *Now what?* Miami, FL: The Center for Dialog of Dade County, Inc., 1977.

Jay, K., & Young, A. *The gay report*. New York: Simon & Shuster, 1979.

Kelly, J. The aging male homosexual: Myth and reality. *The Gerontologist* 1977, *17* (4), 329-332.

Kennedy, E. *Sexual counseling*. New York: Seabury Press, 1977.

Kirkpatrick, M., Roy, R., & Smith, K. A new look at lesbian mothers. *Human Behavior*, August 1976, 60-61.

Kopay, D., & Young, P.D. *The David Kopay story*. New York: Arbor House, 1977.

Lauritsen, J., & Thorstad, D. *The early homosexual rights movement*. Albion, Ca: Times Change, 1974.

Leo, J. Homosexuality: Tolerance vs approval. *Time*. 1979, *113* (2), 48-51.

Macroff, G.J. Should professional homosexuals be permitted to teach? *New York Times*, June 24, 1977.

Marmor, J. Homosexuality and sexual orientation disturbance. In B.J. Saddock, H.I. Kaplan, & A.M. Freedman, (Eds.), *The sexual experience*. Baltimore: The Williams and Wilkins Company, 1976.

Martin, D., & Lyon, P. *Lesbian/Woman*. New York: Bantam Press, 1972.

Masters, W., & Johnson, V. *Homosexuality in perspective*. Boston: Little Brown & Co., 1979.

McNeill, J.J. *The church and the homosexual*. Mission, KS: Sheed Andrews and McMeel, Inc., 1976.

Miller, B. Adult sexual resocialization: Adjustments toward a stigmatized identity. *Alternate Lifestyles*, 1978, *1* (2), 207-234.

Mombello, R. *To come out, an alternative for the young male homosexual*. Laguna Beach, CA: Author, 1977.

Morin, S.F., & Garfinkle, E.M. Male homophobia. *Journal of Social Issues*. 1978, *34* (1), 29-47.

National Gay Task Force. *Corporate survey results*. New York: Author, 1977.

National Gay Task Force. *About coming out*. New York: Author, 1978.

National Institute of Mental Health. *Report of commission on homosexuality*. Washington, D.C., Author, 1969.

Norton, J.L. The homosexual and counseling. *Personnel and Guidance Journal*, 1976, *54*, 374-377.

Oberstone, A.K., & Sukoneck, H. Psychological adjustment and life style of single lesbian and single heterosexual women. *Psychology of Women Quarterly*, 1976, *1* (2), 172-188.

Peplau, L.A., Cochran, S., Rook, K., & Padesky, C. Loving women: Attachment and autonomy of lesbian relationships. *Journal of Social Issues*, 1978, *34* (3), 7-27.

Peplau, L.A., Rubin, Z., & Hill, C.T. Sexual intimacy in dating couple. *Journal of Social Issues*, 1977, *33* (2), 86-109.

Riddle, D.I. Relating to children: Gays as role models. *Journal of Social Issues*, 1978, *34* (3), 38-58.

Riddle, D.I., & Morin, S.F. Removing the stigma: Data from individuals. *APA Monitor*, November 1977, pp. 16; 28.

Saghir, M.T., & Robins, E. *Male and female homosexuality: A comprehensive investigation*. Baltimore: Williams and Wilkins, 1973.

Silverstein, C. *A family matter*. New York: McGraw Hill, 1977.

Tripp, C.A. *The homosexual matrix*. New York: McGraw Hill, 1975.

Vida, G. (Ed.). *Our right to love: A lesbian resource book*. New York: Prentice-Hall, 1978.

Weinberg, G. *Society and the healthy homosexual*. New York: Anchor/Double Day, 1972.

West, D.J. *Homosexuality re-examined*. Minneapolis: University of Minnesota Press, 1977.

5

Indian American: The Reservation Client

Marilyn Jemison Anderson, B.A.

Human Services Administrator
Seneca Nation Health Department
Cattaraugus Reservation
Seneca Nation of Indians
Irving, New York

and

Robert H. Ellis, Ph.D.

Assistant Professor of Educational Psychology
Department of Secondary Education
and Educational Foundations
State University of New York
College at Fredonia
Fredonia, New York

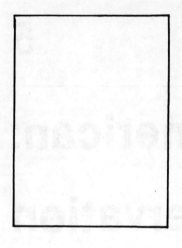

No photographs are included because Seneca Tribal culture would be violated with such an individualistic portrayal.

Marilyn Jemison Anderson, B.A.

Marilyn Anderson is currently the Human Services Administrator of the Seneca Nation Health Department, which includes Social Services, Mental Health and Substance Abuse, Community Outreach, and Medical Transportation. She has been actively involved in the delivery of health services on the Cattaraugus Reservation, where she lives with her husband and two children, since 1973. Mrs. Anderson received her Bachelor's Degree in Sociology from D'Youville College, Buffalo, in 1969. At present, Mrs. Anderson is Editor of Si Wong Geh, the Reservation Newsletter. She is on the Advisory Board for a number of local mental health institutions and she is on the Advisory Board to the National Indian Food and Nutrition Resource Center. In 1974, Mrs. Anderson was named an outstanding young woman of America from New York State.

Robert H. Ellis, Ph.D.

Bob Ellis is currently an Assistant Professor of Educational Psychology in the Department of Secondary Education and Educational Foundations at the State University of New York, College at Fredonia. He completed a Bachelor's and Master's Degree in Psychology at San Diego State University in California and completed his Ph.D. in Educational Psychology at the University of California, Santa Barbara, in 1974. He worked at Idaho State University for a year on a federal mainstreaming project before moving to western New York with his wife and two daughters in 1975. Dr. Ellis is a licensed psychologist in the State of New York and, besides his interests in the Indian culture, is conducting research in the areas of problem solving, creativity, and synthetic processes of the brain. He is presently Project Director of an NSF Project on Creative Problem Solving in Mathematics and has been funded by the Appalachian Regional Commission to develop a Child Abuse Prevention project for Chautauque County in western New York.

No photographs are included because Seneca Tribal culture would be violated with such an individualistic portrayal.

INDIAN AMERICAN
THE RESERVATION CLIENT

Marilyn Jemison Anderson
and
Robert H. Ellis

AWARENESS INDEX

Directions: These questions are to help you to evaluate your under-
standing of the Indian and Indian culture.
Mark each item as true or false.
Compute your score from the scoring guide at the end of
this awareness index.
A post test is provided at the end of this chapter.

T F 1. The Indian behaves differently from non-Indians because of
the poverty in which the great majority of Indians must
live.

T F 2. The non-Indian counselor is at such a severe disadvantage
when working with Indian clients that the attempt should
not be made.

T F 3. Indians are at a disadvantage because their social consciousness has not yet developed to the point where they
can enjoy the "advantages" of the non-Indian life.

T F 4. Because of their different culture, Indians do not have the
western concepts of right and wrong, truth and falsehood.

T F 5. Relatively more alcoholics are on the reservation than are
in the dominant non-Indian society.

T F   6. The notion of change to an Indian is negative because of its implication that the present order of things is inadequate.

T F   7. An Indian can live off the reservation without compromising any basic cultural values.

T F   8. Because of their sense of tribal integration, an Indian student may cheat on a test when asked to do so by another member of the tribe.

T F   9. Indians are not punctual because they do not respect non-Indian peoples.

T F   10. The Indian culture could be classified as primitive.

T F   11. In terms of perceived confidentiality, a non-Indian counselor has an advantage over Indian counselors when working with Indian clients.

Scoring Guide for Awareness Index

1. F	4. F	7. F	10. F
2. F	5. F	8. T	11. T
3. F	6. T	9. F	

A CASE EXAMPLE

The use of ardent spirits amongst the Indians, and the attempts which have been made to civilize and Christianize them by the white people, has constantly made them worse and worse; increased their vices, and robbed them of many of their virtues; and will ultimately produce their extermination. (Seaver, 1925, p. 48).

Mary Jemison, a white woman, had been living with the Seneca Indians in upstate New York for over 60 years when she wrote the above. Although this description was written more than 150 years ago, it appears as valid today for this group of Indians as it was then. Her remarks eloquently and succinctly illustrate the Indian's two major problems in American society today: the attempt to interpret Indian behavior in terms of cultural norms and expectations not shared by the Indian; and, secondly, the continuing attempt to convert the Indian to a "better" culture.

This chapter offers several suggestions for helpers who might provide counseling services to the Indian client; suggestions that will assist counselors in not committing those errors commonly made and thus losing a client in trouble and damaging the counselor's own credibility as helping professionals.

Too often, non-Indians are admonished to be sensitive to cultural differences when concerned with Indians, but one can look far and wide before finding a list or specific statement of those differences. The usual suggestion is for the individual to go and live among the Indians for a while. But, as many workers in the Bureau of Indian Affairs will attest, mere association is not enough. What is needed is a point of view, a new perspective from which to observe problems. To help you, the reader, to develop that perspective, two areas are discussed:

1. the relationship of the Indian and the tribe with a listing of some of the implications of that relationship that have proven confusing and foreign to most non-Indian observers; and
2. the particular problem of alcohol abuse which is identified quite closely with the Indian, showing how it is not really the same type of problem as alcoholism is in the dominant non-Indian culture.

The point which will be emphasized several times is that counselors who interpret an Indian's problems in terms of understanding the problem among non-Indians may most likely be making a serious error which will be reflected in the counseling effectiveness.

The authors recognize the danger of treading in these extremely sensitive territories, especially because a great diversity exists among tribes and individuals both on and off the reservation. The interests, needs, and culture of the re-

111

servation Indian may vary greatly from those of the urban Indian. A similar difference may be found between Indians living in the eastern, midwestern and western parts of the United States. However, we feel that the difficulties for Indians, in general, that are presently being caused by well-meaning helpers justifies the risk. We ask, therefore, that the following be read in recognition that our comments, based on experiences of Seneca reservation Indians, are offered to heighten awareness and not to be used as a final document.

Several basic points should be recognized and accepted before one begins working with an Indian clientele. The Indian American has a culture, a cultural heritage, and a right to that culture as inalienable as any other basic human right. Accordingly, any discussion or suggestions with regard to assimilation, i.e., the suggestion, implicit or otherwise, that an "inferior" culture be abandoned for a "superior" culture, may be viewed, rightly so, as a direct insult and slur.

Most Indians do not prefer assimilation; they do not want all of the "advantages" of the non-Indian life. For the very same reason, it is critical that the counselor not take the attitude that an Indian's problems are "merely cultural." The themes of "cultural disadvantage" and "cultural poverty" have been popular and widely disseminated in the social services literature and suggest, as noted previously, that one culture is richer than another. Although it may be true that an Indian is having difficulty in resolving expectations based on apparently incompatible cultural values, to suggest that the conflict can be resolved by viewing one of those systems as weaker, especially if it is the Indian culture, is a form of cultural arrogance that should be abandoned.

Indians do have problems and Indians do require help and, like everyone else, they are best served by a helper who considers them and their problems individually and with sensitivity to the context of the problem. No one is helped when a problem is dismissed with a simple label, "Oh, it's just cultural"; nor can the individual be helped when his/her basic values system is dismissed casually.

The point that we would like to make is that the *dynamics* of the problems faced by Indians are no different from those faced by any other human being; i.e., a temporary inability to resolve conflicting pressures in a successful and satisfying way. The difference between Indians and others, however, is in the *kinds* of pressure with which they have to contend given their particular culture and the dominant society in which they live.

Importantly, the human services counselor who intends working with Indians must take at least the following preparatory steps so that his/her training can be used most effectively with Indian clients:

1. *Recognize* that Indians approach life with a different set of expectations, values, and interpretations of events and that their approach can be as satisfying and as rich to them as any other culture is to any other person.
2. *Become familiar* with those cultural values so that one can begin to understand and appreciate the pressures being faced by Indian clients.
3. *Resist* the temptation to interpret a particular behavior or problem as if it were caused by the same kinds of pressures that may cause that problem in a non-Indian middle-class society.
4. *Converse* with Indians with an attitude of respect rather than paternalism.

THE TRIBE

A first step in understanding the Indian's cultural differences is to begin to appreciate that the relationship between the Indian and his/her tribe is different from the relationship between the non-Indian middle-class person and his/her society. The Indian sees himself/herself as an extension of the tribe in the sense that he/she is a part of a whole and the wholeness of the tribe is what gives meaning to the part. For example, a flower petal has little beauty by itself but, when it is put together with the other parts of the flower,

113

the whole, which includes the petal, is a thing of great beauty. This relationship stands in contrast to the non-Indian middle-class position where society operates primarily as a set of rules to promote individual accomplishment. Stated somewhat differently, the tribe provides the meaning and justification of existence for the individual from the Indian's point of view, while the individual provides the justification for society in the non-Indian western perspective. As a consequence, Indians will judge their worth primarily in terms of whether their behavior serves to better the tribe, while the non-Indians will judge their worth in terms of accumulated property and power. While these generalizations are clearly too simple, they do serve to show that the Indian uses a value system that is fundamentally different from that of the dominant culture; basic worth is judged in terms of tribal enhancement and not individual enhancement. On the other hand, the Indian is not against individual accomplishment when it reflects positively on the tribe, such as in craft work or sport. In short, it is a mistake to assume, as so many have, that the concept of tribe for the Indian is synonymous with the concept of society for the non-Indian.

Many pressures exist for the Indian to leave the reservation. At this time, approximately 650,000 of the one million American Indians still live on a reservation or very close to it. Pressures for the Indian to leave the reservation have been as direct as the explicit "termination" policy used during the Eisenhower Administration, for assimilating the Indian and, of course, to acquire the now valuable reservation property by providing social services support only if the Indian left the reservation. The reservation, however, is the physical embodiment of the tribe and to leave the reservation the individual must in a sense reject the tribe. Such a separation, if it is not complete and accompanied by the adoption of an "individual" point of view, for an Indian will be traumatic and leaves the potential for psychological insecurities and conflicts unfamiliar to the great majority of non-Indian human service counselors. In order to leave the reservation, an Indian has to assert his individuality for no supporting tribe exists outside the reservation. Furthermore, to leave the reservation, the Indian will have had to adopt one or more of the values of the non-reservation world and that may lay the groundwork for potential future problems. Conflicts may arise when values

114

from basically incompatible cultures are mixed, and, unless resolved, the resulting anxiety and stress will interfere with the performance of day-to-day tasks, just as it would for any other human being. The counselor who wishes to work successfully with the Indian client must dismiss the notion that Indians have problems because they lack certain cultural values; that is, because they are "culturally deficient" or "culturally disadvantaged." Rather, they have problems when they do for the same reasons that others have problems **plus** they have the added stress many times of trying to live happily and successfully within an incompatible value system.

The counselor will find, then a different set of problems depending on whether he/she works with reservation Indians or non-reservation Indians. The non-reservation Indian may show a much greater variety of problems because of the partial transition to an individual culture, a variety that merges into the typical array of problems found in the dominant culture. For example, alcoholism, per se, seems more common among non-reservation Indians living in urban areas than it is among reservation Indians.

Differences among tribes are enormous as are the differences among individual Indians, a fact that must be recognized by counselors. On the other hand, the authors believe that common sets of values are shared by the great majority of Indians to a varying degree that can be identified and discussed as a family of characteristics without suggesting a stereotyped image of the Indian. Furthermore, the fact that these values are discussed within the context of problems that may bring an Indian into contact with a counselor or human services provider is not meant to suggest that these values are negative or in any way inferior to other values. As a matter of fact, these values contribute to the Indian's problems many times only because helpers fail to recognize that the Indian has a different, yet legitimate, way of approaching the world. The following, then, is an attempt to clarify some of the ramifications of a tribal society without suggesting either that they are shared in the same degree by all Indians or that they reflect negatively on the tribal culture.

115

As can be imagined, the tribal culture places a high value on the harmonious relationship between an individual and his/her peers, i.e., *all* the other members of the tribe. A high value is placed on behavior which advances harmony and cooperation in the tribe; to do otherwise is to assert one's individuality and suggest that one is better than the tribe. To be a member of the tribe, then, means that the individual is honor bound to defer to the wishes of others, to be polite, to be unassertive, and to work hard to prevent discord. Because of this value for promoting harmony almost at the cost of everything else, many counselors have been led to believe that because Indian clients fail to disagree, they must agree with the counselor. Occasionally, nothing could be further from the truth, as the counselor is bound to learn from subsequent behavior, and then the counselor assumes that the Indian lied to him/her.

The tribal culture does not support lying and the Indian is not a liar regardless of myth or stereotype. The Indian, however, will go to great lengths to develop misdirections and ambiguities to avoid having to disagree or contradict another person. To the western point of view, such behavior is viewed as synonymous with telling untruths (lying) because it does not clarify the truth. Of more value to the Indian is the fact that contradiction and disagreement are disharmonious and are to be avoided whenever possible. Furthermore, to disagree with someone is in one sense an assertion of ego and individuality and, for that reason also, the Indian works hard to appear to be in agreement.

As a variation of the same phenomenon, consider the dilemma of the Indian student who is called upon to answer a question in front of the group in a class with other Indian students and a non-Indian teacher. To answer it correctly as an individual would be an act of individuality and superiority while to answer it incorrectly or to stand mute in indecision is to bring humiliation to the individual and to the tribe; a classic no-win situation brought on by the cultural insensitivity of a non-Indian.

By the same token, an Indian student cannot refuse showing his/her test paper to another Indian student from the same tribe when he/she is requested to do so. To do so would be to violate the mutual dependence, cooperation, and politeness held valuable by the tribal culture. To anticipate somewhat, the Indian is put in rather the same dilemma when he/she is asked to have a couple of beers; to refuse would be again an assertion of individuality and a social *faux pas*.

Another deeply misunderstood consequence of the tribal culture is the Indian's apparent disregard for the concept of punctuality, planning for the future, and time in general. The Indian's disregard for time has given rise to the stereotype of the Indian as being shiftless, lazy, and undependable. Time is a fairly recent invention on the part of the western civilization and is necessary only in a culture that values change. If no change occurs, time to measure that change is not needed. Change exists only within the context of time and for a culture that values stability and actively discourages change, as the tribal culture does, time becomes an unimportant consideration. Therefore, no support exists for future plans because such plans would imply that the individual is trying to better himself/herself at the expense of the tribe.

Accordingly, most Indians live in the here and now with little concern for long-term projects that require delayed gratification and sacrifice such as education or vocational training. In a sense, Einstein's conceptualization of time as a relative phenomenon that could be affected by other events is much closer to the Indian's conceptualization than the absolute, quantifiable, and linear conceptualization of the western man in the street. The same holds for the western concept of punctuality: Why would one do something solely for the sake of finishing at a certain point in time? Is not something that is worth doing, worth doing well regardless of how long it takes? In short, when a conflict exists between quality and punctuality, punctuality is sacrificed.

The counselor also must recognize that a tribal culture is inherently resistant to change and very conforming from a western perspective in terms of the social and peer pressure toward conforming to tribal custom and tradition. One way to understand this relationship is to remember that all behavior is evaluated in the here and now and in terms of how it contributes to the present welfare of the tribe. This concept is changing slowly, but long-term plans such as going to college, which also involves leaving the reservation, are seen as acts of egoism and individuality and suggest that the tribe is inadequate and so things must be done differently. In very general terms, to suggest doing something different is to suggest that you as an individual may know more and may be better than the tribe as a whole. This is not to say that tribes do not change, rather that they do not value and promote change as inherently valuable. As noted previously, behavior is evaluated in the here and now and, if it does not contribute to harmony and to the tribe, it most likely will be seen as an act of individuality and egoism and a behavior to be frowned upon and censured. As a consequence, the Indian client is very sensitive to the expectations of the tribal peer group and the counselor must recognize and accommodate those sensitivities in his/her work with an Indian if cooperation and a trusting relationship is to develop.

Another example that may be a helpful introduction to the cultural orientation of the American Indian is to consider the relationship between the Indian and personal wealth as distinct from the relationship between the Indian and tribal wealth. The Indian tends not to cultivate a life style directed toward either conspicuous consumption or the accumulation of personal property. From what has been reported previously, it is easier to begin to visualize and understand why the Indian does not subscribe to those behaviors which are fundamental to the economy of the dominant culture; conspicuous consumption clearly smacks of individual egoism and a means of communicating superior individual worth. The accumulation of personal wealth requires as well both delayed gratification, saving for tomorrow what you could consume today, and active future planning, behaviors that are as foreign to the tribal culture as the cut-throat competition which also is implicit in the struggle to accumulate wealth and power. To the Indian, cut-throat competition between individuals is an alien and destructive process because of its disruption to harmonious relations between individuals, the implication that things can be and need to be made better, and because of its explicit advocacy of individual superiority at the expense of another's inferiority.

These otherwise admirable cultural characteristics have been interpreted negatively by the dominant culture and as a consequence have resulted in prejudice against the Indian. The primary reason that this interpretation has been made, as far as the authors can determine, is because non-Indians tend to assume that the tribal behaviors developed out of an individual-oriented culture. That is, Indian behavior has been and continues to be evaluated in terms of standards held by the evaluator and not by the tribal culture. The consequence is that the tribal behaviors are viewed as manifestations of individual pathology or cultural inferiority. For example, counselors are trained that breakdowns in ego functions are key symptoms of impending mental illness; e.g., schizophrenia. Probably, this interpretation is true for an individual reared within a western culture, but a so-called "weak ego" is normal within the dynamics of a strong tribal system and therefore is not necessarily a symptom of mental illness for members of a tribal system. This interpretation would constitute a major error if a counselor confuses common tribal phenomena, nonassertiveness and disregard for punctuality, with symptoms of western individual pathology such as time disorientation and loss of the concept of "I," because a client with real problems would then receive inappropriate therapy.

ALCOHOL ABUSE

One way to illustrate the problem of evaluating behavior in one culture with standards derived from another culture is to look at the problem of the Indian and alcohol. The point is that the misuse of alcohol may occur in one cultural setting for reasons completely different from the reasons that alcohol would be misused in another culture. Likewise, techniques developed to deal with alcohol abuse for one situation may, more than likely, be inappropriate for dealing with it when it arises within a different cultural context.

Such is the case with the Indian and alcoholism. An alcoholic generally drinks both continuously and in isolation. This type of alcohol abuse generally operates to insulate the drinker from both responsibility and a stressful environment. Anyone's familiarity with alcohol use and abuse among

Indians will demonstrate that such a syndrome is considerably rare among reservation Indians although its incidence increases dramatically as the Indian becomes isolated from the tribe. Rather, the Indian who drinks to the extent that his/her health is put into danger drinks in "binges" and in groups. The Indian does not drink to "get through the day" but rather to have a good time with his tribal brothers.

In developing a treatment program then the counselor should not expect a program designed for non-Indian alcoholics to be useful with the Indian problem drinker; rather, the counselor should begin to look at the personal and social mechanisms which maintain that behavior. For example, drinking and drinking to the point of stupefication and unconsciousness for men is usually not frowned on by the tribe and for some Indians a certain degree of social approval is associated with an ability to tolerate large quantities of beer. The notion that Indians have a lower tolerance for alcohol has never been demonstrated physiologically or psychologically and in fact the opposite may be closer to the truth especially if one has ever attended an Indian beer party.

For the Indian, drinking is often a social event done in groups where it acts as a social facilitator. Many individual Indians are shy and withdrawn as one would expect in a culture where social behavior is such a key component to an individual's determination of self-worth. As a consequence, the Indian may use alcohol to overcome that reticence. Furthermore, the sociability caused by the first several drinks also heightens the sense of tribe and brotherhood, both of which then operate as powerful reinforcers to maintain group drinking behavior. Also, because many Indians feel it is bad form to disagree or contradict another person, it would be socially impossible for them to turn down an offered beer—to do otherwise would disrupt group harmony. Refusal could be viewed as an act of individual autonomy and would most likely be interpreted as one individual saying he/she is better than another.

One also must remember that without a concern for the future and with an orientation more to the here and now, an individual Indian may be unconcerned about some future, long-term consequence that may result from too much drinking. In

120

addition, excessive drinking may not interfere with the Indian's life style if he/she generally does not work at a job where punctuality is paramount so that when the binge is over he/she can return to work with no problems whatsoever. Within that context, it is easy to understand how alcohol abuse and, increasingly, drug abuse can become a widespread health hazard. To deal with it though the counselor must first recognize that it most likely develops within the tribal culture and may be maintained by a context different from western style alcoholism, and that whatever kind of program is developed it must be sensitive to the social context dictated by the Indian's tribal culture.

THE PERSONAL AND CAREER GUIDANCE NEEDS OF THIS SPECIAL POPULATION

Clearly, the American Indian has special personal and career guidance needs. For one thing, many Indians are rarely career oriented because of the necessary long-term planning implied, past oppression by non-Indians, and the fact that, in many areas, few career options are open on or near the reservation. In addition, most careers require some college training which again requires long-term planning and an early off-reservation move. Career planning and/or active planning for a college education also carry overtones of personal betterment and egoism.

These perceptions or biases against personal development are changing but the counselor can help if he/she provides guidance in terms of the tribe and how the tribe will be better able to protect its special values and environment if its members are trained to deal directly with the non-Indian world rather than relying on missionaries and the Bureau of Indian-Affairs (BIA). The career guidance counselor also should be aware that many college-bound re-servation Indian students rarely stay a full month on campus. Their first trip away from their home is shock enough but the alien culture, regardless of the television revolution, and its apparent individual coldness can be too much for the adolescent Indian. What is necessary is that the career

121

guidance counselor make an effort to identify those colleges with a significant Indian population which will provide an environment that is not too alien and hostile.

If one primary career and/or personal guidance need of the reservation Indian exists in either the schools and/or society, it is to feel a part of the tribe. Given that the individual Indian may evaluate his/her own personal worth in terms of how he/she contributes to the tribe, then decisions, suggestions and recommendations must be qualified in terms of how they affect the relationship of the individual to his/her tribe.

The following is a list of what might be described as cultural barriers that must be recognized and accommodated by the helper if he/she is to be effective. Again, these items and characteristics are not universal, they do not characterize all Indians nor do they characterize even the Indians from the same tribe. They do, however, provide a list of cultural differences that should be kept in mind and used to evaluate behavior before they are discarded as being inappropriate for a particular client.

1. The Indian client will most likely be shy, not assertive, passive, and very sensitive to the opinion and attitude of his/her peers.

2. The Indian client may actively avoid disagreement or contradiction and, if allowed, will appear to agree or conform even though he/she has no intention of behaving in that way. Note that the best response in this situation is not to try to outwit your client but ask him/her directly so that he/she has no opportunity to be evasive.

3. Many Indians do not like being singled out and made to perform as in school, especially when peers or Indians from other tribes are present except if it is an athletic competition where the tribe as a whole will benefit.

4. Respect must be earned by the helper. Degrees, experience, reputation carry no weight on the reservation; counselors must demonstrate their respect and sensitivity to the needs of their Indian clients before

122

it will be returned. Given the passivity and non-assertiveness of many Indians, one finds difficulty in knowing when that respect has been earned. One indication may be the care your client takes in preparing for your meeting; the more he/she prepares, e.g., has on neatly cleaned shirt and pants or dress even though others would consider the clothes the type one would wear to work, and has brushed hair, the more he/she respects you.

5. Most Indian clients have little tolerance for long-range planning and delayed gratification. The counselor therefore must not become impatient nor expect a major commitment to a complex treatment plan. Take things one step at a time, demonstrate your own commitment to planning, and emphasize and stress direction at every opportunity.

6. The Indian client may not view time as a linear, ordered process that exists as an objective entity that can be chopped up and organized. Patience is absolutely essential as is the recognition that punctuality is not a highly valued behavior.

7. Property and possessions are most often valued only to the extent that they can be used in the present. Possessions are not used in the sense of reflecting personal worth, as in the concept of conspicuous consumption, nor as a protection against some future calamity.

8. Alcohol plays a positive role in the social functioning of the tribal society and is easily abused because of its social acceptability.

HISTORY OF COUNSELING AND OTHER SERVICES AVAILABLE

Essentially, no counseling services have been available to the Indian client on the reservation and, except for a few rare cases, that remains true today. The primary experience of the Indian American with help services has been in the form of either missionaries or bureaucrats (euphemism for BIA workers) whose philosophy of counseling was to tell the Indians that they were uncivilized savages, and that they *must* change. The attitude that Indians are and must be treated as children (paternalism) is not yet history and potential counselors must always avoid giving that impression if they hope to be accepted and effective on the reservation.

THE HELPING PROFESSIONAL'S ROLE

The authors suggest that the non-Indian counselor has certain advantages in working with Indian clients and, given sensitivity to that potential, can provide effective help.

Because of the close social relationship inherent to the tribal culture, Indian clients may not want to open up to Indian counselors. They fear (unwarranted) that whatever they say will be broadcast over the whole reservation by sundown. Although a professional counselor regardless of background, would not break confidentiality in so blatant a way, the Indian client knows only that on the reservation everyone seems to know everything about everyone else and therefore would be extremely reluctant to discuss his/her personal problems with another Indian. Accordingly, a non-Indian counselor has the advantage of not being considered as part of the reservation social communication system and should take advantage of that perception at the beginning of a session by emphasizing that all communications will be held in confidence. The Indian counselor by the same token is put at a decided disadvantage and must demonstrate by his/her behavior over quite a long period of time that confidences will be respected.

A new Indian counselor will find his/her job very trying because in addition to the resistance to opening up to an Indian counselor the tribal members will be suspicious of the counselor who has just returned to the reservation. The best advice to both the new Indian and non-Indian counselor is to keep a low profile and demonstrate through actions that they can be trusted and with that trust respect will grow.

Given the advantage on confidentiality, non-Indian counselors must nevertheless recognize that they will be approached with suspicion and distrust by a great many of their Indian clients. Suspicion and distrust are not unique to an Indian clientele. All counselors are familiar with it, but the non-Indian counselor must be prepared to undergo testing by clients who resist counseling assistance and who will use the counselor's non-Indianness as an excuse to avoid or prevent counseling. The testing may be used to intimidate to a certain extent, but testing will primarily be used to probe the counselor's understanding of the Indian culture with the purpose of finding and exploiting ignorances as a defense to effective counseling. How does the non-Indian respond to the direct challenge: "You're not Indian, you do not understand Indians, you cannot help Indians, leave me alone"? Inform the client that you are not there to help Indians but to help an individual help himself/herself and that the burden of responsibility for change lies on the client's shoulders and not the counselor's.

As a general model of counseling, a good idea is to make sure that the clients assume as much responsibility as they are capable of assuming. In working with Indian clients that goal becomes much harder to achieve because of the Indian's general non-assertiveness, noncommunicativeness, and tendency to promote harmony through apparent agreement. A strategy that has been effective in overcoming this agreeable passivity is to ask questions that allow the client to assume some authority in the situation. For example, a noncommital and/or ambiguous statement can be challenged in such a way that the client is given the opportunity to assume the role of teacher and, implicitly take on the responsibility of providing a clear communication. Specifically, indicate that you do not understand what the client is saying and ask if it could be explained in more detail or in a different way.

In summary, emphasize your perceived advantage of confidentiality, explain that although you are not an Indian (if you are not) your goal is not to help all Indians but to help a single individual, and ask questions in such a way that clients are allowed to assume both authority and responsibility in dealing with their problems. With time you will find that your clientele will begin to respect and trust you and to come to you on their

125

to respect and trust you and will begin to come to you on their own. When that begins to happen it will no longer matter that you are not a member of the tribe. You will have demonstrated that you are both a sensitive and competent helping professional.

With regard to goals counselors may help Indians establish, consideration of cultural values must be taken into account. Therefore, we conclude with an observation made by a Chief of the Six Nations (of New York) as written in Benjamin Franklin's *Remarks Concerning Savages of North America* (Smyth, 1970):

You who are wise, must know that different nations have different conceptions of things; and you will not therefore take it amiss, if our ideas of this kind of education happen not to be the same with yours. We have had some experience of it; several of our young people were formerly brought up at the Colleges of the northern provinces; they were instructed in all your sciences; but when they came back to us, they were bad runners, ignorant of every means of living in the woods, unable to bear either cold or hunger, knew neither how to build a cabin, take a deer, nor kill an enemy, spoke our language imperfectly, were therefore neither fit for hunters, warriors, nor counselors; they were totally good for nothing. (p. 99, Vol. X).

POST TEST

Directions: After reading the chapter, mark each item as true or false.

T F   1. The Indian's relationship to the tribe may interfere with an Indian's plans to attend college or vocational training programs.

T F   2. Only an Indian counselor can effectively help an Indian client.

T F   3. Indians, if anything, are more sensitive to peer expectations than the average middle-class non-Indian.

T F 4. Indians have a lower tolerance for alcohol than non-Indians.

T F 5. Indians view time as a western invention that is unnecessary in a changeless society.

T F 6. To the Indian possessions are of value only to the extent that they can be used in the here and now.

T F 7. Alcohol consumption is frowned upon by the great majority of reservation Indians.

T F 8. Indians remain on the reservation against their will and would prefer, if they had the financial resources, to be assimilated into western culture.

T F 9. An Indian will behave so as to appear as if in agreement with another individual even though there may be total disagreement.

T F 10. Harmony in personal relations is valued by the Indian culture above such western values as punctuality, cut-throat competition, and self-aggrandizement.

T F 11. The newly trained Indian counselor will be welcomed back to the reservation and tribe with open arms.

Scoring Guide for Post Test

1. T	4. F	7. F	10. T
2. F	5. T	8. F	11. F
3. T	6. T	9. T	

Reference List

Seaver, J.E. *A narrative of the life of Mary Jemison: The white woman of the Genesee* (22nd edition). New York: The American Science and Historic Preservation Society, 1925.

Smyth, A.H. *The writings of Benjamin Franklin: Volume X, 1789-1790.* New York: Haskell House Publishers, 1970.

6

Women Entering Or Reentering The Work Force

===

Helen B. Wolfe, Ed.D.

Executive Director
American Association
of University Women
Washington, D.C.

Helen Wolfe, Ed.D.

Dr. Helen Wolfe is currently Executive Director of the American Association of University Women which is head-quartered in Washington, D.C. In this role, she has served as a catalyst, consultant, and clarifier of women's concerns throughout the United States and foreign countries. Prior to her present employment, Dr. Wolfe was actively involved in counseling, research and evaluation, and teaching. She holds degrees from New York State University College at Buffalo, Cornell University, and State University of New York at Albany. Dr. Wolfe is included in **Who's Who of American Women** *and* **Who's Who in the East.** *She and her husband, The Reverend Charles E. Wolfe, reside in Washington, D.C.*

WOMEN ENTERING OR REENTERING THE WORK FORCE

Helen B. Wolfe, Ed.D.

AWARENESS INDEX

Whether consciously or unconsciously, we have all absorbed an attitude towards the phenomenon of large numbers of women entering or reentering the labor market. This attitude has been shaped by our past experiences, by the feelings of others around us, and by the mythology of a previous generation concerning women as well as by any reading or serious reflection we may have done. The following awareness index has been designed to assist the reader in separating fact from fiction in that specific attitude which he/she brings to the consideration of the problems and the reality that confronts this segment of American women.

Directions: Mark each item as true, false, or don't know.
Compute your score from the scoring guide at the end of this awareness index.
A post test is provided at the end of this chapter.

T F ?   1. Women now receive equal protection under the law.

T F ?   2. The changed social climate has produced a significant diversity in the jobs which women choose.

T F ? 3. The unemployment rates for professionally trained women are significantly higher than for men with the same credentials.

T F ? 4. The Federally mandated equal pay for equal work provisions have now evened out the differences between most male and female salaries and the pay gap is narrowing.

T F ? 5. Estimates from the U.S. Department of Labor predict that the average woman will be gainfully employed for almost one-third of her life expectancy.

T F ? 6. If state law forbids the employment of women in a given job, an employer is free to employ only males.

T F ? 7. Most women work because of economic necessity.

T F ? 8. Extending the mandatory retirement age to 70 is likely to have a favorable effect upon employment of women.

T F ? 9. Approximately 10% of employed women have incomes of over $15,000 yearly.

T F ? 10. The Federal government has enforced consistently the laws aimed at ending discrimination against women.

Scoring Guide for Awareness Index

1. F	4. F	7. T	10. F
2. F	5. T	8. F	
3. T	6. F	9. F	

A CASE EXAMPLE

The young woman, with bruised and swollen face as a result of a battering from her husband, with a frightened child clinging to her, is an increasingly heart-breaking sight. Especially wrenching is her desperate conclusion as she counts up her options. "I can't leave him because I can't do anything to make a living for myself and my child." And so she returns to crouch in fear until the next battering. She had prepared herself to be a wife and mother. She had achieved her goal. There had been no need to prepare herself psy-

132

chologically or vocationally for the labor market. Had she married the right man, she might never have felt the crushing weight of the mistake she had made in not acquiring a marketable skill. Perhaps a counselor had urged her to take this step and she had refused. More probably, the counselor had never considered the need at the crucial stage in the young woman's life and would not even feel a "sin of omission" trying to roost upon his/her shoulder.

The day after the funeral of her husband, when friends and relatives have gone back to work or to their own homes, and when the children are away at school, the middle-aged widow sits alone in an empty house. Coupled with the grief process and the trauma of burying the man she had loved, is the crushing realization that he had not left her financially secure. Confronted by stark necessity of going to work, she reaches for the want ads, and with a growing sense of panic she begins to realize that she cannot qualify for any of the jobs she might want. She does not have the financial resources to acquire a marketable skill now. She cannot return to school. She can cook for her family, but she is not really qualified to be a chef in a restaurant. She can clean house, but there is a great difference between cleaning her own house for her loved ones and being compelled to clean other people's houses for wages. She can care for children, but babysitting for others seems to be a somewhat limited career. And so the search goes as her despairing finger inches its way down the columns of the want ads. If only she had prepared herself differently, but she had not thought her husband would die without providing for her. And she turns the page to read another column of the ads.

DEFINITION

The focus in this chapter is upon the problems and needs of those women who become part of the work force, whether willingly or under compulsion. This special population falls outside of many of the traditional societal structures which provide counseling services. Because they are 40 million strong, however, they will increasingly require our attention in the coming years. Economist Carolyn Shaw Bell (1975) has assessed this changing status of women: "With irreversible changes in the culture in response to all facets of the woman's movement, the revolution in the status of women can most simply be summarized in the fact that these women won't go home again." Many of them won't go home again because they can't. Many others won't go home again because they want more out of life than they had before they went to work. But for whatever reason they don't go home again, 40 million working women are no longer content to be second-class workers.

This fact of American sociological and economic life has been recognized in the National Plan of Action (1977), which was adopted at the National Women's Conference in Houston in 1977. Among the 25 issue planks of the Plan adopted by elected delegates from every state and territory and presented to the President and Congress as the official recommendations for implementing Public Law 94-167, is the requirement to provide nonsexist counseling at every level of education, with encouragement of women to increase their range of options and choices to include both non-traditional and traditional occupations and to increase understanding of women's rights and status in various occupations.

Significant improvement has occurred in the status of women over the course of the past one hundred years. During this time, however, women's expectations have risen so enormously that there is no greater congruence between expectation and achievement today than there was one hundred years ago in spite of the gains. This ratio between expectation and achievement is not understood when frustrated women are expected to be grateful for the gains which have been made and not to continue pressing for full equality at once. The sex role stereotypes under which many women chafe today are relics of the American frontier. Sex roles made sense under those conditions, for the division of labor into carefully prescribed male/female roles in cooperation was necessary for family survival. As the American physical environment changed, however, the roles no longer made sense. The growing understanding of roles inappropriateness to a new environment makes women increasingly impatient about their retention. The U.S. family basically has shifted from a producing unit to a consuming unit and this fundamental change in function must be followed by change in social sex roles of an equally fundamental nature. Elizabeth Janeway (1974) has said: "The social changes that we are trying to cope with do not arise from some fiendish plot of bra-burning females, but from our old, old friend the Industrial Revolution. It has remade work, remade society, and now it is remaking the family" (p. 141). We therefore see a new picture of women, children, and family taking shape. We see the trend towards smaller families, working women, and women as increasingly the heads of households.

CURRENT PROBLEMS CONFRONTING EMPLOYED WOMEN

Statistics from the United States Department of Labor (1978) reveal that in 1960, 37.7 percent of all women between the ages of 16 and 70 were employed outside the home. In 1977, in sharp contrast, the figure was 48.4 percent. By 1990, the projections are that 60 percent of all women will be employed outside the home. If these projections continue to hold true, the average woman can now expect to spend 33 years of her life in the work force. Some of this increase is due to the greater number of women voluntarily seeking careers, but the vast majority of women are in the work force out of economic necessity rather than by personal choice. They must support themselves and their children, or the husband's income is not sufficient to satisfy both the basic needs and desires of the family. An estimation is that 80 percent of these women who must work occupy low-paying jobs (U.S. Department of Labor, 1978).

During the same time frame, the number of working women with children has tripled. There are now 7 million children under the age of six whose mothers work outside the home. The average family income for 15 percent of these working women with children under six is only $7,000 a year. Another 43 percent of these same mothers have family incomes between $7,000 and $15,000 a year (U.S. Department of Labor, 1978). In spite of such hard cold facts, we still hear the fiction that women go to work in order to escape the responsibilities of motherhood or to buy luxuries beyond the ability of their husbands to provide.

135

Many women are increasingly being hurt by the inability of our society to come to terms with basic facts. On the one hand, the role of the full-time homemaker is held out as the ideal for women; but on the other hand, society has not seen fit to extend to full-time homemakers the same protection that is extended to other workers in our society. Once a woman decides to become a full-time homemaker, her future rests upon her husband's health, upon the soundness of his financial planning, or upon his continued willingness to provide for her. Her work in the home has no legal recognition, and therefore, she accumulates no pension rights and no Social Security benefits of her own. If she is forced to enter the labor market because of the breakdown of the protective systems for the homemaker, she is pretty much on her own. She finds herself locked into low-status and low-paying jobs and denied access to high-status and high-paying jobs. She has the same economic need to advance vocationally as any of the men in the labor force have.

Women have recognized this basic injustice as revealed in the widening gulf between male and female salary levels. Currently, a male with a seventh-grade education earns more on the average than does a woman with a college degree. (U.S. Department of Labor, 1978). Since the male-dominated workplace still equates occupation and pay scale with sexual stereotypes, women are increasingly turning to the law and to the courts to force the concept of equal pay for work of comparable value which has been denied them in the marketplace.

The problem is even more severe for minority women. In addition to all of the problems faced by other women, they must also face monolingual education and services, high infant and maternal mortality rates, inadequate housing, insensitive psychological and employment testing, and uneven enforcement of affirmative action programs.

Some evidence that women are catching the ambiguity of the mixed signals which society is sending is found in the growing percentage of younger women who are choosing to remain single for a longer period of time. Since 1970, the proportion of the total American households in which the typical husband/wife configuration is found has declined,

136

while the proportion of single person households has increased to 21 percent of the total (U.S. Department of Labor, 1978).

An insistent need faced by working women is the care of the 7 million children who are under the age of six. Great potentials for meeting this need are the concepts of part-time work, job sharing, and flexible working hours. Private and public employers who have shown a willingness to move in these directions should be commended while others should be encouraged to initiate similar policies. The other potential for meeting this need is the day care center. The premise that children are the sole responsibility of the mother needs to be reexamined in cases where the systems of societal support for her role as mother have broken down and she is forced into the labor market. The critical shortage of day care centers is another index of our society's inability to forge and implement a consistent policy towards women. This inconsistency in turn continues the ambiguity of the signals transmitted to American women. The most basic cause of this inability is our failure to change the frontier sex role stereotypes into models which will work in a technological age.

One consequence of the technological age has been the increasing dependence of the family upon the automobile. The sprawl of suburbia of course has indirectly contributed to the plight of the urban minority woman by eroding the vitality of the central city. The dependency also curiously has hurt suburban women by fixing them ever more firmly in their cages even if gilded. The suburban woman has lost more of her potential for an independent life style because of the distances created by the sprawl. She is farther from the centers of work, probably does not have an adequate public transportation system available to her, is a prisoner to a massive house even when she can find household help, and finds her time consumed by the dependence of her entire family upon the automobile and frequently upon her to transfer them.

Working women continue to receive unequal treatment because of the lack of an over-riding consistent national public policy concerned with improving their lot. The United States Supreme Court has not yet defined women as a "suspect class" and the Equal Rights Amendment is not yet part of the United States Constitution. In addition, the Supreme Court has refused to apply the 14th Amendment to women in a consistent manner. Feminists have had some success in the course of the past dozen years in spearheading some important legislative advances for women, but women have not always experienced the expected benefits. Courts have rendered inconsistent interpretations which have encouraged noncompliance. White males who feel themselves threatened by a tightening economy have successfully directed a backlash at women. An increasingly competent and well trained labor pool in a constricted labor market has made it difficult for women to make significant vocational progress. Obviously our society is not able to employ all of its people who want to work. More and more, however, women are demanding that they not be expected to shoulder a greater share of this employment problem than other segments of the population.

PERSONAL AND CAREER NEEDS

We are slowly beginning to realize that yet another dimension is behind the battle of the sexes for an economic place in the sun in the labor market. The restrictive image of women in our society has dictated a type of training for girls which does not equip them for the freedom of choice which is the true aim of the women's movement. Hennig and Jardim, in *The Managerial Woman* (1977), portray one corporate chief executive who was extremely close to his daughter and proud of the way she had turned out. He was asked, "If your daughter had to work for a living, would you have done anything different in the way you reared her?" A long silence preceded his response as he thought about it. Then he hung his head and said, "If she *had* to work for a living, then I've done it all wrong" (p. 204).

Hennig and Jardim (1977) stress as their primary point that perception rather than ability marks the chief difference between men and women in the job market. Boys know from an early age that they must be gainfully employed, but hardly any girl is taught to face this issue. Instead, the girl is systematically taught to look for someone to support her. The

138

difference in mind-set which develops from this basic crossroads in childhood is enormous. Men can't even remember when as boys they began their journey towards employability. Their training is to do something, to master their environment. The girl is started on a different road. Is she pretty enough to attract someone to support her? The woman has been trained to use her individual attractiveness and her winsome attributes to make an effect upon others. Because men and women perceive differently and have since childhood, they frequently are not aware that these differences in perception are due to conditioning. This conditioning leads them to think of the essential differences between the sexes. When women find themselves in the world of work, this conditioning operates to their detriment.

At an early age, boys begin to learn about cooperation through team games, for they win or lose as teams more than as individuals. They soon learn that task specialization is necessary in order to build an effective team. Finally, they learn the all-important lesson that a lone individual does not win—the team as a whole wins or loses. There are stars on the team, but also there are average players. There are people the boy likes on the team, but also there are people he does not like. He learns that he himself does not win unless his team wins, and therefore he must play both with his friends and with those he does not like if he wants the satisfaction of winning. The team sport instills the qualities of cooperation and competition. The boy shares the success of the team, but failure also is easier to absorb because it is shared among the teammates.

When the boy grows up and as a man enters the world of work, he again finds the two qualities which are most important for success: the necessity to win in competition, but the necessity of cooperation in order to win. The man does not have to think consciously about these principles, for he has already learned it by playing baseball or football or hockey or basketball. These principles became a part of his basic personality without his even knowing it. Boys learn to tolerate each other and to use each other in order to put together a team that will win. As men, therefore, they are able to sit in meetings and tolerate each other and use each other to put together a team that will win. A man knows that he does not have to like another man in order to work for him or with him. Women find these attitudes incomprehensible.

The girl by contrast has not been taught to cooperate on a team to win. Most usually she has never been taught that she must get along with others. She has tended to participate in individual sports such as tennis, golf, and swimming. When she has on occasion played on a volleyball team or a girls basketball team, there has not been the intensity of play which is characteristic of boys sports. Girls do not have to tolerate each other to the degree boys must. Girls have been taught that relationships are more important than activities. These relationships define her personal worth. She bases relationships upon the personal qualities she has developed for herself. Because the relationships tend to be important as ends in themselves, the matter of personal liking is important. Men tend to hope that a friendship might come out of a working relationship, but women tend to insist upon it as a prerequisite. Women tend to fall into dangerous traps in the world of work because of this difference in perception. Either they are too painfully vulnerable to criticism because their sense of personal worth has too great an investment in the opinion that others have of them, or they are intolerant to the point where they cannot work well with or for people they do not like or respect.

Planning process is a second major area in which men perceive differently from women. In general, women tend to have difficulty with long-range sequential planning, preferring to live and work in more immediate time frames. Men plan more successfully in long-range patterns. Hennig and Jardim (1977) have isolated three factors in the careers of women which make it difficult for them to develop this skill.

1. Women do not plan a lifetime career, they do not take advantages of possibilities to move in new directions. Instead, they concentrate on the day-to-day job and do it very well. They have not developed, however, to the stage beyond the immediate job.

2. Women have a passivity which inhibits their career development. They are taught to wait to be chosen in the

140

marriage market and therefore it is logical that they should wait to be chosen in the job market. The problem is that women have not been taught how to move freely between successful past experience and demands of a new situation. Because women wait to be chosen, they have difficulty in predicting future success from their past. This waiting to be chosen limits their self-confidence and therefore their potential for taking risks.

3. Because they wait to be chosen, women tend not to recognize perhaps the most important element of all in the business world—the informal network of obligations and loyalties, of favors owed and received, of mutual benefit and protection—"the Old Boy Network" which men always take into account. Often the case is that men are not deliberately excluding women, but that they know the network is operating and that it is important. They assume that the women also know it but ignore it. The fact is, more often than not, that women do not know that the network is operating or do not know how to use it. This weakness relates to the fact that women were not forced to learn cooperative competition on teams.

The femininity issue is probably the most persistent problem which women face in the world of work. Our culture basically defines femininity in terms of passivity, as the ability to attract a man who is an achiever to support her, to stay home and have his children. There is something threatening, therefore, about a woman who wants something different out of life. Other women resent her as one who has rejected their traditional role model, and men frequently perceive her as a woman who is not quite a woman. A dichotomy is developing among women in the labor force. There are the married women who have to work for a time out of economic necessity, but they don't expect anything out of the labor market except wages. In contrast, are the women who have an internal drive to succeed. Typically in our culture, they must do this succeeding at the expense of marriage and home life. In reaction, they often deny their own femininity and devote themselves to careers. The resulting "Boss Lady" syndrome cuts into the wholeness of their personality. Because they

141

have discarded the "woman," they suffer internally. Both younger and older women need assistance in coping with this problem of integrating active achievement into their womanhood.

If women are ever to break out of the low-paying jobs which have traditionally imprisoned the vast majority of them, they need career information which is gender free. Hilliard (1975) has made the point that "it is necessary to recognize and deal with the concept that bias against women is often held by the professional to whom she turns for help" (p. 146). The use of computers to dispense occupational data has proven to be useful because properly programmed computers are gender blind, while unfortunately many human intermediaries are not. Many counselors, both men and women, perpetuate the problem with their stereotyped approaches to the occupational choices open to women. Many recent studies show that women have not greatly diversified their career choices, for they continue to be guided towards and to choose the traditional feminine occupations. A classic example is the domination of women in education and library science, except for the highest paying administrative jobs.

Many of the women in this special population who could benefit greatly from counseling and guidance services are not students. Therefore, they must find these services outside of the traditional educational settings. Over the past few years women's centers have appeared in many communities as a response to these unmet needs for counseling. In these centers, women who attempt to enter or reenter the job market are able to find a supportive emotional climate and to obtain practical assistance through career development workshops, job hunting techniques, and resume preparation. Effective linkages between the educational settings and other social service agencies must be established and nurtured, however, if women in this category are to be served effectively.

HISTORY OF COUNSELING AND OTHER SERVICES AVAILABLE FOR WOMEN

The traditional sex role stereotyping of the past has inhibited most women from seeking significant careers in the world of work. Although women always have been forced into the labor market, it generally was considered as a result of economic or national necessity. These women frequently were not enrolled in the schools which offered counseling and guidance service, and so for the most part they received no counseling from any source. For women not in educational settings, the availability of counseling services for working women has tended to follow the Federal dollars. The money has been spent in varying intensities according to whether the country needed "Rosie the Riveter" during a war-time economy or not. Janeway (1974) said that "one aspect of the war between the sexes not often noted is its manipulative use of women by the State and the Establishment. Wars put women into the labor market and recessions and depressions put them out of it." (p. 79)

As a profession, guidance counselors too often have allowed Federal dollars to establish their priorities, and therefore frequently they have followed, infrequently pioneered. After World War II, a great effort was made to integrate veterans into a post-war society, but no one was concerned about the working women who were pushed out at the same time. The launching of Sputnick dictated that counselors master the techniques required to produce scientific and technocratic career decisions. In the early 1960's, some legislative advances for women were achieved such as the Equal Pay Act, and a few governmental commissions were appointed to focus upon the changing roles of women. In 1965, I attended a pilot conference sponsored by the Women's Bureau of the Labor Department to examine the counseling needs of women and girls. Women counselors and women counselor educators interacted with the Women's Bureau, but the profession as a whole showed no interest.

The civil rights movement helped rekindle the women's movement, but the funding basically emerged for the blacks rather than for women. The drive for passage of the Equal Rights Amendment generated enough energy to create some potentially helpful legislation for women. In 1975, Title IX of the Educational Amendments Act of 1972 was passed. It was intended to eliminate sexual discrimination in college admissions, financial aid, physical facilities, curriculums, sports, counseling, and employment in educational insitutions receiving Federal funds, but lax enforcement resulted in minimal effects for women in educational settings.

The Comprehensive Education Training Act (CETA) has provided programs to retrain women who suddenly find themselves in the work force after many years as homemakers. The program is designed to address the particular educational and/or training needs women have if they are to become self-sufficient. CETA programs often are available, but frequently they are flawed in the way they tend to perpetuate the occupational segregation which has clustered women at the lower end of the job market. Without the CETA programs women remain at the bottom, and with the CETA programs they remain at the bottom.

The most effective counseling programs for these women is currently being offered not by trained counselors, but by active feminists who have worked to increase women's self-confidence through women's studies at universities, and who have to make long-range changes in the sex role stereotyping by providing the impetus for changing the role models of women in the standard elementary school textbooks. These feminists have been instrumental in opening the service academies to women and women's colleges to men. Specifically, however, they have worked on this particular population in the establishment of centers for the prevention of rape, for abused wives, and for vocational counseling. These centers have provided new arenas in which trained counselors can work to reach these women. Feminists, themselves have provided services for women because no one else would.

THE HELPING PROFESSIONAL'S ROLE

Counselors and those professionals engaged in counseling women do need to change their response. The problem, however, is not limited experience with women or even with working women. The numbers of women and working women are too great for this to be the problem. The need for change in awareness, in training, and in the behavior of counselors is due to the archaic stereotypes which have blunted perceptions. It is important to help women to see real alternatives so that they can begin to move beyond what has always been traditional.

Women need the reassurance that their aspirations are not atypical, and group counseling is an effective technique for providing this assurance. The mutual encouragement and support of other women similarly engaged is important. Women need to be encouraged to discuss what they can do. They need to understand that revealing this information is not boastful, but that self-promotion and the ability to communicate the skills which a person has are all part and parcel of labor force participation. Women have been conditioned by society to minimize their qualifications. It is important to help them move towards greater self-awareness and to refine their ability to project this confidence.

Women tend to have accumulated a host of skills through their voluntary activities. A growing awareness on the part of public and private employers is that these skills are potentially marketable. Voluntary experiences which have involved a woman in communications, planning, budgeting, management, and legislation are just as valid in producing competence, though acquired without salary, as more readily understood job experience. It requires a sensitive counselor who also is knowledgeable to hear "I haven't worked in a dozen years" and guide the speaker to realize that she has indeed worked and acquired new skills, even if not for a pay check. These mature women who are entering or reentering the labor force tend on the whole to have a very strong work ethic and they tend to be intelligent and compassionate.

Diversity in occupational choice should be presented to women by counselors through meaningful career orientation courses. The diversity is especially important because the job outlook in some of the traditional occupations for women tends to be bleak. The counselor must be careful, however, not to do the woman a disservice by guiding a less secure woman into a field where she would find herself a distinct minority. The Labor Department suggests 25 percent may be a cut-off figure of one sex or the other to indicate that those areas are nontraditional fields. Counselors must make women aware of the resistance they are likely to encounter in non-traditional fields, while at the same time encouraging women to move into these areas. The awareness of potential problems and psychological pressures will better equip women who do want to try.

Career planning is just as important for women as it is for men. Because women tend to deal with short-range planning and have trouble with sequential planning, however, the counselor may encounter a barrier to long-range career planning. The counselor who understands that this attitude is the result of the acculturation process for women rather than "just the way women are" will be able to overcome this attitude. Women can be taught to look ahead to the next job based upon current and past experiences, but the counselor cannot assume this skill. Careful discussion of life stages should be supplemented by suggested readings to provide factual data. Because these women did not absorb the necessity for long-range planning in their earlier years, the counselor must help them learn it as women.

Interest, aptitude, and ability tests seem to have less relevance for mature women than they have for mature men. The presuppositions behind the test construction perpetuate the sex role stereotypes. Until revisions are made, the validity and usefulness of many of the tests must be questioned. Therefore, the decision of use must be an individual decision made by counselor and counselee together. In general, the sensitive counselor will find that the pro-forma battery of tests is not helpful for older women.

The counselor should be cautious in his/her assessment about whether the woman needs further formal education. In some cases, it may be appropriate to seek additional credentials desired through nontraditional avenues such as "the university without walls," in which academic credit is assessed on the basis of life experience. In other cases, however, it may be advisable for the woman to enter a college or university. The institutional climate towards mature women has become much more favorable since the falling birth rate has affected college enrollments. Now women are seen as a desirable market by the academic community. The recent proliferation of courses and services available to them, of course, also are due to the agitation of women and continuation of these courses seems assured by the satisfactory achievement of the women who continue to enroll. In still other cases, however, formal college training is not indicated as part of the career planning process. The skilled counselor can help the woman separate out the relevant from the irrelevant in educational approaches to meet her career goals.

The counselor must be able to help the woman learn to develop an effective resume. Many women tend to include too much data, such as date of birth, marital status, and number of children. They need help in assessing their skills adequately and then expressing them on paper. Many good materials are published to assist her, including "The Resume Preparation Kit," available from Catalyst in New York.

"The Superwoman Syndrome" is a problem which faces the married woman who enters the work force. The sensitive helping professional can help her cope with it. Because of the sex role stereotypes, many women feel a trace of residual guilt when they go to work, and this guilt must be dealt with. This guilt is manifested in the tendency to compensate by becoming Superwoman, the need to do it all—the job plus all of the myriad of tasks that the wife and mother performs who is not employed outside the home. A few exceptional women are able to do these tasks without damage to themselves, but most women will need to share tasks with their husband and/or children. The employed mother also may seek to assuage this guilt feeling by over-indulging the children and should have an opportunity to work through this problem. Counselors can help women define their priorities and to live with a series of compromises involving preparation of meals, housecleaning, and social life. The Superwoman Syndrome often is precipitated by pressure which the husband brings to bear. The husband is as much a prisoner of the sex role stereotypes as is the wife. The counselor must be able to help the working wife deal with the threat of her income to his masculinity.

POST TEST

James Michener wrote a book entitled *The Quality of Life*. In reflecting upon educational and occupational opportunities for minorities he made the telling point that we cannot afford as a society to cut anyone short of his/her full potential for we all have too much at stake. What great novel has not been written because we blocked the full potential of someone through destructive stereotypes? What cure for cancer might have been discovered by a woman or a black? What improvements in the quality of life have we lost by this suicidal cutting off of the brain of such a large part of our population? Because of their sensitivity to human personality, and their skill in surmounting problems, counselors as a group are in a position to pioneer in the task of helping women achieve their full potential without destructive side effects. The post test may provide a convenient attitudinal check list for the counselor who would assist women in this area of growth.

Directions: After reading chapter, mark each item.

T F ?   1. Women have a natural instinct for long-range planning.

T F ?   2. One of the chief differences between men and women in the labor market is their perception about employment.

T F ?   3. One of the reasons feminists have sought equal funding in athletic programs for men and women is the valuable training it provides for coping with work situations.

T F ?   4. The "Superwoman Syndrome" among employed women is solely a result of the woman's guilt feelings.

T F ?   5. Standardized tests are useful in counseling the vast majority of mature women.

T F ?   6. Group counseling sessions are generally an effective technique in working with mature women.

Scoring Guide for Post Test

1. F	3. T	5. F
2. T	4. F	6. T

Reference List

Bell, C.S. The next revolution. *Social Policy*, 1975, *6*, 5.

Hennig, M., & Jardim, A. *The managerial woman*. New York: Anchor Press/ Doubleday, 1977.

Hilliard, M.E.V. Expanding opportunities for the re-entry woman. In *Issues of sex bias and sex fairness in career interest measurement*. Washington, D.C.: National Institute of Education, 1975.

Janeway, E. *Between myth and morning; Women awakening*. New York: Morrow, 1974.

Michener, J. *The quality of life*. New York: Fawcett, 1972.

Resume preparation manual: A step-by-step guide. New York: Catalyst, 1976.

International Women's Year Commission. *National plan of action*. Washington D.C.: 1977.

U.S. Department of Labor. *Twenty facts on women workers*. Washington, D.C.: 1978.

7

The
Black
Client

Roderick J. McDavis, Ph.D.

Associate Professor of Education
Department of Counselor Education
University of Florida
Gainesville, Florida

Roderick J. McDavis, Ph.D.

A native of Dayton, Ohio, Roderick J. McDavis received his B.S. degree from Ohio University in 1970, his M.S. degree in student personnel administration from the University of Dayton in 1971, and his Ph.D. degree in counselor education from the University of Toledo in 1974. While at the University of Dayton, he served as Director of the Center for Afro-American Affairs. He is currently Associate Professor of Education in the Department of Counselor Education at the University of Florida. He served as President of the Florida Association for Non-White Concerns in Personnel and Guidance and recently was awarded the Presidential Citation for Exemplary Service to the Association and the Concerns of Minorities in the field of Counseling and Guidance. He co-hosts a television program, "The Black Family," aired on public television in Jacksonville, Florida and was presented with the Distinguished Service Award for Community Outreach through TV Media by the Florida Association for Counselor Education and Supervision. He also was named as one of the Outstanding Young Men of America by the U.S. Jaycees. His primary interests and publications are in counseling ethnic minorities and student personnel work. His articles have appeared in **Counselor Education and Supervision, Journal of Non-White Concerns in Personnel and Guidance,** *and* **Journal of College Student Personnel***. He has served as consultant in public school systems, universities, community colleges, and community mental health agencies.*

THE BLACK CLIENT

Roderick J. McDavis, Ph.D.

AWARENESS INDEX

Directions: These questions are to help you evaluate your understanding of the Black Client.
Mark each item as true or false.
Compute your score from the scoring guide at the bottom
of page 154.

T F 1. Being called a stereotypical name is the most negative effect of discrimination.

T F 2. The Supreme Court ruled that racial segregation in public
and private schools was unconstitutional in the Brown
versus Board of Education case.

T F 3. The least of the problems confronting Black people today
is being able to utilize public facilities.

T F 4. Blacks are not included enough in mainstream society.

T F 5. Today, many Blacks are in non-traditional careers.

T F 6. Many Blacks are not aware of the counseling services that
are provided by counselors and counseling agencies.

T F 7. The client-centered counseling approach is most effective
with Blacks.

CASE EXAMPLE

When Derick was very young, his parents told him that he was a good person, intelligent, and capable of achieving anything if he was willing to work hard. Derick believed his parents and when he started school, was eager to learn as much as he could about science since he wanted to become a medical doctor. During his elementary school days, Derick did very well in his studies, but his scores were low on the standardized aptitude tests. His white classmates made jokes about how "dumb" Derick was and started telling him that their parents said that Blacks could never do as well on these tests as whites. Derick did not believe them but nevertheless was disturbed and concerned about their comments. When he discussed this concern with his teachers and counselors, they avoided telling him some of the negative effects that standardized tests can have for many Black students.

One day when Derick was walking home from elementary school, a car passed him and he heard someone in the car yell, "Hey nigger, you and your kind should go back to Africa!" When he got home, Derick asked his parents what the person meant. They told him that some white people are prejudiced and say things like that because this is one way they can show their dislike for people of other races. They said also that he should not worry too much about being called bad names by white people. This was Derick's first encounter with being called a "nigger." He did not know whether he should ignore it, get mad about it, or worry about it at all.

Derick completed elementary school with a "B" average in his studies but he continued to score poorly on standarized aptitude and achievement tests in high school. He began to think about what his classmates in elementary school had said to him and thought that maybe they were right—Blacks could not score as well as whites on standardized tests. He discussed his results with his counselor who suggested to him that he might consider a career in some area other than

Scoring Guide for Awareness Index

1. F	3. T	5. F	7. F
2. F	4. T	6. T	

medicine because his standardized test scores were so low; he continued to make "B's" in most of his courses, especially in science classes.

During his junior year, Derick decided to try out for the school baseball team. He had played little league baseball, been on the little league All-Star team, and played junior league baseball for three years. On the first day of tryouts, Derick noticed he was the only Black competing for a position on the team. The manager asked the candidates to catch fly balls and ground balls and to practice throwing the ball. Derick was the only one who caught every ball hit to him and he made accurate throws to the proper bases. The next day, however, Derick's name appeared on the cut list, even though he and some of the other candidates knew he had performed well enough to survive the first tryout. That summer, Derick played baseball on the same junior league team as a student who had played on the high school team. Derick started in every game for this team while his fellow classmate sat on the bench. His experience in the summer league confirmed that a probable reason he was cut from his high school team was because he was Black.

Derick graduated from high school with a "B" average in his courses and went to college. His parents told him that if he continued to work hard in college his dream of becoming a medical doctor would come true. His major was pre-med and he maintained a "B + " average in his courses. In most of his classes after his sophomore year, Derick was the only Black student. This situation did not concern Derick until he enrolled in an advanced zoology course during his junior year. He noticed that the professor never called on him to answer a question in class although his hand was raised. Several times he attempted to make an appointment to talk about this avoidance with the professor, but the professor was always too busy. At the end of the term, he received a "C" grade in the course although his test scores and projects averaged a "B" grade. Again, Derick tried to arrange a meeting with the professor but he was never available. He thought about appealing the grade but was afraid he would create more problems for himself. Derick became even more aware that some people will harm, ignore, and/or avoid helping you because your skin is Black. He began to realize that he probably would be discriminated against in some form the rest of his life.

Derick scored low on another standardized test required for entrance to medical school, but was admitted anyway because of his good grades. He worked hard, finishing in the top third of his class. Ironically, some of his white classmates had initially told him that the only reason he was admitted to medical school was because he was Black. Derick had been through many trials and tribulations to become a physician and yet he knew to some people he was and would always be "just a nigger." As Derick began to plan the rest of his life, he wondered if he would ever live long enough to see the day when he and other Black people would be fully accepted by white society.

THE BLACK POPULATION

In March, 1977, the 24.5 million Blacks living in the United States comprised the largest ethnic minority group in the country and 11.5 percent of the total population (U.S. Bureau of the Census, 1978). The 1977 census also determined the following for the Black population: 74 percent lived in the central cities of the metropolitan areas, 39 percent were less than 18 years old, 54 percent were between 18 to 64 years old, more than 50 percent of the families were husband-wife families while 37 percent had a female head of household, and approximately 30 percent had two person families while 29 percent had five or more persons in the family.

With regard to education, about 46 percent of the Black adults, 25 years and over, were high school graduates and 17 percent had completed one or more years of college. However, 75 percent of the Blacks between 20 and 24 years old were graduates of high school and approximately 32 percent had completed one or more years of college. Of the 9.7 million Blacks over 16 years old in the labor force, about 14 percent were unemployed, 39 percent had blue-collar occupations, approximately 33 percent white-collar occupations, and 26 percent were working in service occupations. The median income of Black families in 1976 was $9,240 with 26 percent of

Black families earning under $5,000, 27 percent between $5,000 and $9,999, 19 percent between $10,000 and $14,999, and 28 percent earning over $15,000.

Blacks were first brought to the United States in 1619 when a Dutch ship landed at Jamestown, Virginia, with 20 slaves of African descent (Sloan, 1971). During the first 244 years of their presence in this country, Blacks were used exclusively as slaves in most parts of the country, especially the South. Most Blacks lived on plantations and worked in the fields or houses of whites without receiving wages. On January 1, 1863, President Lincoln signed the Emancipation Proclamation which freed all Blacks from the bondage of slavery. The 13th Amendment abolished slavery, the 14th Amendment gave Blacks the right to be citizens, and the 15th Amendment gave Blacks the right to vote.

Since the 1860's the history of Blacks in the United States has been affected significantly by court decisions and congressional legislation. In the Plessy versus Ferguson case in 1896, the Supreme Court upheld the doctrine of "separate but equal" educational facilities for Blacks which resulted in over 50 years of segregated education. This doctrine also contributed to the migration of many Black people from the South to the North in the early 1900's.

Another outcome of this decision was the development of more predominantly Black colleges and universities. During this period Black people were influenced by two significant figures in Black history, Booker T. Washington and W. E. B. DuBois. Washington's contention was that Blacks could be more progressive if they learned skills or trades in agricultural and mechanical fields and continued to work and live in rural areas of the South. DuBois, on the other hand, believed that Black people should pursue education in professional fields and become leaders of the race. Both men inspired Black people to acquire more education in a wide variety of occupations during the period between 1900-1950.

Segregated school systems lasted until 1954 when the Supreme Court declared that racial segregation in public schools was unconstitutional in the Brown versus Board of

Education case. For the first time in 335 years, Blacks were permitted to attend the same schools as whites. This integration led to a larger number of Blacks being educated in such professional fields as law, medicine, business, and engineering. The Civil Rights Act of 1964 provided Black people with basic human rights that they had been previously denied. Blacks were able to eat in any public restaurant and stay in any public motel. In 1965, through the Voting Rights Act, Congress gave Blacks in the South the right to vote, a right which they had been denied in past years. In the Bakke decision of 1978, the Supreme Court ruled that race can be used as a factor in admitting students to colleges and universities; these institutions are permitted to use affirmative action measures to increase the numbers of Black students admitted to undergraduate and graduate programs.

These court decisions and congressional acts have had a positive and negative effect on Blacks. Psychologically Blacks are beginning to perceive themselves as people who are equal to majority group members under the law. Yet, many Blacks wonder if they as a people will ever be seen as equals since there remain some majority group members who have not accepted recent court decisions and congressional acts and still view Blacks as inferior.

The history of Black people in the United States has been dismal. It has been filled with oppression, discrimination, and unfair treatment. While it is true that the plight of Blacks in 1979 is better than it was in 1619, Blacks still find themselves in a society that does not fully accept them. This fact continues to be in the minds of Blacks and results in mistrust and dislike for some majority group members.

PROBLEMS CONFRONTING BLACKS

Labeling

A problem that all Black people face is being labeled as a minority group member by society. While the word "minority" is not necessarily negative, the term causes many Blacks to wonder if they are perceived as equals by majority group members. As Black children grow older, they soon realize that they are labeled as minorities by majority group members. This label imprinted on their minds by society becomes another stigma that Black people must learn to accept and cope with throughout their lives.

One effect of this label is that many Black people develop negative self-concepts and do not strive to fulfill their potentials. An example of this would be Black students who begin to believe that being a member of a minority group means not being able to achieve as do majority group students. A second effect is that many Blacks develop a mistrust of majority group members. As Black children learn the history of how Blacks were treated by whites, they begin to doubt that members of this group will ever understand, accept, and respect them. Hence, they start to wonder if they can or should trust any majority group member. Third, the minority label causes many Blacks to dislike members of the majority group. If a person cannot be trusted, it is difficult to form a friendship relationship with that person.

Discrimination

Another problem that faces all Black people is discrimination. In spite of all the legislation and court decisions that have provided human rights to Black people, they are still discriminated against in society and schools because of the color of their skins. One area in society that provides an indication that discrimination still exists is housing. The vast majority of communities in the urban centers of society are still segregated or minimally integrated. In other words, most Black people live in one part of the city and most whites in another. Many whites do not want Blacks living in their neighborhoods and when Blacks move into these communities white flight occurs. Further, some real estate companies will not sell homes in some white neighborhoods to Blacks. Thus, as the year 2000 approaches many Blacks and whites continue to live in separate communities.

Discrimination in our society also affects the employment rate among Blacks. While many factors contribute to the high unemployment rate among Blacks, one of those factors is racial discrimination. Many Blacks have had the experience of applying for a job, being told they were not qualified, and discovering that the only difference between them and the person who received the job was the color of their skins.

Discrimination in schools is reflected in the attitudes of many administrators, teachers, and counselors toward Black students. In order to perform well in school, students must believe that those responsible for their education are genuinely interested and concerned about them as people. Unfortunately, many educators have negative attitudes toward Black people and are unable or unwilling to work with Black students effectively.

Standardized and competency tests are other examples of discrimination in schools. Research indicates that Black students score lower on these tests than their white counterparts. When Black students learn this fact, they begin to doubt their intelligence and potentials. Many of these students lose interest in their school work and begin to look for other ways to become successful. While many educators are aware that these tests are biased against Blacks, they continue to use them to judge the knowledge and potentials of Black students. It is very difficult for students to be motivated or believe in themselves if they know that they are being tested unfairly in school.

Career Role Models

A third problem that faces all Black people is the lack of Blacks in nontraditional fields or careers. There are no Black senators or governors, no significant numbers of Blacks in chief executive positions of major corporations or television networks, few Black administrators in predominantly white colleges and universities, and a relatively small percent of Blacks in medicine, dentistry, law, college teaching, engineering, pharmacy, architecture, and aeronautics. Black students in school begin to perceive these and other such technical professions as career areas that Blacks do not enter when the only role models they see in these areas are whites. The lack of Blacks in nontraditional fields causes many Black parents not to encourage their children to seek careers in these areas. It also causes many educators and counselors not to advise Black students to take courses that are prerequisites to entering many of these professions.

Being labeled a minority group member, discrimination in society and schools, and the lack of Blacks in nontraditional fields are three problems that confront Black people. These problems cause many Blacks to not have faith in the American system. These problems make the meaning of the words "equality" and "human rights" difficult for Blacks to understand, much less experience. These problems will continue to face Black people until a concerted societal effort prevails to seek solutions to them.

PERSONAL AND CAREER GUIDANCE NEEDS OF BLACKS

Personal Needs

Black people need to be understood, accepted, and respected in society and schools as well as other people. Many whites have had limited contact with Blacks as individuals and minimal involvement in activities sponsored by Black organizations. Hence, whites have not been exposed to some of the differences in the culture, lifestyle, and communication patterns of Blacks. For example, some whites criticize and penalize Blacks for using Black dialect when they do not understand that this style of communication is accepted in the home and community. The experience of many Blacks is that they have not felt respected or accepted by white society. This feeling of lack of respect has led Blacks to think that they are being ignored or rejected by whites with the end product being mistrust and hatred leading to further separation of the groups.

Negative stereotypes about Blacks have existed since Africans were brought to America as slaves. Many whites learn these stereotypes at a young age, believe them, and never challenge them. Sensitive to negative stereotypes, some Blacks may consent to the attitudinal and behavioral expectations of whites and assume certain roles for survival. Others may learn to rationalize or deny the existence of negative stereotypes, while still others may absorb it as a negative self-concept. Thus a second personal need of

161

Blacks—they want to be perceived as individuals who are judged by the content of their character rather than the color of their skins. In other words, Blacks do not want whites to have expectations of them that are based on stereotypes, they want to be seen as individuals who have different as well as similar needs to those of whites.

A third personal need of Blacks is that they want to be treated as equals rather than unequals. As Blacks become aware of their history in America, they learn that Blacks have always been treated as second class citizens by most whites. The effect has been that Blacks expect to receive unfair treatment in their associations with majority group members. Black children learn from their parents at an early age that they should be very cautious about trusting whites. Most of these parents can share personal experiences of their unfair treatment by whites. For instance, some Black parents have told stories about having to drink from separate water fountains, sitting in the balconies of movie theaters, not being able to stay in certain hotels or motels, and not being able to obtain loans to start businesses.

A fourth personal need of Blacks, one that perhaps encompasses the others, is to be included in the mainstream of society. Blacks rarely have been able to feel an integral part of society. The effect of this is that Blacks have learned to live in two worlds, one Black, the other white. Black parents teach their children that they must learn to function in white society as well as they function in Black society. Developing a "dual personality" is necessary for Black children so that they can survive in both worlds. For Blacks, there is no choice; they must learn to relate to and live with whites to avoid being isolated and segregated in society. Blacks want to be included in the mainstream of society without having to sacrifice those qualities that make them different. In other words, Blacks want to be themselves and to be perceived by majority group members as people who have something to offer society.

Career Needs

Black students need to be provided information about nontraditional careers, including examples of Black males and females who currently are working in nontraditional fields. These nontraditional careers would include engineering, architecture, pharmacy, computer science, and medicine, career areas that historically, Black have not entered for a variety of reasons. One of the main reasons is the lack of exposure to information describing the different types of career opportunities available in areas such as these.

One means of providing this type of information is to develop culturally relevant career guidance materials. Included could be a slide/tape presentation that shows Blacks working in some of the nontraditional career areas and an audio tape in which they are discussing how they became interested in their careers. A career scrapbook could be compiled that contains pictures of Blacks in nontraditional career areas and a description of each career next to the pictures. A third idea is to invite Blacks in some of these careers to speak to Black students about the career opportunities in their areas. The purpose of all three ideas is to demonstrate to Black students that other Blacks have entered these career areas and experienced success.

Black students may perceive these nontraditional career areas as unrealistic for them, and therefore, counselors need to provide encouragement that these are realistic career choices. Some Black students will need to be advised to take course work in math and science. Encouragement from counselors not only may motivate Black students to seek additional information about these career areas, but also encouragement can have a positive effect on the Blacks' self-concepts in that they will begin to believe that they can succeed in these areas.

Black students will need alternatives in their career choices. This means helping them to identify several major career areas such as science or engineering, to select a variety of possible career choices within these respective areas, and to explore the requirements for each career. Thus, a person can better understand the education necessary to acquire the skills needed to do the job, the amount of time involved in preparing for this career and the career options available within an area of interest.

Because many Black students respond well to challenges, counselors should not be afraid to challenge them to explore and to enter nontraditional as well as traditional career areas. This challenge is especially true if the grades and motivation level indicate that they can succeed in these types of careers. Many times these students will select a traditional career area over a nontraditional career area simply because they do not want to take a risk on entering a career field where Blacks have not been known to succeed. Challenging these students to enter nontraditional careers communicates in a positive way that counselors believe it is possible for Blacks to achieve in these areas.

COUNSELING SERVICES
FOR BLACKS

Many Blacks of the older generation are not aware of the services that counselors provide. Thus, many of them do not utilize the counseling services that currently are available in their communities and do not encourage their children to seek the help of a counselor at the schools attended. Most younger Blacks, however, have become familiar with counseling and counselors through attendance at the public schools. Some younger Blacks have positive attitudes toward counseling as a result of their experiences with school counselors; some, on the other hand, have negative attitudes. The important point is that those Blacks who have not had positive experiences with counselors in schools are most likely not to seek the help of counselors in the community when Blacks really need help. Based on these observations, it is not surprising that counseling services in the community are underutilized by many older and younger Blacks.

Significant others in the Black community such as ministers, relatives, friends, and elderly persons have been used as counselors by Blacks. The assumption made by many Blacks is that these persons are more interested and qualified to help them than are professional counselors. Another reason Blacks have not utilized counseling services is that many of the agencies in the community that provide counseling services expect clients to come in and ask for help; the traditional way that counseling has been made available to all people. In Black communities, however, this system does not work well because Blacks are not accustomed to sharing their personal problems with strangers. Thus, in spite of the increased mental health services, available to Blacks, a substantial increase in the utilization of such services by Blacks has not occurred.

The increase in the number of Black counselors in schools and community mental health agencies during the 1970's is beginning to have more of a positive effect on the utilization of counseling services by Blacks. These counselors are aware of the perceptions held by many Blacks toward counseling and counselors because they have lived in Black communities. They understand why many Blacks have negative attitudes toward counselors and counseling and what must be done to change these attitudes. These Black counselors are informing Blacks in the communities of the many ways that counselors, both Black and white, can help with personal concerns and problems.

The recent trend of establishing many community mental health agencies directly within the Black community also has improved the availability of counseling services to Blacks. The fact that these agencies are very visible means that Blacks will begin to perceive them as a part of their community and thus will begin to make better use of them. It is important to recognize that it will take some time before these agencies become totally accepted by Black communities because of the negative stigma that has been attached to these types of agencies in the past. It is, however, a step in the right direction in terms of increasing awareness of such services, of more Blacks making use of agencies, and of establishing the overall need and purpose of counseling services.

ROLE OF HELPING PROFESSIONALS

One problem that faces many helping professionals in their attempt to provide better counseling services for Black clients is the lack of experience in working with Black people.

This problem is caused by the fact that many individuals who enter the helping professions have not lived around or developed friendly relationships with Blacks. Thus, many helping professionals who leave preparation programs are unsure of how to approach and counsel Black clients. It is not an uncommon practice for these professionals to refer Black clients to Black helping professionals if the inexperienced professionals find themselves unable to work effectively with Black clients. While this practice may seem plausible, it is nonetheless limiting and unprogressive. Counselors must learn to work with different clients and not provide less than adequate or appropriate counseling services for Black clients.

The question that might be posed is "Are helping professionals responsible for being able to counsel Black clients effectively?" Without hesitation, the answer to this question is "Yes." Helping professionals are responsible for being able to help Black clients. Being aware of how one thinks and feels about Blacks is a necessary first step in learning how to counsel with them. Awareness of attitudes can help individuals to determine if, as counselors, there is a need for increased experiences with Blacks in general to learn more about their culture, lifestyles, and communication patterns. Experience also can serve as a vehicle for individuals to dispell any myths or stereotypes that counselors may hold about Blacks. A second step is to use some of the concepts and techniques from existing counseling approaches with Black clients.

Existentialism

Existentialism is a school of thought that is concerned with individuals and their attempt to retain their identities, to make their own choices, and to provide their own self-directions (Strickland, 1966). In a practical sense the existential counselor tries to understand clients as they exist in their own worlds (Shertzer & Stone, 1974). For helping professionals, this means viewing Black clients as unique and different. The approach also means learning the culture, lifestyle, and language of Black clients as well as trying to understand what these clients are experiencing.

How can helping professionals do this? The most effective way is for these professionals to place themselves in situations which enable them to feel what it is like to be different. Attending social affairs sponsored by Black organizations, such as dances, parties, and picnics is one way to better understand how it feels to be a member of a minority group. Also, by eating meals with Blacks at Black community restaurants and having informal conversations with Blacks, helping professionals can begin to learn the culture, lifestyle, and language of Blacks. These professionals also can use these existential concepts to eliminate whatever negative attitudes they hold toward Blacks and to develop positive attitudes toward Black clients. The aim is to become a professional who believes that all people have an inherent right to retain their identities, make their own choices, and be self-directed individuals.

Client-Centered Counseling

Carl Rogers, originator of the client-centered approach, believes that helping professionals should bring acceptance, understanding, and congruence to the counseling relationship and communicate these characteristics to the client in order to establish rapport and an effective counseling relationship (Cunningham & Peters, 1973). Professionals must communicate acceptance and understanding to Black clients during the first counseling session to demonstrate the professional's sincere and genuine interest in these clients and their personal concerns. It is just as important for these professionals to be congruent, meaning no contradiction between what they say and what they do (Cunningham & Peters, 1973). Congruent professionals are open, honest, and not afraid to be themselves with Black clients.

How can helping professionals communicate these concepts to Black clients? By sharing some personal information or making small talk, professionals can verbally communicate these concepts to Black clients. This approach shows the client that the helping professional is a real person. A warm smile, a firm handshake, and a relaxed manner are nonverbal ways of expressing these concepts to Black clients. Essentially, the idea is to make Black clients feel comfortable and secure when they come for counseling so that they are more willing to discuss their personal concerns. Unless rapport has been established with the client, the chances of developing an effective counseling relationship are slim.

Helping professionals who are able in some way to communicate acceptance, understanding, and congruence during the initial interview are better able to establish rapport with Black clients.

Reality Counseling

The reality counseling approach developed by William Glasser provides three concepts that helping professionals can use to develop more effective counseling relationships with Black clients. One concept of the reality approach is that the professional should be involved in counseling relationships (Glasser & Zunin, 1973). Basic to reality counseling is the idea that helping professionals discuss their own experiences with the client. A second concept is that the professional should not make value judgments about the client's behavior (Glasser & Zunin, 1973). Reality counseling asks clients to make a value judgment as to whether their behavior is responsible and therefore good for them and those with whom they are involved (Glasser & Zunin, 1973). A third concept is that the professional should encourage the client to be committed to execute a plan of action (Glasser & Zunin, 1973).

How can helping professionals use these concepts with Black clients? First, use of the pronouns I, you, and we by the professional and client is encouraged because it facilitates their involvement in the counseling process (Glasser & Zunin, 1973). Professionals must share their own experiences with Black clients because these experiences serve as models for these clients and show them that professionals are willing to disclose themselves. Thus, it becomes less threatening for Black clients to self-disclose their own experiences. Second, helping professionals should not make value judgments about Black clients' behavior but rather guide them to an evaluation of their own behavior. Because Black clients may hold values different from those of the professional, professionals should not judge Black clients' behavior as good or bad but rather seek to help clients understand how their values can lead to a happier life. By not making value judgments about Black clients' behavior, helping professionals are able to facilitate personal growth. Third, if professionals have shared some of the behavior changes they have made in their own lives and have accepted and not judged the behavior of Black clients as good or bad, these clients may be open to commit themselves to a plan of action to change their behavior.

Behavioral Counseling

The behavioral counseling approach contains three techniques that helping professionals can use to help Black clients find solutions to their personal concerns. Goal setting, role playing, and modeling can help Black clients learn to acquire those behaviors that they believe will help them become better individuals. For example, many Black clients perceive the counseling relationship as a process in which both the professional and client are actively involved in seeking solutions to the clients' concerns. By assisting Black clients to set realistic goals for the counseling relationship, professionals can demonstrate that they are willing to share their thoughts and feelings with those clients and that the clients' concerns can be resolved. Role playing and modeling are effective ways in which professionals can help Black clients acquire new behaviors because these techniques emphasize demonstrating appropriate behavior. Through these techniques professionals and clients are actively involved in the counseling process. Helping professionals can use these behavioral techniques to counsel Black clients if the techniques are used in a spirit of cooperation.

Gestalt Counseling

Frederick Perls' theory of Gestalt counseling offers some techniques that helping professionals can use to help Black clients understand themselves and their environments. The aim of Gestalt counseling is to assist individuals to discover that they need not depend on others but can be independent (Shertzer & Stone, 1974). A major focus of Gestalt counseling is to help the individual make the transition from environmental support to self-support (Shertzer & Stone, 1974). In counseling Black clients, professionals must keep in mind that although society may provide obstacles or impasses for Black clients, it is necessary for them to overcome these impediments and become fully functioning, responsible individuals.

Gestalt counseling contains several techniques that can help Black clients to become more aware of themselves and their environments. Enhancing awareness is a Gestalt technique that helps clients focus their attention on immediate behavior (Shertzer & Stone, 1974). Helping professionals can help Black clients become aware of their present behavior by asking "how" and "what" questions. Many Black clients' concerns are a part of their immediate past experiences and these need to be resolved during the first counseling session. By enhancing Black clients' awareness toward their concerns, professionals demonstrate that they are ready to offer immediate help.

Sharing hunches is a Gestalt technique that encourages clients to explore inner feelings (Shertzer & Stone, 1974). By introducing statements about clients' concerns with such phrases as "I see you as being" or "I imagine that you feel," professionals can help Black clients discuss their feelings and concerns in more depth. Because many Black clients are emotional and want' helping professionals to become actively involved in the counseling relationship, sharing hunches can help Black clients understand that professionals are listening to them, are aware of their emotions, and want to hear more about their concerns.

Rational-Emotive Counseling

Albert Ellis' theory of rational-emotive counseling provides two techniques that helping professionals can use to help Black clients become more rational problem-solving individuals. These techniques are the ABC method and the use of homework assignments. The ABC method is the application of principles from rational-emotive counseling that helps clients to change their irrational thinking or beliefs to rational thinking or beliefs (Cunningham & Peters, 1973). This method encourages clients to use rational thinking to control their emotions. Professionals' active roles in this method can motivate Black clients to think in ways that help them solve their own problems. For Black clients who seek concrete ideas and suggestions for resolving their concerns, the ABC method can be quite effective.

Use of homework assignments with Black clients also provides ways for them to work on solutions to their concerns

170

outside counseling relationships. These assignments should be practical, that is, assignments that clients can accomplish (Cunningham & Peters, 1973). Assignments should be jointly agreed on by professional and client to ensure that both parties understand what is to be done by the client. Both the use of the ABC method and homework assignments are techniques that helping professionals can use to help Black clients reach practical solutions to their concerns and develop rational ways of thinking.

General Information

No time can be specified during the counseling relationship when the concepts or techniques discussed previously should be used. Rather, the primary aim is for helping professionals to consider individual differences among Black clients, to understand the nature of the clients' concerns, and to be prepared to respond by using one or more of these concepts and techniques. These approaches and techniques are flexible in that they can be adapted to meet individual needs of Black clients. These concepts can be used to help verbal and nonverbal Black clients resolve their personal and nonpersonal concerns. Use of most of these concepts and techniques requires that helping professionals be active participants in the counseling process. Because of the hesitance of many Black clients to disclose themselves in counseling relationships, professionals must be willing to take risks and become actively involved in the counseling process. Active involvement by professionals demonstrates to Black clients that the professionals are genuinely interested in the clients as people and in their concerns. Therefore, it is important for professionals to remember that being actively involved in counseling relationships can help them become more effective with Black clients.

Helping professionals can learn to use these approaches and techniques with Black clients by first learning to apply each approach—behavioral, client-centered, existential, Gestalt, rational-emotive, and reality counseling. If professionals can effectively apply each of these six approaches, then they can begin to use a combination of the concepts and techniques with Black clients. For some helping professionals, this application means learning or relearning

171

how to use these approaches and techniques effectively. For other professionals who already know how to use these approaches, it means being more eclectic when they counsel Black clients.

POST TEST

Directions: After reading the chapter mark each item.

1. If you had to walk in the skin of a person of another race, which of these would be the most damaging to self:

_____a. being called a stereotypical name by a member of another race
_____b. being the only member of your race in a classroom setting
_____c. constantly failing standardized tests
_____d. being judged by the color of your skin rather than the content of your character

2. This Black leader encouraged Black people to pursue higher education in order to cultivate knowledge and leadership:

_____a. Booker T. Washington
_____b. W.E.B. DuBois
_____c. Frederick Douglass
_____d. Harriet Tubman

3. Which of the following is not a major problem confronting Black people today:

_____a. being labeled as a minority group member
_____b. being able to utilize public facilities
_____c. the lack of Blacks in nontraditional fields or careers
_____d. discrimination in housing and jobs

4. Being seen as people who have the capacity to contribute to society remains a dream to Blacks because:

_____a. Blacks are not understood, accepted, or respected
_____b. Blacks are stereotyped
_____c. Blacks are not treated fairly
_____d. Blacks are not included enough in mainstream society

5. Which of the following is not a method of providing Black students with role models in nontraditional career areas:

_____a. developing a slide/tape presentation that shows Blacks in nontraditional career areas discussing how they became interested in these areas
_____b. compiling a career scrapbook that has pictures of Blacks in nontraditional career areas
_____c. inviting Blacks in nontraditional career areas to speak to Black students about career opportunities in their areas
_____d. encouraging Black students to explore a variety of nontraditional career areas

6. Older Blacks do not utilize counseling services because:

_____a. they are not aware of the services that are provided by counselors and counseling agencies
_____b. they do not believe that counseling works
_____c. too few Black counselors are working in Black communities
_____d. many of the counseling agencies in the community that provide counseling expect clients to come in for help

7. Which of the following counseling approaches is most effective with Black clients:

_____a. behavioral
_____b. client-centered
_____c. rational-emotive/reality
_____d. eclectic

Scoring Guide for Post Test

1. d	3. b	5. d	7. d
2. b	4. d	6. a	

Reference List

Cunningham, L., & Peters, H. *Counseling theories*. Columbus, Ohio: Charles E. Merrill, 1973.

Glasser, W., & Zunin, L. Reality therapy. In R. Corsini (Ed.), *Current psychotherapies*. Ithaca, Ill. F.E. Peacock, 1973.

Shertzer, B., & Stone, S. *Fundamentals of counseling* (2nd ed.). Boston: Houghton Mifflin, 1974.

Sloan, I. *Blacks in America 1492-1970*. Dobbs Ferry, N.Y.: Oceana Publications, Inc., 1971.

Strickland, B. Kierkegaard and counseling for individuality. *Personnel and Guidance Journal*, 1966, *44*, 470-474.

U.S. Bureau of the Census, *Current population reports*, Series P-20, No. 324, "Population Profile of the United States: 1977," U.S. Government Printing Office, Washington, D.C., 1978.

8

Asian—Americans

David Sue, Ph.D.

Associate Professor of Psychology
University of Michigan
Dearborn, Michigan

David Sue, Ph.D.

David Sue, Ph.D., is currently an Associate Professor of Psychology at the University of Michigan-Dearborn. He received his undergraduate degree at the University of Oregon and completed his doctorate at Washington State University in 1973. Dr. Sue has research and clinical interests in Asian-Americans, Behavior Therapy, and Human Sexuality. He is a licensed psychologist in the State of Michigan and actively engages in consultation and psychotherapy. Dr. Sue frequently collaborates on articles concerning Asian-Americans with his brothers, Derald and Stan, who also are psychologists.

ASIAN—AMERICANS

David Sue, Ph.D.

AWARENESS INDEX

Directions: Mark each item true or false.
Compute your score from the scoring guide at the end of this awareness index.
A post test is provided at the end of the chapter.

T F 1. Most Japanese voiced strong objections to the United States government to their forced evacuation to detention camps during World War II.

T F 2. The incidence of poverty among elderly Chinese is much higher than that for elderly black and Spanish-speaking populations.

T F 3. College enrollment rates for Chinese and Japanese between the ages of 18-24 is quite high, but the percentage of these individuals who actually complete college is surprisingly small.

T F 4. Most studies indicate that Chinese and Japanese groups have highly similar values and family structure.

T F 5. Asian-Americans appear to have as varied a choice of careers as their caucasian counterparts.

Scoring Guide for Awareness Index
1. T   3. F   5. F
2. T   4. T

PERCEPTIONS, SENSITIVITY, FEELINGS

The following poems were written by fifth and sixth grade children from Franklin School in Berkeley, California as part of a class project and they illustrate the perceptions, sensitivity, and feelings of being a member of a minority group in American. (D.W. Sue, 1973, pp. 397-399.)

I'm an Asian and I'm proud ot it. I'm a person although some people don't look upon me as one. They call me names and think it's funny! Sure I get called names. Do you think I like it? After all, how would you feel if someone called you a "Ching, chong Chinaman" or a "Nip"? They can't even tell us apart.

They say things about our culture like, "They write so funny." Even our language they make fun of by going Ching, cho chu.

I'm an Asian. I've got dignity but the thing I don't have is friendship.

Robert Chung

Asians are silent people
Never speaking of distress
Bearing much in their heart
The burden of the silent one.

Standing up to their rights
Trying to prove loyal by working hard.
America, a place of hopes . . .
For white people only!

Leah Appel

178

I am an Asian. Asians are proud people and I am proud to be Asian. Many people call me Caucasian, especially blacks. I have been called names, as many people have. Asians have been placed in concentration camps, discriminated and bombed. Yet at this moment, they are fighting and dying for their country in Vietnam.

People who don't know the Asian history say things like "All Chinese are laundry men" and "All Japanese are gardeners." Of course, I know it was the only menial labor available when the immigrants first came to America.

I hate that song with, "Japanese eyes slant down and Chinese eyes slant up." Last year I was the only Asian in my class. As an insult they called people "Chinese spies." It is enough to make you sick.

But, I am proud to be Asian and I want all to know.

Naomi Nishimura

Material written by children on pp. 178-180 is reproduced from Derald Wing Sue, "Asians are . . . ," *The Personnel and Guidance Journal*, Vol. 51, No. 6, Feb 1973, pp. 397-399, with permission from American Personnel and Guidance Association.

Yellow is the sun coming
up in the morning
And the sun coming down
in the evening
Yellow is a house being painted
Yellow is the color of
some pencils
Yellow is the sunset,
Yellow is the sunrise.
Yellow is the color of some paper.
It's the peeling of a
grapefruit or lemon,
Yellow is the shine of
a light.
Yellow is a banana.
Yellow is a color that
is very bright to
everyone.
Yellow is me!

Jon Mishima

POPULATION

Difficulties arise in the attempt to characterize Asian-Americans because this population is comprised of so many different groups (Chinese, Guaminas, Japanese, Korean, Malays, Philipinos, Samoans, Vietnamese, and so forth), each with its own language and cultural history. Compounding the problem are the differences that exist within specific Asian-American groups in terms of acculturation and primary language or generational status in the United States. For example, the primary language in Chinese groups may be Cantonese, Mandarin, or English. Asian groups are continually bolstered by immigrants and an estimation is that by 1980 the Asian-American population will reach three million, double the 1970 census figure (Owan, 1975). Since 1975, 220,000 refugees from Indochina have been granted permanent residency ("The Home of the Brave," 1979) and in June, 1979, President Carter doubled the number of Indochinese refugees allowed to enter the United States to 14,000 a month.

CHINESE AND JAPANESE AMERICANS

The diversity of Asian-American groups, each with different cultural norms and values, means that adequate representation of the groups is simply not possible. The focus of the present chapter, therefore, will be primarily on the Chinese and Japanese groups, who currently comprise the two largest Asian-American populations in the United States and who have the earliest history of entry into this country. According to the 1970 census, the Japanese are the largest Asian-American subgroup with a population of 591,000, 72 percent of whom live either in Hawaii or California. The rate of immigration of this group is low, averaging about 5,000 a year. The Japanese group will be characterized more and more as American born. The second largest subgroup is the Chinese with a reported 1970 census figure of 435,000, the majority of whom live in the Western United States. Another large percentage of this population (20%) lives in the state of New York. Approximately 20,000 Chinese immigrate to the United States each year. In contrast to the Japanese population, the Chinese are increasingly becoming an immigrant group and, by 1980, will number 800,000, to become the largest Asian minority in the United States (Owan, 1975).

Brief History of Chinese and Japanese in America

Asian-American groups immigrated to the United States for much the same reasons as other immigrant groups—seeking a financial security and an improved standard of living. The first Asian group to immigrate heavily to the United States was the Chinese in the 1840's. The immigration was triggered by the discovery of gold in California coupled with a disasterous crop failure in China. In contrast to other immigrant groups, the Chinese were "sojourners"—individuals who did not seek to settle permanently but to earn some money and return to China. The Chinese immigrants, who were primarily males, worked as laborers in gold mines and railroads or were employed at other less desirable jobs such as laundry work. They were subjected to massive discrimination and prejudice soon after arriving. These attitudes resulted in the Exclusion Act of 1882 which prevented the legal immigration of Chinese from 1882 until 1944, when the act was repealed. This ban resulted in the separation of husbands from their wives for decades and a highly unequal sex ratio. In 1890 over 100,000 Chinese males and only 3,868 Chinese women were in the United States (Wong, 1973). Not until the 1960's was a closer balance attained. Today the elderly males still form a higher percentage than their female counterparts (Office of Special Concerns, 1974).

Currently, the Chinese are considered a successful minority. However, they form a bimodal distribution with one mode composed of a highly successful group and the second mode encompassing much less successful individuals. Over 40 percent of the Chinese-Americans earn an annual income of less than $4,000, which is a higher percentage of poverty than the average for the United States (Office of Special Concerns, 1974). Recent immigrants who gain employment in low paying and unskilled work will increase the percentage of poor Chinese. The immigrants migrate to New York City and the larger cities in California aggravating the ghetto-like conditions in the Chinatowns.

Immigration of the Japanese in large numbers began in the 1890's from Hawaii and Japan. They also were lured by the promise of better conditions and wealth in the United States and filled the demand for a cheap source of labor to replace the Chinese. Many Japanese males came to the United States to live and later sent away for picture brides from Japan. As laborers, they worked on railroads and in canneries. Because the great majority of them were from the farming class, many turned to farming and worked on unwanted lands or found work as agricultural laborers. Although the Japanese were considered as more desirable than the Chinese because they brought their families, prejudice and discrimination quickly followed. In 1906, the San Francisco Board of Education issued an order segregating Japanese from white school children (Masuda, 1973). The Gentlemen's agreement limited immigration and the Alien Land Act of 1920 which was directed primarily against the Japanese prevented them from purchasing land. An editorial in the San Francisco Chronicle in 1920 reflected the attitude of white Americans at that time (Ogawa, 1973):

The Japanese boys are taught by their elders to look upon . . . American girls with a view to future sex relations

. . . What answer will the fathers and mothers of America make . . . ? The proposed assimilation of the two races is unthinkable. It is morally undefensible and biologically impossible. American womanhood is far too sacred to be subjected to such degeneracy. An American who would not die fighting rather than yield to that infamy does not deserve the name . . . (p. 7)

Feelings against the Japanese culminated in the location of over 110,000 persons of Japanese ancestry into detention camps during World War II. Effects of these camps resulted in financial ruin for many Japanese families, disrupted the family structure, and served to break up Japantowns (Kitano, 1969). Currently, the Japanese are considered a model minority. However, evidence is clear that they tend to be underemployed (Office of Special Concerns, 1974).

SPECIAL PROBLEMS

As a group, Asian-Americans have not received widespread attention from educators, counselors, nor state and federal officials. The prevailing view that Asian-Americans are model minorities and problem free has resulted in limited financial and moral support. Although special concerns sessions were held for Blacks, Spanish speaking, and Native Americans at the White House Conference on Aging in 1971, Asian-Americans were not included until a request was made by Asian-American groups (Asian-American Elderly, 1972). This exclusion was in spite of statistics from the Office of Special Concerns (1974) that the incidence of poverty among elderly Chinese is much higher than that for elderly black and Spanish-speaking populations. Similarly, Asian-Americans were originally not included in the National Institute for Mental Health Center for Minority Group Programs, since problems among this population were unknown (Brown & Ochberg, 1973). Asian-Americans frequently are not categorized as minorities and not often eligible for affirmative action programs. One Asian-American applying for admission to graduate school was told that in order to qualify as a minority

183

group member he would have to furnish information indicating that he came from a disadvantaged background. Members of other minority groups were not required to furnish this information (Sue, Sue, & Sue, 1975).

Housing

Problems among Asian-Americans are not highly visible because many of them occur in Chinatowns. Twenty percent of all Chinese housing is overcrowded. This percentage is 33 percent in New York City. San Francisco's Chinatown spans 42 square blocks and contains 885 persons an acre, which is ten times the national average (Yee, 1970). Exacerbating the problem is the continued influx of Asian immigrants to already overcrowded communities.

Counselors and educators tend to feel that Asian-Americans experience few adjustment difficulties and this view has been supported by the popular press ("Success Story: Outwhiting the Whites," 1979; "Success Story of One Minority Group," 1966). The *Newsweek* article "Success Story: Outwhiting the Whites," (1979) pointed out the "success" of the 220,000 Indochinese refugees who have settled in the United States since 1975; nearly 95 percent are either employed or attending school. The article also pointed out, however, that 40 percent of those who had white collar jobs were underemployed. This success myth masks the discrimination and prejudice that Asian-Americans still face (Governor's Asian American Advisory Council, 1973) and has resulted in a lack of financial and government interest. Reflecting the lack of attention placed on Asian-Americans is the finding by Yee (1973), who examined 300 social studies textbooks for elementary and secondary schools. Approximately 75 percent of the books made no mention of Chinese at all, and the rest provided minimal coverage involving Chinatowns, the development of silk, and Oriental customs.

Testing and Education

For many Asian-Americans, entering school with strange and confusing surroundings can be a frightening experience. A lack of facility with English provides an additional

184

disadvantage. Information from the Office of Special Concerns (1974) indicated that 62 percent of the Japanese in the United States for three or more generations will speak predominantly Japanese as children. Among Chinese children under the age of fourteen, 96 percent of those who are foreign-born speak Chinese and 70 percent of the second generation children speak Chinese in their homes. Facility with English will continue to be a problem for future generations of Asian-Americans. Because of this difficulty, Asian-Americans may be at a disadvantage with respect to tests such as the Graduate Record Examination or the Miller Analogies Test which depends heavily on familiarity with English. Watanabe (1973) reported that at the University of California at Berkely, over one-half of the students of Asian descent failed to demonstrate competence in college-level reading and composition which is twice the failure rate of the general campus population.

Personal Stress and Conflict

Constant exposure to the values and norms of the host culture as well as the lack of information on the culture of Asian-Americans in schools and society may produce stress and conflict. Japanese-Americans have been found to be more tense and apprehensive than their caucasian counterparts (Meredith & Meredith, 1966). Both Chinese and Japanese students are characterized as internalizing blame, and experiencing feelings of isolation, anxiety and nervousness (Ayabe, 1971; Fenz & Arkoff, 1962; Sue & Kirk, 1973). Chinese-American college students also display a higher fear of negative evaluation and lower assertiveness than caucasian college students (Sue, Ino, & Sue 1979). Self-esteem problems have been found in Asian elementary students. They are twice as likely as whites to endorse a statement that "good luck is more important for success than hard work," an indication that they had less sense of control over their environment (Coleman, Campbell, Hobson, McPartland, Mood, Weinfeld, & York, 1972).

PERSONAL AND COUNSELING NEEDS OF ASIAN-AMERICANS

Traditional values have had a very significant impact on the psychological characteristics of Asian groups. A variety of studies comparing caucasian and Asian students have found that the latter experience value conflicts, more loneliness, passivity, conformance, deference, reserve, and humbleness (Ayabe, 1971; Meredith & Meredith, 1966; Sue & Frank, 1973). An examination of test results involving 154 Chinese and Japanese males attending the University of California, Berkeley also found that these Asian students avoid abstract theoretical approaches, have low tolerance for ambiguity, demonstrate a liking for structure and tend to evaluate ideas in terms of practical applications (Sue & Frank, 1973). Although indications are of increasing assimilation and changes in social roles (Fong, 1973; Levine & Montero, 1973), Asian-Americans will continue to show unique personality and interest patterns for generations to come.

Values

The result of personality tests are attributable to Asian values and probably the exposure to an oppressive society. Because it would be difficult to determine the effects of prejudice and discrimination, the discussion will focus on Chinese and Japanese values which are highly similar. In both cultures, the families are patriarchal with the father in control of authority. Parent to child communications are formal and flow downward. Relationships between family members as well as role expectations are well defined and each member's position is highly interdependent. Good behaviors such as filial piety, achievement, and obedience are defined clearly and an individual's behavior reflects upon the entire family. Control of the children is maintained by fostering feelings of shame and guilt. These values can account for the importance of structure and deference in Asian-Americans.

Independence and Self-Reliance

Chinese and Japanese children feel a much greater sense of obligation towards the family and parents than do caucasians. As Hsu (1953, p. 72) observed, "The most important thing to Americans is what parents should do for the children; to Chinese, what children should do for their parents". In Chinese stories, personal sacrifices for the sake of filial piety are rewarded while in stories such as Cinderella and Hansel and Gretel to which Americans are exposed, the children defeat evil adults. Family expectations of unquestioning obedience often produce problems when Asian children are exposed to American values emphasizing independence and self-reliance. These conflicts may be revealed during counseling sessions:

> John's parents had always had high expectations of him and constantly pressured him to do well in school They seemed to equate his personal worth with his ability to maintain good grades. This pressure caused him to spend endless hours studying, and generally he remained isolated for social activities . . . John's more formalized training was in sharp contrast to the informality and spontaneity demanded in caucasian interpersonal relationships . . . his cirlce of friends was small and he was never really able to enjoy himself with others. John experiences much conflict because he was beginning to resent the pressure his parents put on him and also their demands. His deep seated feelings of anger toward his parents resulted in his passive aggressive responses of failure in school and his physical symptoms . . .

As Sue and Sue (1972) pointed out, the case of John illustrates possible conflicts faced by Asian students between their loyalty to the family and desires for personal independence, learned patterns of emotional restraint and formality which interfere with social interactions, and feelings of guilt and depression when failing to live up to parental expectations.

Educational Expectations

The pressure to succeed academically among Asians is very strong. From early childhood, outstanding achievement is emphasized because it is a source of pride for the entire family. Chinese mothers are more likely than white mothers (41 percent versus 11 percent) to rate school achievement as "very important" (Sollenberger, 1968). This finding was surprising since 47 percent of the mothers and 52 percent of the fathers in the study sample had received no more than elementary school education and were from the lower socioeconomic class. Reflecting the emphasis on education is the finding that college enrollment rates for Chinese and Japanese between the ages of 18-24 and the percentage completing college is higher than any other group in the United States. Parental expectations for achievement can be an additional stress factor in young Asian-Americans.

Emotional Restraint

In Chinese and Japanese cultures restraint of emotions is emphasized because emotions are viewed as potentially disruptive forces on the family structure. Because of this restraint, emotional expression is considered a sign of immaturity and is suppressed. Most Americans, however, feel that the expressing of emotions is indicative of individuals who are mature and accepting of themselves. The conflict produced by these differences in values is illustrated in this example of an Asian placed in a group situation.

> The Japanese group member is deterred from directly confronting other group members because he has been taught that it is impolite to put people on the spot . . . the admission and display of personal inadequacy, even in a counseling group is a sign of familial defect . . . In most situations the Japanese person tends to be non-expressive. He has been raised [reared] since childhood not to show his emotions. Thus, although he may be moved by what is occurring in the group, he is almost instinctively restrained from revealing his concern, and facial expression remains passive. . .One Caucasian characterized this behavior as a sign of noncaring, and it brought forth this exclamation from him "Doesn't this have any effect on you? Don't you care at all?" (Kaneshige, 1973, pp. 408-410)

Kaneshige suggested that, in group situations involving Asians, extra effort has to be made to produce a non-threatening climate. Confidentiality must be stressed and responses from Asians should be actively elicited while minimizing interruptions by other group members.

Career Choices

Sue and Frank (1973) also found differences in choice of career fields. In contrast to the general student body, Chinese and Japanese students were more likely to show interest patterns and career majors in non-social science fields such as engineering and sciences of chemistry, biology, and physics. Similar findings were obtained on a sample of Chinese-American students attending a large midwestern university (Sue, Ino, Sue, 1979). Watanabe (1973) hypothesized that the under-representation of Asians in the social science areas may be due partly to culture since forceful self-expression is not reinforced or it may be because of discrimination and prejudice that Asians are more likely to face in the social science fields. Many well meaning counselors may unintentionally restrict the career choices of Asians in the social sciences because of the stereotypic notions that Asians are "good in the physical sciences" and "poor in people relationship areas." As with any group that has faced restricted career choices, careful exploration of all possible fields must be presented to the individuals.

IMPLICATIONS OF CULTURAL VALUES ON TRADITIONAL COUNSELING

Many counselors do not understand why Asian-American clients do not actively participate in the counseling process, and often label them as "repressed" or "resistant" (Sue & Sue, 1972). Such a reaction illustrates the problems that exist when the helping professional and the client differ in racial and ethnic backgrounds. Differences in value orientations and expectations may be responsible for premature termination of minority group members. Sue and McKinney (1975) found in their study of 17 mental health centers that over 50 percent of the Asian-American clients dropped out of therapy after only one session versus a rate of 29 percent for caucasian clients. To obtain an adequate understanding of the effects of cultural values on counseling, one needs to examine some of the characteristics of traditional forms of counseling and contrast them with the values of Asian-Americans. Sue and Sue (1977) identified three types of goals or expectations in counseling which may be a source of conflict with minority group members.

First, most counselors expect their clients to exhibit openness and psychological mindedness. To do so, however, the client must be fascile with the standard form of English. Because many Asian-Americans come from a bilingual background, they may be disadvantaged in this form of verbal expression. Asian clients also have learned to restrain emotional expression and feel that this repression represents a sign of maturity. These factors can hinder verbal communication and a counselor who is inexperienced with clients from minority Asian groups may conclude erroneously that the individual is resistant or repressed.

Second, the process of counseling involves the revelation of intimate details on the part of the client. The cultural upbringing of Chinese and Japanese clients may be in opposition to this goal. Discussion of personal problems is difficult because such disclosure is felt to reflect not only on the individual but also on the whole family. The pressure from the family not to reveal personal matters to strangers is strong. In addition, the Asian client comes to the counseling situation expecting advice or practical solutions rather than to gain insight into the nature of his problem. Many Asian-Americans feel that mental health is due to the avoidance of morbid thoughts and that mental illness has an organic basis (Tsai, Teng, & Sue, 1979). Problems may be presented in the form of somatic complaints or in educational and occupational difficulties. A focus on personality dynamics at the beginning may be misunderstood and serve to drive the client away.

Third, the counseling environment is often an ambiguous one for the client. The therapist listens while the client talks about the problem. In many cases, little direction is given. The unstructured nature of the counseling environment adds additional stress to Asian-American clients who prefer concrete, tangible, and structured approaches to problems. The pattern of communication also may be unsettling. Asian-Americans may have been reared in an environment in which

190

communication flows down from an authority figure. The counselor is expected to initiate a conversation. Placed in a situation where the Asian-American client is asked to initiate conversations, the counselor will likely receive only short phrases or sentences. A counselor may respond negatively to Asian-American clients not knowing that for them, silence and deference may be a sign of respect.

These factors indicate the importance of flexibility on the part of the counselor and helping professional in working with Asian-Americans. Because an Asian-American will already feel much ambivalence in seeking therapy, a helping professional needs to use a gradual approach. Confrontation will increase already present feelings of guilt and shame. Instead of immediately focusing on personal matters, the counselor may follow the lead of the client and discuss the presenting problem even if it is considered to be "superficial." Sue and Sue (1972) presented a case in which meaningful material was obtained after the individual completed the Edwards Personal Preference Schedule. The presenting problem revolved around vocational counseling. The counselor's impression was that the client was encountering conflict over parental type expectations of him as the oldest son. Direct approaches to discuss this problem were not successful. However, a discussion of test results in a nonthreatening manner provided the opening.

COUNSELOR: Let's explore the meaning of your scores in greater detail as they relate to future vocations. All right?

CLIENT: Okay.

COUNSELOR: Your high score on achievement indicates that whatever you undertake you would like to excel and do well in. For example, if you enter pharmacy, you'd do well in that field (client nods head). However, your high change score indicates that you like variety and change . . . You may tend to get restless at times . . . Maybe feel trapped in activities that bore you.

191

CLIENT: Yeah.

COUNSELOR: Do you see this score (Abasement score)?

CLIENT: Yeah, I blew the scale on that one . . . What is it?

COUNSELOR: Well, it indicates you tend to be hard on yourself . . . For example, if you were to do poorly in pharmacy school . . . you would blame yourself for the failure . . .

CLIENT: Yeah, yeah . . . I'm always doing that . . . I feel that . . . it's probably exaggerated.

COUNSELOR: Exaggerated?

CLIENT: I mean . . . being the oldest son.

COUNSELOR: What's it like to be the oldest son?

CLIENT: Well . . . there's alot of pressure and you feel immobolized. Maybe this score (points to change scale) is why I feel so restless. (pp. 642-643)

This approach led to a discussion of his resentment toward his parents for the pressure to succeed which was followed by a successful resolution to the problem. The provision of structure as well as a careful explanation of the counseling process will do much to facilitate mutual understanding. Once rapport and trust have been formed, a counselor will have greater freedom in exploring more potential areas of conflict.

Finally, some words of caution should be presented. Most Asian-Americans are able to handle the cultural conflicts and adequately resolve them. This last section has dealt with only those encountering difficulty. Greater variability also exists among Asian-Americans in the degree to which they are influenced by cultural values. Many Asian-Americans are as assertive as caucasians. A counselor, educator, or other human service worker should not automatically assume Asian-

192

Americans will have conflicts over emotional or assertive expression. Rather, the understanding of Asian values should sensitize individuals to potential conflicts and conflict areas. Counselors will still have to rely on their clinical judgement and knowledge of cultural differences.

POST TEST

Directions: After reading the Chapter, mark each item either true or false.
Compute your score from the scoring guide at the end of this post test.

T F 1. Asian-Americans can be considered a model minority group, with a very low incidence of poverty and under-employment.

T F 2. The psychological characteristics of Asian-American college students have been found to be virtually identical to those of Caucasian college students.

T F 3. Most Asian-American clients may feel more comfortable in a structured counseling environment than one that is unstructured.

T F 4. Most second and third generation Chinese and Japanese children in the United States use English as the primary language in their homes.

T F 5. Asian-American clients often terminate prematurely from therapy.

Scoring Guide for Post Test
1. F   3. T   5. T
2. F   4. F

Reference List

Asian-American Elderly, The (White House Conference on Aging, 1971). Washington, D.C.: U.S. Government Printing Office, 1972.
Ayabe, H.L. Deference and ethnic differences in voice levels. Journal of Social Psychology, 1971, 85, 181-185.

Brown, B.S., & Ochberg, F.M. Key issues in developing a national minority mental health program at NIMH. In C. Willie, B. Kramer, & B.S. Brown (Eds.), *Racism and mental health: Essays.* Pittsburg: University of Pittsburg Press, 1973.

Coleman, J.S., Campbell, E.Q., Hobson, C.J., McPartland, J., Mood, A.M., Weinfield, F.D., & York, R.L. The locus of control and academic performance among racial groups. In S.S. Gutterman (Ed.), *Black psyche.* Berkley: The Glendessary Press, 1972.

Fenz, W., & Arkoff, A. Comparative need patterns of five ancestry groups in Hawaii. *Journal of Social Psychology,* 1962, *58,* 67-89.

Fong, S.L.M. Assimilation and changing social roles of Chinese-Americans. *Journal of Social Issues,* 1973, *29,* 115-128.

Governor's Asian American Advisory Council. *Discrimination against Asians.* Seattle: State of Washington, 1973.

Home of the brave. *Newsweek,* July 2, 1979, p. 48.

Hsu, F.L.K. *American and Chinese: Two ways of life.* New York: Abeland-Schuman, 1953.

Kaneshige, E. Cultural factors in group counseling with interaction. *Personnel and Guidance Journal,* 1973, *51,* 407-412.

Kitano, H.L. *Japanese Americans: The evolution of a subculture.* Englewood Cliffs, New Jersey: Prentice-Hall, Inc., 1969.

Levine, G.N., & Montero, D.M. Socioeconomic mobility among three generations of Japanese Americans. *Journal of Social Issues,* 1973, *29,* 33-48.

Masuda, M. The Japanese. In Governor's Asian-American Advisory Council, *Discrimination Against Asians.* Seattle: State of Washington, 1973, 6-9.

Meredith, G.M., & Meredith, C.G.W. Acculturation and personality among Japanese-American college students in Hawaii. *Journal of Social Psychology,* 1966, *68,* 175-182.

Office of Special Concerns. *A study of selected socioeconomic characteristics of ethnic minorities based on the 1970 census, Volume II: Asian-American.* Washington, D.C.: Department of Health, Education, and Welfare, 1974.

Ogawa, D. The Jap Image. In S. Sue & N. Wagner (Eds.), *Asian-Americans: Psychological perspectives.* Ben Lomand, Ca.: Science and Behavior Books, Inc., 1973.

Owan, T. Asian-Americans: A case of benighted neglect. Paper presented at the National Conference of Social Welfare, San Francisco, 1975.

Sollenberger, R.T. Chinese-American child rearing practices and juvenile delinquency. *Journal of Social Psychology,* 1968, *74,* 13-23.

Success story of one minority group. *U.S. News and World Report,* December 26, 1966, pp. 32-34.

Success story: Outwhiting the whites. *Newsweek,* July 21, 1979, p. 27.

Sue, D.W. Asians are . . . *Personnel and Guidance Journal,* 1973, *51,* 397-399.

Sue, D.W., & Frank, A.C. Chinese and Japanese American college males. *Journal of Social Issues,* 1973, *29,* 129-148.

Sue, D., Ino, S., & Sue, D.M. Assertiveness in midwestern Chinese Americans. Unpublished manuscript, 1979. (Available from author of this chapter.)

Sue, D.W., & Kirk, B.S. Differential characteristics of Japanese-American and Chinese-American college students. *Journal of Counseling Psychology,* 1973, *20,* 142-146.

Sue, S., & McKinney, H. Asian-Americans in the community health care system. *American Journal of Orthopsychiatry,* 1975, *45,* 111-118.

194

Sue, D.W., & Sue, S. Counseling Chinese-Americans. *Personnel and Guidance Journal*, 1972, *50*, 637-644.

Sue, D.W., & Sue, D. Barriers to effective cross-cultural counseling. *Journal of Counseling Psychology*, 1977, *24*, 420-429.

Sue, S., Sue, D.W., & Sue, D. Asian-Americans as a minority group. *American Psychologist*, 1975, *30*, 906-910.

Tsai, M., Teng, L.N., & Sue, S. Mental health status of Chinese in the United States. In A. Kleinman & T.Y. Lin (Eds.), *Normal and deviant behavior in Chinese culture*. Hingham, Ma.: Reidel Publishing Company, 1979.

Watanabe, C. Self-expression and Asian-American experience. *Personnel and Guidance Journal*, 1973, *51*, 390-396.

Wong, K.C. The Chinese. In Governor's Asian-American Advisory Council, *Discrimination against Asians*. Seattle: State of Washington, 1973, 2-5.

Yee, A. Myopic perceptions and textbooks: Chinese Americans' search for identity. *Journal of Social Issues*, 1973, *29*, 99-113.

Yee, M. Chinatown in crisis. *Newsweek*, February 23, 1970, 57-58.

9

Older
Persons

Harold C. Riker, Ed.D.

Professor of Education
Counselor Education Department
University of Florida
Gainesville, Florida

Harold C. Riker, Ed.D.

Harold C. Riker is professor of education, Counselor Education Department, University of Florida, Gainesville. He is a faculty associate of the Center for Gerontological Programs and Studies and a member of its steering committee. Dr. Riker received his B.A. and MA. degrees in English literature and history from the University of Florida; his Ed.D. degree in student personnel administration from Teachers College, Columbia University.

Active in local, regional, and national professional associations, he is currently chairperson, Advisory Council, Gainesville Area Agency on Aging, covering 16 counties; past chairperson and member, Gainesville Housing Authority; vice president, Florida Council on Aging; member, planning committee, 1980 Governor's Conference on Aging; member, Advisory Board, Gainesville RSVP; member, American Personnel and Guidance Association's Committee on Adult Development and Aging, and editor of the Committee's quarterly newsletter; member, the Gerontological Society, National Council on Aging, and NRTA-AARP. His publications include **College Housing as Learning Centers** *(1965); "Learning by Doing," a chapter in* **Perspective on the Preparation of Student Affairs Professionals** *(1977); "Potential Crisis Situations for Older Persons," a chapter in* **Counseling the Aged** *(1978); and "Residential Learning," a chapter in the* **Future American College** *(in press). His continuing interests are in human development over the lifespan.*

OLDER PERSONS

Harold C. Riker, Ed.D.

AWARENESS INDEX

Directions: Mark each item as true or false.
Compute your score from the scoring guide at the end of this Awarness Index.
A post test is provided at the end of the chapter.

T F 1. An older person is one who is 55 years of age.

T F 2. Older persons are very much alike.

T F 3. The numbers of older persons are increasing rapidly.

T F 4. Older persons represent 29% of all persons with incomes below the poverty level.

T F 5. Physical impairment is largely limited to those who are 65 years of age and above.

T F 6. Stereotypes of older persons often become self-fullfilling prophecies.

T F 7. Counselors are likely to have some degree of prejudice against older persons.

Scoring Guide for Awareness Index
1. F   3. T   5. F   7. T
2. F   4. T   6. T

OLD OR NOT?

Age is a quality of mind.
If you have left your dreams behind,
If hope is cold,
If you no longer look ahead
If your ambition fires are dead,
Then you are old.

But if from life you take the best,
And if in life you keep the just,
If love you hold;
No matter how the years go by
No matter how the birthdays fly,
You are not old.

—Author Unknown

TWO CASES

Two delightful women illustrate the range of differences among older persons. The first, Mrs. G., is 72 years of age and lives alone in a college town where her husband was a member of the faculty before his sudden and unexpected death. She is representative of white, professional, middle-class families.

Mrs. G. has lived through her grief and has joined a small group of widows who, after a short training period, are active in assisting older, recently widowed women to work through their sense of loss and fear of the future.

A vivacious, attractive woman, who looks much younger than 72, Mrs. G. participates in a variety of community activities. She attends her church regularly and is a member of several of its committees. She has joined the Retired Senior Volunteer Program (RSVP) and spends four hours each week at the City Hall Information Desk.

Mrs. G. usually is busy, and usually with other busy women of about her same age. Together, they are involved in helping others through a number of community agencies. Mrs. G. has a son and his family living in the same town; she enjoys a warm relationship with them. She has a number of friends in other communities where she and her husband have lived, and maintains an active correspondence.

Mrs. G. is an active person who finds happiness and support in her family, her friends, and her service for others. She finds that age has brought new opportunities.

Mrs. C., on the other hand, represents a very different segment of U.S. society. In her mid-nineties, she is black, poor, and dependent for her existence on food stamps and supplemental security income provided by the Federal Government. When her two sons were very young, her husband deserted her and she assumed the full burden of the sons support. Now in their 70s, these sons remain strongly attached to their mother who has helped to rear their children and their children's children. Both sons have returned to live with Mrs. C., their time seems to be spent mostly in playing cards and drinking liquor.

Mrs. C. spends much of her time in bed, watching television. When she leaves the house, it is to see the doctor or attend church. Somewhat hard of hearing, she has a slight tremble in her voice and arthritis in her hands. Her physical environment is incredibly bad. The three room house in which she lives is in poor condition; there is no running water or inside toilet. Near the house is a water pump and old wooden privy. The house and yard are unkempt; flies and other insects abound. For her meals, Mrs. C. relies on her neighbors and junk foods.

For over 60 years, Mrs. C. worked as a house maid; for most of those years she was with one family and was regarded as a family member. Although life for Mrs. C. has been far from easy, she has been sustained and supported by the affection of her former employer and the bonds of love and loyalty which have held her family together.

WHO ARE OLDER PERSONS?

In the sense that every person is older than someone else, all persons are older. In the sense that attitudes toward life and living influence aging, those persons who habitually look backward to the past rather than forward to the future are older, regardless of their chronological age. By stating that persons sixty years of age and over are eligible for benefits under the Older Americans Act, the U.S. Congress has so defined older persons. Because retirement from jobs has traditionally been set at 65 years of age, those who are 65 and over often are described as older persons.

In order to define older persons as a special population, the chronological age of 65 and above is used in this chapter, principally because much of the demographic information about older persons is based on this age group. At the same time, one should recognize that those who are 40 years of age or more are often classified as older, particularly by employment agencies which are aware that those in this age group experience longer periods of unemployment than those who are younger.

Several points should be made about older persons. First, they are a very diverse group, with wide variations in family background, education, income, abilities, and interests. Second, each person is a unique individual, very much like he/she has always been, only more so. In other words, arrival at a certain age, whether forty, sixty, or sixty-five, in no way marks any fundamental change in personality, interests, or abilities. And, third, the rapid rise in numbers of older persons has created a special and growing segment of the total population, with particular needs, interests, and concerns which demand attention and response on the part of the U.S. society.

THE AGING OF AMERICA

U.S. citizens are living longer. As early as 1800, the median age was 16; by 1970, it was just under 28; by 2000, it will reach 35 *(Graying of America*, 1977). Between 1900 and

1976, the average life expectancy of men and women increased by more than 50%, from 47.3 to 72.8 years. For men, life expectancy in 1976 was 69.0; for women, 76.7. Currently, 75% of the U.S. population can expect to reach 75 years of age; in 1900, 40% could do so. Men who arrive at 65 years of age can anticipate living for 13.7 more years; women can expect 18 more years (National Committee on Careers for Older Americans, 1979).

The numbers of older persons are increasing dramatically. In 1900, about 3 million persons age 65 and over were reported by the U.S. Bureau of Census. This number expanded over six times to more than 20 million in 1970 (Atchley, 1977). The 1980 total is about 25 million, and the estimate for 1990 is almost 30 million, a ten-year growth of nearly 20% (*Challenges of the '80s,* 1979).

The population age mix will continue to change during the next decade. The largest percentage increases will occur in the 30-39 age group, up 28.5%, and the 40-49 age group, up 37.4% by 1990. The 65 and above age group will follow with a 19.6% growth in numbers (*Challenges of the '80s*, 1979). During the 20-year period from 1980 to 2000, those persons in the 75 + age group will increase in numbers by 52.5%, from about 9.5 million to almost 14.4 million. At the same time, the 65 and over age group will grow by 27.7% (National Committee on Careers for Older Americans, 1979).

Demographic Characteristics

An appalling fact about this population is the sizeable number who live at or below the poverty level. As of 1975, about 16 of every 100 older persons, or approximately 3.3 million, were below the poverty level, described as an income below $3,200. Although older persons represent only about 10% of the total population, they constitute approximately 29% of all persons receiving an income at the poverty level or below. In an inflationary period, with rising costs and the declining value of fixed incomes, older persons are especially vulnerable to financial difficulties. To assume that a person can maintain a decent standard of living on $3,200 a year, or $62 per week, is, to say the least, unrealistic (U.S. Government Printing Office, 1978).

On the basis of race, approximately 90% of persons 65 years of age and over are white; 8% are black; 2% are other. The sex ratio is weighted toward females who represent 59% of the total, while males represent 41%. Older persons have substantially less formal education than do those under 65 years of age. Sixty-three percent of the older person group has had some high school education or less as compared with 26% of those under 65 years of age (Harris & Associates, 1975).

Employment

The percentage of employed older persons has dropped steadily. In 1900, 63.1% of men over 65 were employed; by 1978, this percentage had fallen to 20.5% (National Committee on Careers for Older Americans, 1979). Among the factors involved was encouragement by the Federal Government for workers to retire early, thus creating more jobs for others. Organized labor also has bargained for pension plans which would permit early retirement, opening up employment and promotion opportunities for others. Inability to find or keep regular work has led some workers to use their retirement options.

Trends toward earlier retirement apparently do not reflect the preferences of a substantial proportion of workers and retirees. According to a 1979 Harris study, 51% of the surveyed employees expressed a preference to keep working rather than to retire; 48% in the 50-64 age group preferred to keep working after age 65; 46% of those who had retired wished they were still working; and 56% of the retired group wished they had not stopped working.

Health

Older persons, about 86% of them, are believed to have one or more chronic or long-term diseases such as arthritis, diabetes, high blood pressure, and heart disease. Yet, in spite of such conditions, these persons remain generally active and independent. At least 95% live in their own communities, with about 5% in institutions such as nursing homes. At the same time, the 65+ age group is responsible for about 25% of our country's health costs and makes use of as much as 25% of all drugs. It should be noted that 72% of those in the 45-64 age group also may have one or more chronic diseases as listed previously (Butler, 1975). Physical impairment, therefore, is by no means limited to those who are 65 years of age and above.

In the past, aging and disease were often regarded as part of the same process. More recently, the importance of distinguishing among changes resulting from aging, disease, and social-psychological factors has been recognized. For example, Comfort (1976) has concluded that about 25% of aging involves physical changes, such as gray hair, wrinkled skin, and weakened muscles. Seventy-five percent, he believes, can be described as "sociogenic aging" which is imposed on individuals by the negative stereotypes about aging maintained through the culture of which they are a part (Comfort, 1976). If indeed aging is, to some considerate extent, socially imposed, changes in negative stereotypes should receive high priority.

STEREOTYPES OF OLDER PERSONS

A basic problem experienced either directly or indirectly by older Americans is discrimination because of age. By means of discrimination, younger persons place older persons in a category of inferiority and describe older persons as different from themselves. This kind of discrimination enables younger persons to deny the possibility of their own aging. The irony of this situation is that these younger persons eventually find themselves the victims of their own prejudice.

An insidious effect of ageism, as Butler (1975) has described prejudice against older persons, is that many older persons accept and believe in their inferiority and the weaknesses attributed to them. What, then, are some of the common stereotypes?

The Stereotype of Unproductiveness

Older persons are believed to become unproductive and, hence, useless, a point of view long supported by the concept of mandatory retirement. However, the facts are that, given the opportunity, many older persons continue to be productive and actively involved in work and/or community life.

Contrary to popular belief, older workers can be as effective as younger workers, except perhaps in jobs requiring prolonged physical stamina or rapid response behaviors. Older workers are dependable, maintain excellent attendance and safety records, and require minimum supervision after job requirements are learned.

In terms of creativity, some persons remain active in their 80s and 90s. Examples include Pope John XXIII, working at church reform; Christopher Wrenn, designing St. Paul's Cathedral in London; and Michelangelo, completing St. Peter's Cathedral in Rome.

The Stereotype of Disengagement

One theoretical explanation of the behavior of older persons is that they gradually withdraw from customary life activities and become more concerned with self. Such withdrawal can be selective, so that relationships with some persons are retained; but the emphasis is on less interaction with others and on living with memories of the past.

While this theory of disengagement explains the behavior of some older persons, it by no means has general application to all. The facts are that many older persons are very much involved in the life of their communities, to the extent that an "activity theory" has been stated to account for this type of behavior. A "continuity theory" suggests that individuals tend to continue in retirement the behaviors they have followed throughout their lifespan. The problem is, of course, that the stereotype of disengagement can mislead older persons to believe that they should withdraw from others after active work experience.

The Stereotype of Inflexibility

Older persons are commonly believed to be set in their ways, insistent on following specific patterns of behavior, and unwilling to consider change. At least two factors may be involved. The first could be preference for what is familiar and customary. The second could be fear resulting from awareness of a slowdown in personal reaction time coupled with an acceleration in the tempo of life in the world around them.

However, the facts are that healthy older persons do respond positively to change, shifting points of view and altering life styles as part of their continued personal growth. The ability to change and adapt seems to be related more to lifelong behavior patterns than to age.

The Stereotype of Declining Ability to Learn

The notion that persons can no longer learn when they grow older is expressed by the popular saying, "You can't teach an old dog new tricks." Also the belief is that intelligence slides downward from adult years through old age.

The facts are that healthy older persons can continue to increase their ability to organize their thinking and successfully complete a college degree program with notable efficiency. There is some evidence that older persons can be helped to improve their response speed on intelligence tests (Baltes & Schaie, 1974). The possibility is that reduced learning speed may be related to environmental deprivation.

The Stereotype of Senility

The term, senile, is loosely and inaccurately applied to older persons who are forgetful, confused, or unable to maintain attention to one topic for any period of time. Both older and younger persons experience anxiety, grief, and depression, yet when the former give evidence of these problems they are sometimes assumed to have brain damage! Overuse of drugs, malnutrition, and undiagnosed physical ailments may produce behavior labelled senile.

Permanent brain damage, correctly described as senility, is irreversible. However, the facts are that much of what is called senility can be successfully treated. Regrettably, this possibility might be ignored for the unstated reason that older persons are sometimes regarded as dispensable.

The Stereotype of Declining Interest in Sexual Activity

This stereotype has two elements. The first is the frequent belief that sexual relationships for persons over 65 years of age are improper. A typical description of older men involved in sexual activity is "those dirty old men." Lustiness in younger men becomes lechery in older ones. Older women who reveal a sexual interest in men may be labelled as suffering from emotional problems.

The second element is the common impression that older men and women lose with age their physiological capacities for sexual activity. The facts are that healthy older persons who have maintained some degree of continuity in their sex lives continue to enjoy sexual relationships throughout most of the lifespan. Physiological changes do occur, but they tend to be gradual and the body usually accommodates to them. At the same time, because of the emotional problems which can develop in this area of sexual relationships, accurate information and warm understanding are important to the mental and physical health of those involved.

The Stereotype of Serenity

Popularized by fiction and the news media, untroubled serenity often is pictured as the reward of those who grow old. Grandma bakes cookies in the kitchen while Grandpa rocks contentedly on the front porch. The apparent conclusion to be reached is that the storms of active life are over.

The facts are that older persons often face more stressful conditions than any other age group. Yet they have a remarkable ability to endure crises, and their resilience suggests that living longer has prepared them, somehow, to handle new stress.

The youth-oriented society of this country has effectively segregated its older membership, perpetuating a host of false beliefs about aging, and dooming many older persons to life with little hope and declining enjoyment. The stereotypes about aging seem to undermine important personal qualities of self-confidence and self-worth, and to forecast a dismal, decaying future which hardly seems worth the effort. The social prejudice confronting older Americans implicitly denies the possibilities for continued personal growth and explicitly imposes barriers to those striving to develop their own capabilities.

COUNSELING NEEDS OF OLDER PERSONS

Counseling needs vary widely among older persons. For sizeable numbers, these needs are minimal. For some, perhaps as many as 30% of the 65+ population, needs for counseling range from moderate to great. There are two general areas of needs.

The first concerns accurate information about the normal aging process. Such information is essential as a basis for countering inaccurate and incorrect information represented by the stereotypes of aging and older persons. Another important type of information covers the various forms of assistance which are available for older persons from federal, state, and local governments as well as privately operated agencies.

The second general area of counseling need is assistance in resolving personal problems and/or in continuing or renewing progress toward self-fulfillment. Personal problems often grow out of personal losses such as loss of spouse, friends, job, status, health, and youth, and generalize to feelings of loneliness, worthlessness, and depression. The passage of time awakens the older person to the realization that youthful dreams remain unfulfilled and that death is inevitable. Two frequently asked questions are: Who am I? and Why am I here?

As older persons find and are helped to find answers to these questions, additional needs arise. Such needs revolve around the development or renewal of realistic, short-term goals for living. Of particular value is training in decision-making skills which will enable older persons to consider

209

alternative courses of action and resolve problems with a greater sense of purpose. An important element of purpose is focusing on the present in terms of lifestyle.

Categories of Needs/Concerns

Myers (1978) classified needs or concerns into four major categories. The first category, personal, includes the psychological concerns of death and dying, mental health, and independence; and the physical concerns of health, accepting the aging process, and accepting self as one who is aging.

The second category is social which covers psychosocial concerns, such as relationships with significant others, and group membership which involves overcoming social isolation and identification with peers.

Within the third category, labelled activity, are concerns related to work, leisure time, and utilization of skills. Work involves the needs arising out of gainful employment and retirement. Leisure time encompasses hobbies, service, and recreational activities. Skill utilization includes vocational evaluation and learning new skills.

Environmental concerns, the fourth category, are basic because they relate to independence in meeting environmental demands and obtaining needed services.

The primary purpose of Myers' study was to develop and test the "Older Persons Counseling Needs Survey," an instrument which can now be used to measure the counseling needs of older persons, because it was found to have reliability and validity. In the process of testing this instrument with a sample of 850 older persons, Myers identified a number of priority needs. High priorities appeared to be assigned by the sample population to
1. transportation needs,
2. needs for self-acceptance,
3. needs to learn about physical changes which accompany aging,
4. needs relating to physical health,

5. needs for social services and legal assistance, which may be associated with the need for independence,
6. needs for group activity with peers, and
7. needs to feel useful.

A number of these need areas seemed to have favorable potential for intervention by counselors. This particular sample population was developed to mirror the general characteristics of older persons in Florida. Included were representatives of rural and urban areas, higher and lower socioeconomic levels, and the black and white races.

A 1977 study by Ganikos investigated the expressed counseling needs of older adult students. Her sample population included 155 older persons, ranging in age from 59 to 86, who were enrolled in courses at one of five community colleges in Florida. Based on a literature review and interviews with community college students who were 60 years of age and over, Ganikos developed six categories of counseling needs: vocational, educational, personal adjustment, family relationships, social-interpersonal adjustment, and adjustment to life situations.

About half of the subjects in the Ganikos study indicated some need for counseling in the six categories. Educational needs were regarded as most important by this sample and, perhaps, naturally so because each was participating in an educational program. Of least importance, in terms of assigned ratings, were needs relating to vocation and family relationships. Given high ratings of importance were needs concerned with personal adjustment, social-interpersonal adjustment, and adjustment to life situations.

Of interest are the demographic variables which were found to have some influence on expressed needs. Age was one. The younger subjects, with an age range of 59 to 65, reported greater educational and vocational needs than the older subjects, age 65 and above. Younger widowed persons seemed to have greater educational needs than older widowed persons.

Other variables which appeared to affect expressed counseling needs were sex, marital status, and educational level. Subjects who were married and in the lowest education group (0 to 11 years of schooling) indicated more counseling needs related to personal adjustment than married subjects in the highest education group (college and graduate school). In terms of adjustment to life situations, females reported greater needs than males, with both groups being at the middle educational level (high school and college).

To be noted is the fact that both studies report high levels of counseling needs for self-acceptance, which can be related to personal adjustment; group activity with peers, or social-interpersonal adjustment; and feelings of usefulness, or adjustment to life situations.

Needs of Older Women

Older women have some special problems. They live longer than men so that 50% of the women 65 years of age and over are widowed (Butler, 1975, p. 5). Because society frowns on their dating and marrying younger men, widows generally continue to live alone. Many have never worked except as housewives; those who have worked usually have received low wages. As a result, older women often are living on limited incomes with few, if any, opportunities for social activities.

Social roles of older women may become indeterminate, particularly with the loss of the husband. Self-identity may develop as a central issue. Loneliness is a common problem. Relationships with sons or daughters may change, with conflicts arising from differences of opinion regarding degrees of responsibility for each other. Women at lower socioeconomic levels are likely to experience greater feelings of isolation and loneliness than those of the middle-class because the latter often have more friends and more community interests. Widowhood seems to be less of a problem among working class black women than among white women (Atchley, 1977).

Older Persons' Needs for Employment

For many Americans, retirement from a full-time job has been viewed as the beginning of the end of life. For some, this view has been correct; they have declined rapidly in associations with others, in activities, in interests, and in health. Why? High among the possible factors is loss of the sense of personal worth which has been derived from the job. In the U.S. society, employment has long been the focal point for self-definition, association with others with similar interests, social contacts, and a development of a personal value system. To deny employment to those who want to keep working and have the capabilities for doing so is, in fact, to destroy a significant support for life itself.

Fortunately for older persons the reasons for enforced retirement are changing and conditions favorable to continued employment, at least on a part-time basis, are improving. Individuals are living longer and are in better health than in years past. Research supports the fact of continued intellectual capacities of older persons, and their qualities of dependability, loyalty, and effectiveness on the job are confirmed by employers' experience.

Decline in the availability of labor is leading business and industry to encourage employees in various categories to remain on the job rather than to retire. Dramatic increases in the costs of pension plans and special services for older persons are leading planners to suggest that the age for retirement be raised beyond the traditional 60 to 65 years. Inflation has added so much to living costs that income to supplement pension payments is becoming essential.

Older persons tend to have a variety of common needs in today's world. Their common problem is that they have been largely ignored. This situation is changing and will continue to change.

DEVELOPMENT OF SERVICES FOR OLDER PERSONS

The principal vehicle for federal, state, and local government assistance to older persons is the Older Americans Act passed by the Congress in 1965. This Act defined a national policy for older persons and included these specific objectives:

an adequate income; the best possible physical and mental health; suitable housing; full restorative services; opportunity for employment without age discrimination; retirement in health, honor, dignity; pursuit of meaningful activity; efficient community services when needed; immediate benefit from proven research knowledge; and freedom, independence, and the free exercise of individual initiative . . . (Butler, 1975, p. 329)

Provided for by this Act was the Administration on Aging which, for at least the first seven years of its existence, suffered continually from insufficient funds and limited authority.

During fiscal year 1966, Congress appropriated $6.5 million to carry out the provisions of the Older Americans Act. By the end of the first year of operation most of the States had qualified for grants based on approved state plans. In a number of the years following 1966, this Act was amended and funding increased. For fiscal year 1969, appropriations amounted to $31.9 million; for 1973, $213 million; for 1975, $257.5 million; and for 1978, $720.4 million. Thus, during a twelve-year period, appropriations have grown tremendously (Administration on Aging, 1979b).

The 1978 Amendments represented a strong Federal effort to encourage the comprehensive coordination of services in order to better serve older persons. Title III, Part B, was written to include social services, senior centers, and nutrition services. Specified for funding under nutrition services were congregate meals and home-delivered meals. Added to the definitions of social services were those which would make available preretirement and second career counseling for older persons. Legal services, such as assistance with taxes and finances, were continued under the definitions of social services. The Administration on Aging's proposed regulations implementing the 1978 Amendments amplified the term counseling to include "welfare" and the "use of facilities and services" (Administration on Aging, 1979a, p. 45042).

The Aging Network

As part of the recently designated Federal Department of Health and Human Services, the U.S. Administration on Aging is the first element of the Aging Network and is responsible for implementation of the Older Americans Act which authorizes many of the services provided for older persons.

The second element of the Aging Network, after the U.S. Administration on Aging, is the State Unit or Agency on Aging, established by each of the states. Specifically designated by action of state legislatures, this agency is responsible for serving as the advocate for the state's older population and coordinating all activities in the state relating to the Older Americans Act. State Units on Aging were organized during the years immediately following passage of the Older Americans Act of 1965.

Area Agencies on Aging, the third element of the Aging Network, were authorized by the U.S. Congress through the 1973 Amendments to the Act. State Agencies on Aging were required to divide the state into planning and service areas, to decide which areas would have an area plan, and to designate for each of these areas an Area Agency on Aging. Currently more than 600 area agencies are operating in the United States.

Two general purposes of these agencies are to
1. serve as both advocate and focal point for older persons within the area, and
2. develop and administer the area plan for a coordinated and comprehensive system of social and nutrition services.

The number of organizations actively involved in the field of aging probably exceeds the 284 listed in the National Council on the Aging Directory of 1971. Each of these organizations has an impact on a particular group of older persons; some organizations compete for grants funded by public and private agencies; many exert political pressure on elected representatives to support legislation favorable to their programs and concerns. A smaller number are engaged in multiple programs and activities.

Impressive is the jointly operated organization of the *National Retired Teachers Association and the American Association of Retired Persons* (NRTA-AARP). With an approximate membership of 12.5 million, this organization is the largest of its kind in the world. Dedicated to the well-being and active involvement of retired persons, NRTA-AARP is built on a well-developed network of local, state, regional, and national units which maximize membership participation. In each state, a joint legislative committee considers political issues affecting older persons and initiates specific recommendations for legislative action. This organization also makes recommendations concerning federal legislation.

The Gerontological Society is another sizeable national organization which is actively involved in the development and dissemination of information regarding aging and older persons. Its three branches focus on biological sciences, clinical medicine, and behavioral sciences. Its two journals, the *Gerontologist* and the *Journal of Gerontology*, are useful resources in the field of aging.

Variety of Services

Many services provided older persons by federal, state, and community agencies have in common two objectives: the first is to improve and expand quality of life; the second, is to extend personal independence, delaying or avoiding dependence on long-term institutional care. Holmes and Holmes' (1979) study of human services for older persons describes in detail most of the following services.

Information and Referral Services. These services are intended to provide a bridge between older persons needing assistance and the agencies which can provide it. For some older persons access to the service delivery system represents a mystery, or an unknown, or both.

Multi-purpose Senior Centers. These centers are community facilities where older persons can expect to find a number of services relating to health, social, and educational matters, together with facilities for recreational activities. These centers enable the community to take advantage of the skills of older persons, on the one hand, and, on the other, act as focal points for the delivery of services.

Homemaker and Home Health Services. These services are intended to enlarge the possibilities for frail elderly to remain in their community and to reduce feelings of dependency and loss of dignity which can result from serious illness. Homemaker services bring an individual into older persons' homes to help with food shopping and preparation, eating, dressing, light cleaning, personal laundry, bed changing, and possibly, paying bills and escort assistance to other services. Home health services are furnished to older persons under a physician's care by home health agencies. Among these services are nursing, physical therapy, occupational therapy, and medical supplies.

Legal Services. These services are important to older persons not only because they have many of the legal problems experienced by younger persons but also because they often need help in establishing their eligibility for such programs as Social Security and Medicare.

Residential Repair and Renovation Services. These services are intended to assist older persons to continue living in their own homes. As a matter of public policy, the repair and renovation of existing housing to meet basic standards seem to be both economical and realistic, with new public housing regarded as a supplemental effort. It should be noted that about 70% of persons who are 65 years of age and over own their own homes. Remaining in their homes often contributes to older persons' feelings of identity, self-worth, and personal happiness.

Services for Employment and Volunteer Work. These services are intended to provide older persons with opportunities for meaningful activities either with or without pay. As noted in an earlier section, such activities are important to personal feelings of worth and usefulness. Title V of the 1978 Amendments to the Older Americans Act provides for the part-time employment of low-income persons, age 55 and over, whose prospects for employment are poor. This program is carried out by non-profit organizations under contracts with the Labor Department.

217

Daycare for Older Persons. Daycare is provided at centers where frail elderly may stay for varying lengths of time during a day. National studies indicate an average attendance of 2.5 days per week during a five-day week. Services at a daycare center include general nursing assistance; rehabilitative treatment, such as physical, occupational, and speech therapy; personal care; one meal per day, snacks, and special diets, as necessary; social and recreational activities; assistance with social and psychological needs; and transportation. Daycare centers may emphasize restorative health care, maintenance health care, or psychosocial care.

Nursing Home Services. Nursing homes are largely controlled by private industry and provide long-term care for older persons who are unable to remain in their own homes or care for themselves.

Counseling Services. Sometimes counseling services are provided for older persons, particularly if such services are defined as the giving of information and advice. However, the number of professionally trained counselors available for older persons is few. Greatly needed, these services generally are authorized by existing legislation but have yet to be given the priority and support required to insure their effectiveness.

THE HELPING PROFESSIONAL'S ROLES

For many years counseling has been associated primarily with helping younger persons. To consider older persons as possible counselees has been to open up a new area of opportunity for helping professionals. At the same time, problems quickly emerge.

Problems Affecting Role Performance

The first problem is for counselors to recognize that older persons differ from younger persons in several important ways. They have an extended background of experience. Their problems tend to be the result of losses, mentioned previously. Their life tasks may involve a shifting and redirecting of fairly well established attitudes, goals, and behaviors. They probably recognize that life is indeed finite. Their needs are likely to be more often short-term or immediate.

A second problem is to recognize and appraise the degree to which older persons may have been overpowered by some of the stereotypes with which they have been surrounded by society. In some instances, stereotypes about the aging process may have so influenced the behaviors of older persons that change is difficult if not impossible. For example, one stereotype is that older persons are inflexible, unpleasant, difficult, and hard to get along with. At a time when an older person is losing family members and friends who move away or die, that person's conviction may grow that the circle of family and friends is shrinking because of his/her behaviors. This conviction may be reinforced by the stereotype which becomes a self-fulfilling prophecy.

Associated with the second problem is a third, which is the prejudice against older persons likely to be held, often unknowingly, by counselors and others who work with older persons. This prejudice can have a profound influence on the attitudes of helping professionals toward older persons. For example, when older persons are confused, forgetful, or depressed, the helping professional's first reaction may be that these behaviors are typical and to be expected. Yet the facts are that such conditions can often be corrected. Another example is the helper's reaction to the older person who is ill and unlikely to recover: "Nothing I can do will make any difference." Such a reaction overlooks the importance of the older person's emotional state in the immediate present.

Approaches to this problem of ageism include expanding the helper's knowledge about aging and older persons, increasing frequency of association, stimulating sensitivity to older persons as unique human beings, and maintaining personal awareness of the subtle existence of ageism. Despite the best intentions of counselors and other helpers, some degree of prejudice against older persons is inevitable because of the common fear of death and growing up in a society which has long maintained such prejudice.

An additional problem for helping professionals is a definition for counseling, particularly counseling for older persons, and a clear, perhaps frequent interpretation of this definition to both older persons and those who work with them. One useful definition is that counseling is "the process through which a trained counselor assists an individual or group to make satisfying and responsible decisions concerning personal, educational, social, and vocational development" (U.S. House of Representatives, 1977). This definition makes the important points that counseling is a process which involves a relationship, one or more decisions on the part of the counselee, and positive action which can result in the counselee's further development.

Counseling older persons, known as gerontological counseling, is perhaps best identified as helping individuals to overcome losses, to establish new goals in the process of discovering that living is limited in quantity but not quality, and to reach decisions based on the importance of the present as well as the opportunities of the future.

Probably gerontological counseling takes place more effectively within the context of activities which appear to be meeting the immediate needs of older persons. For example, counseling may occur while the counselor is transporting the counselee to the food stamp office. Likewise, counseling may take place when meals are delivered to older persons at home by paraprofessionals trained by professional counselors. It must be remembered that most of today's older persons are unlikely to have had experience with counselors during earlier years. In addition, discussing issues of a personal nature with someone outside the family was, in the past, frequently discouraged.

Perceptions of Counseling

In 1979 Murphey studied counseling services for older persons in Florida, as perceived by administrators, direct service supervisors, and service provider staff associated with aging programs. Based upon questionnaire returns from 373 program personnel, he concluded that counseling should be more clearly defined. He noted apparent differences of opinion about the definition of counseling and what it involves. He discovered that only 10% of the 220 aging projects in Florida included counseling as a program function. At the same time, the direct service staff tended to see most of their work as counseling.

Aging program personnel generally agreed that counseling services should be integrated with other programs rather than organized as a separate and distinct program. In this connection, their feeling was that mental health centers were not meeting the counseling needs of older persons. Program personnel expressed the belief that trained counselors were necessary; however, they also felt, although not strongly, that paraprofessionals could fill counselor roles. Administrative staff stated that current funding for counseling services was adequate; direct service providers disagreed.

Several of Murphey's conclusions should be noted. First, counseling should be closely associated with the life support services of transportation, meals, and homemaker programs, with counselors serving as facilitators. Second, aging program employers in Florida should gain a fuller understanding of the aging process and have additional preparation in working with older persons. And, third, counselor educators should communicate more directly with professionals in aging programs in order to increase awareness of the contributions which counselors can make to the well-being of older persons.

The loose usages of the words "counseling" and "counselors" can leave little doubt that they are perceived in a wide variety of ways by the general public and, in fact, by counselors themselves. Clarification of counselor roles and functions should help to improve understanding.

COUNSELOR ROLES

Perhaps the many roles taken by counselors account for the differing perceptions of their functions. In the case of gerontological counselors, they function like all counselors, as trained helpers equipped with specialized knowledge and skills. These are applied to a diversity of situations and conditions which involve older persons. Gerontological counselors assume a variety of roles.

Facilitators. Counselors, equipped with information about services for older persons, make easier the individual's process of learning about these services, understanding ways in which a particular service will be helpful, and initiating action which will result in satisfying use of the service.

Counselors for Independent Living. In this role, they assist older persons to assess the conditions which may be producing feelings of isolation, loneliness, and depression, to consider ways to counter these conditions, and to take positive, corrective actions.

Counselors for Personal Growth in Aging. Here they concentrate on the developmental aspects of the human lifespan, helping older persons to understand better the special tasks to be accomplished at their particular stage of life, and encouraging them to decide upon a way or ways to carry out these tasks.

Preretirement Counselors. Perhaps better identified as Life Style Counselors, these persons concentrate the attention of older persons on actions to be taken in preparation for the transition from full-time work to greater freedom in the use of time and less than full-time work. Considered by the counselor and counselee are role changes and new roles.

Employment Counselors. In this role, they assist older persons as they consider entering or reentering the labor market on a part-time or full-time basis, or serving as a volunteer worker. To be evaluated are older persons' needs for employment of some kind, for purposes of either personal support or personal development, or both.

Financial Counselors. Such counselors help older persons to evaluate their current financial situation as a basis for improving management. Another important function is planning for changes in income and expenses resulting from such alterations in life style as retirement from full-time employment. To be emphasized is financial planning during earlier life stages.

Leisure Activities Counselors. These counselors focus the attention of older persons on the diversity of activities to be considered for a happier, fuller life, either a part of or apart from employment. The possibilities range from active recreation to solitary contemplation, from group participation to individual creativity, with counselees often building on earlier interests and abilities.

Marital and Family Counselors. These counselors address at least three types of situations when assisting older persons in marital and family matters: first, the role adjustments required of both spouses when either one spends more time at home as the result of retirement, illness, or other circumstances; second, the needs of one or both partners in understanding that continued sexual activity into advanced age is both possible and healthy; and, third, the stresses which can develop when older parents come to live with married children and/or when parents require the services provided by nursing homes.

Counselors for Nursing Home Patients. Such counselors find a wide range of individual needs which often have as common elements the needs for self-worth and love. Particular counselor attention may be required for such problems as reality orientation, adjustment to declining health, and interpersonal communication skills.

Counselors for the Terminally Ill. In this role, counselors serve as impartial persons who care and feel deeply for older persons experiencing doubts, fears, and questions in the face of death. The significant counselor goal is to help the dying person to live each day fully and to gain peace of mind.

Bereavement Counselors. They assist older persons who have experienced the death of a spouse, family member, or close friend to move through the grief process by providing empathy and support which lead to acceptance of the loss. Counselors try to keep counselees from withdrawing and breaking social ties at the very time when friends can be especially supportive.

223

Trainers for Peer Counselors. Counselors function as trainers for peer counselors in order to increase the number of helpers who are qualified by training and attitude to assist other older persons to handle a variety of concerns and issues. Serving as peer counselors also can be tremendously stimulating to older persons, improving their own mental health.

Consultants. Counselors fulfill the important role of consultant for elements of the aging network and related organizations in various ways such as studying organizational problems and assisting in their resolution, reviewing mental health issues and offering recommendations, and suggesting new approaches and/or programs which will enhance the well-being of the older persons concerned.

Advocates. Counselors act as advocates for older persons who may not have the knowledge, energy, or assertiveness to obtain the assistance and support they need. Advocacy also includes informing the public about issues involving older persons, countering negative stereotypes about aging, and promoting programs, such as continuing education for older persons, which may reduce or prevent problems related to aging.

SUPPORT SYSTEMS

To consider roles of gerontological counselors separately is to risk overlooking the fact that these roles are closely interrelated. More importantly, the needs of older persons are intermeshed, with the significant consequence that older persons must be understood and helped in their totality as human beings.

Regrettably, this point of view seldom prevails at the present time. Current federal legislation places heavy emphasis on the physical needs of older persons, with considerably less attention to mental and emotional needs. Thus, the efforts of the aging network have been largely directed toward meeting physical needs. It is entirely possible that a more balanced approach to meeting the needs of older persons might have more effective results over a period of time. From the viewpoint of gerontological counselors, an assessment of total needs is indispensable to corrective action aimed at a total effect. Also indispensable is the development of interrelated support systems.

Educational Support System. One continuing goal for this system is to explain the aging process to young people in order to combat the fear of growing old and the discrimination caused by the negative stereotypes of older persons. A second continuing goal is to develop lifelong educational programs which will enable older persons to keep abreast of social, economic, and political changes in the world and maintain a competence level which will make it possible for them to participate in meaningful ways in the life of their communities.

Social Support System. Because this system tends to become smaller as people grow older, efforts must be made to replenish and revitalize it as necessary. One possibility is to encourage older persons to remain active in part-time employment, leisure activities, civic affairs, and educational programs. Another is to suggest that older persons move into housing projects or form small size living groups which have membership responsibilities.

Health Support System. Health insurance and hospital care are basic elements of these systems. To be further developed are lifetime health care training and lifetime programs for physical exercise. Additionally, medical training should include greater attention to geriatric medicine and close working relationships with professional counselors so that physical and mental health care can be coordinated effectively.

Services Support System. This system currently includes access services such as transportation, information and referral; in-home services, such as homemaker and home health aide, visiting and telephone reassurance; legal services; nutrition services; multipurpose senior centers; and housing. Additional efforts are needed to coordinate these various services in order to maximize their results for older persons. Congregate housing and community care programs represent positive steps in this direction.

For helping professionals who work with older persons one basic requirement is knowledge about the available support systems and access to them. An equally important requirement is recognizing the complexity and diversity of the needs of older persons. Success in helping older persons may well rest on the recognition that emotional needs and physical needs are inevitably interrelated. When older persons are the clients, the helping professionals scope of information and activities must indeed be broad.

POST TEST

Directions: After reading the chapter, mark each item true or false.

T F 1. Among the counseling needs of older persons, one major area is accurate information.

T F 2. Self-acceptance is an important counseling need of older persons.

T F 3. Federal appropriations for services for older persons have increased somewhat during the past 12 years.

T F 4. The Aging Network consists of 3 major elements.

T F 5. Excellent sources of information about older persons are the large national organizations which concentrate on older persons.

T F 6. The number of services available to older persons is rather small, considering the needs.

T F 7. Counseling is one of the major services for older persons supported by federal funds.

T F 8. The helping professional has many diverse roles to fulfil in working with older persons.

T F 9. An important support system for older persons is the educational system.

Scoring Guide for Post Test

1. T	4. T	6. F	8. T
2. T	5. T	7. F	9. T
3. F			

Reference List

Administration on Aging. Grants for State and Community Programs on Aging, *Federal register, part II*. Washington, D.C.: U.S. Government Printing Office, July 31, 1979a.

Administration on Aging. *Older Americans Act of 1965, as amended*. Washington, D.C.: U.S. Department of Health, Education, and Welfare, July 1979b.

Atchley, R. *The social forces in later life*. Belmont, CA: Wadsworth Publishing Company, Inc., 1977.

Baltes, P., & Schaie, K. The myth of the twilight years, *Psychology Today*, March 1974, pp. 35-38; 40.

Butler, R. *Why survive? Being old in America*. New York: Harper & Row, 1975.

Challenges of the '80s. *U.S. News and World Report*, October 15, 1979, pp. 45-80.

Comfort, A. Age prejudices in America. *State Government*, Spring 1976, no pagination.

Ganikos, M. *The expressed counseling needs and perceptions of counseling of older adult students in selected Florida community colleges*. Unpublished doctoral dissertation, University of Florida, 1977.

Graying of America. *Newsweek*, February 28, 1977, pp. 50-52; 55.

Harris, L., & Associates. *The myth and reality of aging in America*. Washington, D.C.: The National Council on the Aging, Inc., 1975.

Harris, L., & Associates. *1979 study of American attitudes toward pensions and retirement*. Chicago: Author, 1979.

Holmes, M., & Holmes, D. *Handbook of human services for older persons*. New York: Human Sciences Press, 1979.

Murphey, M. *Counseling services for older persons as perceived and provided by selected Florida aging program administrators and direct service personnel*. Unpublished doctoral dissertation, University of Florida, 1979.

Myers, J. *The development of a scale to assess counseling needs of older persons*. Unpublished doctoral dissertation, University of Florida, 1978.

National Committee for Careers for Older Americans. *Older Americans: An untapped resource*. Washington, D.C.: Academy for Educational Development, Inc., 1979.

National Council on the Aging, Inc. Directory: *National organizations with programs in the field of aging*. Washington, D.C.: The Council, 1971.

U.S. Government Printing Office. *Poverty among America's aged*. Washington, D.C.: Author, 1978.

U.S. House of Representatives. *HR Bill 1118, Counseling Assistance Act of 1977*. Washington, D.C.: U.S. Government Printing Office, 1977.

10

Persons With A Disability

Nicholas A. Vacc, Ed.D.

School of Education
University of North Carolina
Greensboro, North Carolina

and

Kerry F. Clifford, Ed.S.

Bradford—Union Guidance Clinic
Starke, Florida

Nicholas A. Vacc, Ed.D.

Dr. Nicholas A. Vacc is a Professor in the School of Education at the University of North Carolina, Greensboro. He received his degrees from Western Reserve University, Syracuse University, and State University of New York. His prior employment includes being a teacher, school psychologist, VA Counselor, Director of Counseling, and University Professor. For four years, Dr. Vacc served on the Chautauqua County Mental Health Board and was chairman of the Subcommittee on Mental Retardation. He was a member of the Board of Visitors of the J.N. Adam Developmental Center, a state residential unit for the mentally retarded. In addition, he has served as a consultant to programs and agencies serving special populations. Dr. Vacc has a special interest in research with emotionally handicapped children. He is actively involved in the American Personnel and Guidance Association and the Council for Exceptional Children.

230

Kerry F. Clifford is currently Clinic Coordinator and Counselor for Union County of the Bradford-Union Guidance Clinic with offices in Starke and Lake Butler, Florida. As a scholarship athlete at Kansas State University, he received a B.S. in Mechanical Engineering in 1957. In 1967, as the result of an industrial accident, he became paraplegic. A Masters of Rehabilitation Counseling was received at the University of Florida in 1971, where work toward a Ph.D. continues. In the recent past he has served an an instructor at Santa Fe Community College in the Work Exploration Unit and in the CETA program Vocation Preparation Class. He is a member, and past chairman, of the Gainesville, Florida, chapter of The Governor's Committee on the Employment of the Handicapped. He also serves on the Handicapped Advisory Committee for the North Central Florida Regional Planning Council. Mr. Clifford has been involved in the development of, and has participated in wheel chair athletics in the Gainesville area. He has served as a volunteer consultant on architectural barriers and designed his home. A major hobby is CB radio with which he has assisted in the promotion and organization of the local REACT team, which monitors and assists motorists on the national emergency channel nine on CB radio. He and Suzanne, his wife of 26 years, have three children and their first grandchild.

Kerry F. Clifford, Ed.S.

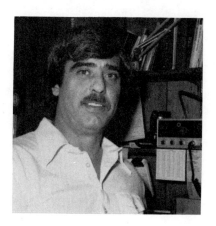

Persons With A Disability

Nicholas A. Vacc
and
Kerry F. Clifford

AWARENESS INDEX

Directions: These questions are to help you to evaluate your understanding of individuals with a disability. Mark each item as true or false. Compute your score from the scoring guide at the end of the awareness index. A post test is provided at the end of this chapter.

T F   1. The term "wheelies" refers to a common expression used for individuals who need to use a wheel chair for mobility.

T F   2. Individuals who have a disability like to be recognized as an example for "normal" individuals.

T F   3. The mass media has been very helpful in assisting individuals with a disability to change the attitudes of others.

T F   4. Generally speaking, society places a high premium on physical perfection.

T F   5. The paraplegic personality can be summarized or characterized by the word angry or hostile.

T　F　6. There is a growing recognition by society of the capability of individuals with a disability to assume competitive employment.

T　F　7. Counselors as helpers need to focus attention on advocacy for helping individuals with a disability.

T　F　8. As helpers, it is important that we recognize those aspects of our behavior and society that provide limits on individuals with a disability.

Scoring Guide for Awareness Index

1. T	3. F	5. F	7. T
2. F	4. T	6. T	8. T

BACKGROUND

The authors of this chapter care deeply for the welfare and productive existence of all individuals. Their interest, however, evolved from two very different sets of events. The first author became conscious of inequities for children with handicapping conditions, in our educational system very early in his professional career and has been involved since then with the education and welfare of individuals with exceptionalities. The second author experienced an accident on the job which resulted in a severed spinal cord and a disability that affected both his professional and personal life immeasurably. Although a paraplegic and a "wheelie," he does not view himself nor does he wish others to view him as a disabled person. Yet, during the twelve years that have passed since he received his injury, he has had many experiences which have conveyed to him that the majority of people regard him as a disabled person. The first person accounts included in quotes in this chapter convey some of his own personal experiences and feelings.

To speak of individuals who are disabled, who differ from the non-disabled in physical, emotional, and/or mental ability, is to speak of a minority group. As with any minority group, this one is, and will continue to be faced with prejudice, hostility, lack of understanding, and indifference.

REFLECTIONS

Many wheelies feel that they really cannot condemn members of the general public for their attitude toward the disabled, because "walkies" (people other than wheelies) have not had the opportunity to learn anything different. Some non-disabled feel that the wheelie and other individuals who are disabled should stay at home, "out-of-sight and out-of-mind," while other non-disabled individuals feel the disabled should be protected from the rough and tumble world. Thus, individuals with a disability have to cope with people who range in outlook from complete ignorance and lack of understanding to the over-sympathetic and protective.

Many individuals cannot camouflage their disability because a wheelchair is not easily concealed. Because one does not stand very tall in a wheelchair, the general public tends to think of a wheelie as something less than a full grown person. The wheelie is literally looked down upon.

One day when I had on my braces and was just about to stand up, a neighbor woman dropped in. She had never seen me standing, only sitting in the chair. I stood up, moved out into the room and stopped. She sort of stared at me with a "funny" look on her face. I immediately checked the air by nose to see if, as often happens when I get up in braces, I had done a "no-no." There were no signs. I then quickly looked to see if my "plumbing" was in order. Everything was all right, but she was still looking at me the same way. Suddenly she smiled, ran over and put her arms around me and said, "Man! You are a big one aren't you." I didn't ask her, "A 'big one' of what?" but after that event, a subtle change was made in her attitude towards me.

CURRENT PROBLEMS

Even in this enlightened age, a stigma is attached to a disability. Some people feel that paraplegics are paralyzed from the neck up as well as the waist down. Some find it difficult to talk directly to anyone in a wheelchair. They talk over their heads and often discuss them as if they were not present. Martin (1974) has characterized the public's response to the handicapped with "They are different, they trouble us in deep, unexplainable, irrational ways, and we would like them somewhere else, not cruelly treated, of course, but out of sight and mind" (p. 150). Many non-handicapped individuals will admit they are uncomfortable in the presence of anyone with a disability. Some try to hide their feelings by over-attention, over-kindness, or maudlin sympathy.

It is difficult for paraplegics to accept the attitudes of others towards them. At first they resent the people who, meeting them for the first time say, "You poor thing, what is wrong with you?" Or, the more common situation of manner and tone of voice when they say, "Boy! You can sure handle that thing! How do you do that?" These same people would never dream of saying to Carlos Alvarez, "Man! You sure can catch that ball! How do you do it?"

The person with a disability wants to be recognized as an individual, not merely a statistic or a case of being a wonderfully courageous person—an example for the world. Or more important, they do not enjoy being pitiful objects used to stimulate fund raising. Probably not a person with a disability does not bristle when he or she sees a campaign picture of a child on crutches, standing in the shadows, with a woeful look as he or she gazes into the distance where other boys and girls are playing. There is little wonder that many people have the idea that individuals with a disability are objects of pity when they see such pictures. How much better it would be to have the same child mixing with playmates and sharing in the fun, even if he or she is only sitting in the sandpile making roads while the rest run and play.

Mass media does little to help the cause of individuals with disabilities. In many plays and novels, the disabled male person has been portrayed as a miserable tyrant, often very wealthy, who makes life unbearable for all who come in contact with him; or an evil villain who seeks revenge for his disability by committing various horrible crimes; or a meek, pitiful creature who suffers greatly and tries to smile, but must spend the rest of his life wrapped in a blanket sipping hot milk. Seldom does the mass media portray a person with a

236

disability as a believable human being. The television series, "Ironside," was a good attempt to show a paraplegic in realistic terms. Ironside, however, did not propel his chair by himself as much as he should have. They have not succeeded completely, but it is an encouraging start, at least.

Society places such a high premium on physical perfection that it views with some doubt, the achievements of any individual who has a disability. It appears that society does not expect people with a disability to function as normal individuals, and is somewhat hesitant to accept their achievements because it makes for an uncomfortable feeling. Therefore, people tend to cover up by being over-lavish in their praise for the disabled's effort, and indeed often are patronizing as if praising a child or someone from whom such a standard of achievement was not expected. In a way, some people look on an achievement by the disabled in the same way that Dr. Samuel Johnston did a dog walking on two legs. Dr. Johnston said, "It is not the fact that he does it well, but the fact that he is able to do it at all that brings praise."

One of the myths that has developed surrounding well adjusted persons who have a disability is that they are always supposed to be happy, or at least pretend they are. However, when paraplegics, for example, act happy just because they are happy and feel good, people sometimes look at them rather suspiciously, as if it is a "front." When they get angry or are just "down" that day, they are often looked upon with pity. And, if they complain or criticize, it is viewed that they are doing it because they are in a wheelchair, not because there might be an actual injustice such as an architectural barrier where none should exist.

If sometime you would like to see and hear a display of anger by a paraplegic, come to the hospital parking lot with me some day. I have, upon several occasions arrived early enough to have a pick of parking spaces. I always choose one that is the last in line at the west end of the lot. This space is chosen so that the door on the passenger side of the car is free to swing wide open, for easy egress and ingress of the car. Several times upon returning to the car, some joker has parked a V.W. sedan next to the passenger side with two wheels up on the

237

grass and the other two almost in my car's fender wells. Of course, I have passed about fifteen empty spaces on the way to the car. The temperature of the air rises about five degrees centigrade and the tar in the road melts from under my wheelchair. Other events arousing similar reactions include exams or a paper being due which I have not yet finished.

An injury that confines one to a wheelchair, does not change a person's personality, but some of the experienced feelings may be lessened, such as fear, anger, and sex drive (Hofmann, 1966). If these feelings are indeed lowered, their manifestation is not. The shy, retiring person will still be shy though confined to a chair, the complainer will still complain, and the aggressive person will still be aggressive. There is no paraplegic personality; each wheelie is an individual. Further, physically disabled people do not want to be viewed as handicapped or disabled, but as individuals with a disability. They can become as well adjusted as anyone else, if they receive love, understanding, and tactful help in meeting problems. They want to be judged competitively in their community, with emphasis upon what they *can* do, not what they *cannot* do.

Today, more than ever before, there is growing recognition of the potential capability of individuals with a disability to assume independent living and competitive employment. With this recognition, change is occurring in the direction of a more comprehensive attack on the problem of providing these resources, facilities, and services which will help integrate the individual with a disability into the community. The following verse by an unknown, presumably paraplegic author aptly conveys the frustration of being separated from society:

I burn the rubber off my wheels.
    I can hardly wait;
My wheelchair's 30 inches wide,
    the john is 28.
Some plead for civil justice
    when they are set upon.
I ask for just one freedom,
    the right to use the john.

I've thought about reforming
 and changing my evil ways;
To be a model of deportment
 for the remainder of my days.
But when I get to heaven
 and face the Pearly Gates,
St. Peter will say, "You're 30 inches wide.
 Our gates are 28."

                                        Unknown

NORMALIZATION

With the requirements of normalization principles as stipulated by law, it has become increasingly important that the schools and other agencies of society find ways of working with and helping individuals with disabilities who may differ from the "normal" population in emotional stability, learning capability, and/or physical capability.

Helping individuals with disabilities to cope with problems in their natural environment so that the handicapping aspects of the disability are minimized and the level of life functioning is maximized, has produced a need for a change in counseling services to include advocacy. At this time, however, there appears to be an inadequate response to this need for extended and strengthened services for individuals with disabilities.

Helpers must be conscious of the present inequities for individuals with disabilities and strive to adjust the "system." Otherwise, we perpetuate the old ways of destruction. As Tennyson so capably put it:

How dull it is to pause
to make an end,
to rest unburnished,
not to shine in use.

It needs to be understood that a disability represents a massive assault on an individual, and how he or she acts will depend on environmental experiences. These environmental experiences are influenced by the nature of the disability, the realistic problem(s) it creates, the person's attitude, material resources, and the attitude of family members and/or people in the immediate environment as well as society. It is toward an understanding of these factors and their manifestations relative to the individual that helpers should be sensitive.

The importance of helpers striving to "adjust the system" when working to assist individuals with a disability can be dramatically illustrated by the case of a Vietnam War veteran whom the second author was requested to assist. The veteran, whom we'll call Joe, was a pleasant, good-looking young man who had attempted suicide two times within a three-month period.

We talked initially of the things that two paras usually discuss, especially in a hospital setting with one person being a relatively novice wheelie and the other more experienced. The subjects included incidence of injury medical/surgical course, hospitals and care, bowel/bladder control, decubiti ulcers, types of chairs, and operations. After a while it became evident that Joe had two major concerns. The most important by far was sexual function and the other was mobility, especially operating an automobile himself without assistance. That these subjects were important to Joe was not surprising. What was surprising was that he had not been offered counseling and information concerning them. According to Joe, his inquiries about the subjects had elicited vague, confusing, and unsatisfying responses.

Counseling after two suicide attempts had never touched upon the subjects of Joe's concern. The question is whether the non-disabled do not view with importance those activities which they take for granted or whether they view the disabled as having no needs other than those directly related to their disability (McBain, 1976).

Joe's ignorance of whether or not he could obtain a reflex penile erection paralleled my own experience seven years earlier. A few suggestions on procedures plus health and safety precautions were offered on determining whether an erection, plus degree of erection, could be obtained. With this, the two-hour visit with Joe terminated. His smile and demeanor during my visit the next day answered the question of whether he had been successful. During the ensuing months, sexual function education and possible procedures were presented and discussed with the veteran. At the same time, Joe obtained an automobile with hand controls and instruction and training on how to use them. Subsequently, Joe became very busy in living. Times for the unofficial counseling visits became increasingly short and finally ceased. When Joe was discharged from the hospital, he rented an apartment which had been made architecturally adequate, set up independent living, and started classes at the community college nearby.

It is sad to report that Joe did not continue to "live happily ever after." He had other handicaps with which to contend in addition to his physical disability. He was young and had experienced a rather protected earlier life. As a result he was psychologically and emotionally immature, lacking experience in coping with the demands of independent living. He developed behaviors indicative of arrogance and pride, spurning further counseling and even friendship. Alcohol and other drugs became more and more part of his lifestyle. He quit school, wrecked his car several times, and finally, due to improperly caring for himself, developed a chronic urinary tract infection as well as a decubitus ulcer on his buttock. He became rather desperate and his parents took him back to the home area. I have not heard from Joe since that time.

In the case of Joe, the system was eventually adjusted so he could function independently in society—he was helped in learning how to function adequately with his disability. In the past, many individuals like Joe who had a disability, in addition to not receiving the type of assistance which is of concern to them, would have been separated from their natural environment based on the rationale that their removal would eliminate the problems and frustrations they might encounter in their everyday life. This latter situation has been especially true for school age children with a disability, a handicapping condition. Fortunately, a change is currently taking place via the significant movement of improving educational programs for school-age individuals with handicapping conditions; a movement which resulted from the full enactment of Public Law 94-142. Perhaps the schools may be the place where bridges can be built between the past and the future; between the old attitudes of separation and passive service, to involvement and aggressive action that will result in relationships with society for which all individuals seem to strive.

SCHOOLS AND CHILDREN WITH A DISABILITY

Even people not immediately affiliated with the education profession seem to be aware of the law recently passed which acknowledges equal educational opportunities for all children. This law is Public Law 94-142, which resulted from the work of parents and other individuals who brought public attention to the handicapped through policy victories won in the nation's courts and state legislatures. It is a law that has been designed to insure that all public education agencies provide an appropriate educational program for a child with a disability or handicap.

Public Law 94-142, the Education for All Handicapped Children Act, applies to all children, ages 3 to 21, who require special education and related services. As defined by this Act, handicapped children are those who are:

mentally retarded, hard of hearing, deaf, orthopedically impaired, other health impaired, speech impaired, visually handicapped, seriously emotionally disturbed, or children with specific learning disabilities who by reason thereof require special education and related services. (Ballard & Zettel, 1977, p. 178)

The major purposes of Public Law 94-142, as summarized by Ballard and Zettel (1977) are to do as follows:

Guarantee the availability of special education programming to handicapped children and youth who require it.

242

Assure fairness and appropriateness in decision making with regard to providing special education to handicapped children and youth. Establish clear management and auditing requirements and procedures regarding special education at all levels of government.

Financially assist the efforts of state and local government through the use of federal funds. (pp. 177-178)

Section 504 which was enacted through the Vocational Rehabilitation Act Amendments of 1973, applies to all Americans with a handicap or disability but has special meaning for school age children because it guarantees them, when appropriate, access to regular education programs. As the statute indicates:

No other qualified handicapped individual in the United States shall, solely by reason of his handicap, be excluded from participation in, be denied the benefits of, or be subjected to discrimination under any program or activity receiving Federal financial assistance. (Ballard & Zettel, 1977, p. 178)

The school in particular has the potential for providing intervention for children with a disability because it is a major part of a child's natural environment. Accordingly, this section of the chapter will focus on the school as an agency that is potentially capable of providing important assistance with helping these individuals achieve preparation for "normalization."

Because children and youth with a disability have a greater period of contact with the school than any other agency, there should be personnel in the schools, who are adequately trained to work with children with a disability concerning their career, personal, and social problems. The goal for significant adults working with children with a disability should be to develop a milieu that prescribes normative behavior and ways of problem solving which these children can follow when facing dilemas in their lives.

HISTORY OF COUNSELING SERVICES FOR CHILDREN WITH A DISABILITY

Relatively speaking, it has only been in recent years that children with a disability have been provided for in the public schools and then it has been done mainly through special education classes. DeBlassie and Cowan (1976) indicated that counseling for the handicapped was first mentioned after 1950 with the formation of the National Association of Retarded Children (NARC), the organization that brought pressures to provide services for the mentally retarded in areas previously neglected. Gowan, Demos, and Kokaska (1972) reported that

> The guidance of exceptional children is one of the last areas of guidance to be developed. Consequently, guidance theory and practice in this area are, in many instances, in a rather primitive state. Typical of this situation is a view which regards guidance as equivalent to vocational information or involved only in the identification of exceptional children. (p. 1)

Counseling assistance in the schools for children with a disability, if available at all, has often been limited to practical information-providing or advice-giving efforts. Most counselors are aware of students in their schools, who have a disability and are concerned about providing appropriate services for them. Yet, it seems fair to conclude that incomplete services are being provided. The counselor's inadequate involvement with children with a disability may be attributed to lack of time and/or apprehension caused mainly by his or her limited knowledge of and experience with children with a disability. Consequently, it appears that many counselors are not meeting the career development and social and personal adjustment needs of children with a disability. There needs to be an operational awareness of the fact that the career and personal-social needs of individuals with a disability are important. Children with a disability, no matter how well trained they may be in academic skills, cannot hold a job if, for example, they cannot get along with their fellow workers or have limited knowledge of career opportunities.

In order to meet the needs of children with a disability, an urgent change must be made in the traditional behaviors of school counselors to counter the results reported by Hanna's (1976) investigation of the role of the counselor in working with educable mentally retarded children. His study revealed that in the past, counselors have been perceived by special educators as failing to assume the appropriate responsibilities with handicapped children.

SERVICES SCHOOL HELPERS CAN PROVIDE

Services which helpers in the school can provide children with a disability can be divided into two areas, advocacy and direct service. These suggested services are as follows:

Direct Service

1. Provide career, personal, and social counseling for students with a disability on an individual and group basis.

2. Assist students with a disability to:
   a. obtain appropriate in-school placement and/or employment.
   b. secure admission for appropriate training.
   c. participate in extra curricular activities.

3. Consult regularly with:
   a. teachers of students with a disability.
   b. administrators.
   c. other staff members of the pupil personnel services.

4. Assist in arranging the transition of a student with a disability:
   a. from one classroom to another.
   b. from school to the training setting.
   c. from school to employment.

5. Identify needs of parents of students with a disability.

6. Evaluate the impact of the guidance program on students with a disability.

Advocacy

1. Sensitize other staff members to educational practices and materials which may be prejudicial to students with a disability.

2. Inform parents of mandates and regulations with regard to the educational rights and opportunities of students with a disability.

3. Assist students with a disability and their parents in seeking and using school-community resources.

4. Participate in identifying at all school levels the needs of students with a disability.

HELPING PROFESSIONAL'S ROLE

Helpers need to examine and realistically appraise their own attitudes that may exist when working with an individual with a disability. They need to be cognizant of not over-simplifying the problems of individuals with a disability as being those which are directly related to the disability only. Mental, emotional, and career problems of individuals with a disability are likely to originate from as wide a spectrum as do those of the non-disabled individual. The individual with a disability is likely to have not only diverse career goals and leisure interests but also limitations concerning life management. Accordingly, it is important that we as helpers do not categorize individuals with a disability and limit our involvement with them to concerns that are only directly related to their disability.

McBain (1976) summarized three facts which helpers need to acknowledge in order to assist a person with a disability:

1. There is great variation in functional limitation among those classified as possessing a particular type of disability.

246

2. Technological change has created vast new possibilities for compensating for physical limitations.

3. The individual's attitude and will to accomplish can bring about achievement that may seem impossible with a given disability. (p. 7)

Assumptions

Four basic assumptions need to be underscored.
1. Each individual with a disability is a "unique" person varying in his or her wish to receive and respond to life's experiences.

2. Elements of a helping relation advocated for the non-disabled are equally applicable to those individuals who have a disability.

3. Individuals with a disability are limited by having to function in a non-disabled world with architectural obstacles, debilitating attitudes, and assumptions which until recently, have separated them from the "normal" world.

4. Because an individual with a disability has more than the usual amount of contact with helping professionals, a necessity will be for the helper working with an individual with a disability to become involved with a number of other helping professionals such as physicians, rehabilitation counselors, and staff members of community agencies.

Helpers working toward possible solutions for individuals with a disability will find it of assistance to gain an understanding of four areas of daily life functioning in which handicapping aspects of a disability come into play. These areas, mobility, time, physical or body requirements, and personal and social disposition, should be considered as a point of departure for helping individuals with a disability work toward a solution of problems in their environment. Although these areas are interrelated, they are separated here to highlight their importance to an individual with a disability. The salient points relative to each area are presented.

Mobility is being able to move freely in one's environment. Each of us, from infants to adults, seems to desire being as physically independent as possible. We hold dear the ability to be able to go wherever we want whenever we want, and the individual with a disability is no exception.

Generally we are not usually concerned with time per se, but rather with its utilization. It is this utilization of time concerning daily living that affects some individuals with a disability. Common functions such as getting dressed, preparing a meal, or other tasks that are taken for granted by the non-disabled, may occupy a place of major importance to an individual with a disability. Time is finite and if daily living requirements involve longer time frames, a person's choices of activities become restricted.

Physical or body requirements of an individual with a disability may vary from those of non-disabled persons, depending on the nature of the disability. The conditions that are of importance include additional safety requirements, avoiding activities that may run the risk of creating injury to the body, and assistance with physical or body care.

The personal and social attitudinal disposition starts at the most basic point of the individual's commitment to growth and a desire to set goals in the search for an improved quality of life. Personal and social attitude is the desire to command the physical environment and to acquire social knowledge of self. The authors' view concerning individuals with a disability is to treat the disability as a challenge; another life problem to be solved. As such, the helper seeks to teach new skills for adapting to one's environment.

Certain needs should be fulfilled in order to provide for more and better services for individuals with a disability. Research needs to be conducted in the area of guidance services for these individuals, our training programs need to be improved to include the development of skills for working with the disabled, and inservice training programs need to be included for helpers in all agencies to improve their skills for direct service roles.

Assistance can be provided with some immediacy by focusing attention on a self-appraisal of existing services. Consideration should be given to whether each of the following services is a part of your current program. If they are not, consideration should be given to incorporating the services into the program. Services which any agency should provide individuals with a disability include:

1. Providing information to the individual with a disability concerning his or her legal rights and opportunities.

2. Using assessment materials to assist individuals with a disability in understanding themselves in relation to educational and career opportunities and requirements.

3. Cooperating with significant others to develop or review and revise programs and plans for individuals with a disability.

4. Conducting workshops on topics such as careers, human relationships, and decision making for individual with a disability and significant others in their environment.

Last Words

In the earlier sections of this chapter, emphasis was placed on the importance of recognizing those aspects of our behavior and society that provide limits on individuals with a disability. Public Law 94-142 and Section 504 of the Rehabilitation Act of 1973 have increased public awareness of the rights of an individual with a disability to have a productive and meaningful life. It is up to us helpers to create ways that will assist the members of this special population and their families to expand control over their own life styles. Passiveness on our part relative to the needs of individuals with a disability is a compromise of our professionalism. Let's evaluate, improve, re-evaluate, and continue to improve our services with the goal of improving the total milieu for all individuals in society. We should keep in mind the words of Szasz (1961) which were spoken in another context, but are applicable to this situation: " . . . although there are certain biological invariants in behavior, the precise pattern of human actions is determined largely by roles and rules" (p. 13).

POST TEST

Directions: After reading the chapter, mark the following items either true or false.

T F 1. Old attitudes of separation for children with a disability will change in the schools in part due to the full enactment of Public Law 94-142.

T F 2. Relatively speaking, only in recent years have children with a disability been provided for in the public schools.

T F 3. In order to meet adequately the needs of children with a disability in the schools, counselors will need to assume more responsibilities for the children.

T F 4. Advocacy by school counselors for children with a disability is a service outside the counselor's role and function.

T F 5. An examination and realistic appraisal of a helper's attitudes is a "first step" when working with individuals with a disability.

T F 6. Elements of a helping relation advocated for the non-disabled are equally applicable to those individuals who have a disability.

T F 7. By conducting a self-appraisal of existing services, helpers can obtain some assistance in providing services to individuals with a disability by focusing attention on elements of service which require improvement.

T F 8. An assumption of this chapter is that as helpers, we should help create ways that will assist individuals with a disability and their families to expand control of their own life styles.

Scoring Guide for Post Test
1. T	3. T	5. T	7. T
2. T	4. F	6. T	8. T

Reference List

Ballard, J. & Zettel, J. Public Law 94-142 and Section 504: What they say about rights and protections. *Exceptional Children*, 1977, *44*, 177-184.

DeBlassie, R. R., & Cowan, M. A. Counseling with the mentally handicapped child. *Elementary School Guidance and Counseling*, 1976, *10*, 246-253.

Gowan, J., Demos, G., & Kokaska, C. (Eds.) *The guidance of exceptional children* (2nd ed.), New York: David McKay Co., 1972.

Hanna, R.C. *The role of the counselor in working with educable mentally retarded students.* Unpublished doctoral dissertation, University of Florida, 1976.

Hofmann, G.W. Some effects of spinal cord lesions on experienced emotional feelings. *Psychophysiology*, 1966, *3*(2), 143-156.

Martin, E. W. Some thoughts on mainstreaming. *Exceptional Children*, 1974, *41*, 150-153.

McBain, S. L. *Enhancing understanding of students with physical disabilities.* Palo Alto, Ca.: National Consortium on Competency-Based Staff Development, 1976.

Szasz, T.S. *The myth of mental illness.* New York: Dell Pub. Co., 1961.

11

The Mexican— American

Donald L. Avila, Ph.D.

Professor
Foundations of Education Department
University of Florida
Gainesville, Florida

and

Antonio L. Avila, Ed.S.

Graduate Student
Counselor Education Department
University of Florida
Gainesville, Florida

ABOUT THE AUTHORS

Both authors are Mexican-Americans born in Los Angeles, California. The chapter has come as much out of their own personal experience as it has from available data.

Donald L. Avila, Ph.D.

The senior author is a professor in the Foundations of Education department at the University of Florida where he teaches personality and specializes in self-concept theory.

Antonio L. Avila, Ed.S.

The junior author is a graduate student in the Counselor Education department at the same university studying for his doctorate in school psychology.

THE MEXICAN-AMERICAN

Donald L. Avila and Antonio L. Avila

AWARENESS INDEX

Directions: Mark each item true or false. Compute your score from the scoring guide at the end of this awareness index. A post test is provided at the end of the chapter.

T F 1. The "Castilian Hussle" is a famous Mexican dance.

T F 2. Mexican-Americans can be easily identified by their physiognomy.

T F 3. Generally speaking, Spanish is Mexican and Mexican is Spanish.

T F 4. Mestizo is the Spanish word for Alien.

T F 5. Studies on the self-concept of minority groups are very useful.

T F 6. Many values of Mexican-Americans and middle-class Americans are in direct conflict.

T F 7. Mexicans often try to "pass" for some other nationality.

T F 8. Mexican-American parents are adamant about inculcating the old values in their children.

T F 9. Fortunately, little discrimination towards Mexican-Americans is found in our public schools.

255

T F 10. The best thing we can do for our Mexican-American children is to get them acculturated as soon as possible.

Scoring Guide for Awareness Index

1. F	4. F	7. T	10. F
2. F	5. F	8. F	
3. F	6. T	9. F	

A LITTLE HISTORY

The best place to start anything is at the beginning, and the Mexican-American begins with one of the most incredible stories in the history of the world—the conquest of Mexico.

On February 19, 1519, Hernando Cortes, eight hundred troops, fourteen cannons and sixteen horses landed on the Yucatan Peninsula of Mexico (Prescott, 1934). In less than three years this handful of men conquered an entire empire numbering millions of people and established not only a *new* nation, but also a new breed of human beings.

How was this feat possible? How could a relatively few individuals have such a tremendous impact on history? Several factors contributed, but three were major ones. The first, understandable; the other two, uncanny.

The first circumstance that allowed this small band to accomplish what seems like an impossible task is not unusual —a state of affairs that has plagued and caused many empires to fall. At the time of Cortes' arrival, Mexico consisted of many separate tribes under the loose control of the Aztec Empire. Although considered a unified people, great disharmony was among the separate tribes. Many of them had been conquered by the Aztecs, and like many of the peoples conquered by Rome, never got over their resentment of and hatred for their conquerers. Consequently, when Cortes came to the Mexican shores, he was often able to recruit fairly large numbers of natives to further his cause.

The next two major factors contributing to the success of the conquistador seem more fictional than real, but they were true. Although the Aztecs were civilized in many ways, in others they were barbaric and crude. One of these factors was in their style of warfare. The native armies consisted of foot soldiers and their weapons were clubs, knives, and swords. They had never heard gun powder ignite nor seen horses. The rumors natives heard of these things made them reluctant to fight. When they did engage in battle with the Spanish, the explosions of rifle and cannon and the awesome sight constituted by huge animals and their riders terrified many of the natives and caused them to flee in fear.

Judging the impact of the third and perhaps strongest factor in Cortes' success is difficult, but the impact was considerable. A strong belief within the Aztec religion was that a white bearded god had once ruled and resided in Mexico and it was foretold that he would one day return. Clearly many of the natives thought Cortes was that god and they either failed to resist the Spaniard or joined his cause because of the belief. The Aztec Emperor, himself, made many blunders that contributed to the downfall of the empire, because, being confused as to whether or not Cortes was a god, the Emperor's judgment was clouded. He neither wanted to give his nation to plunderer's nor offend a god. So, a nation was conquered by what was little more than a group of bandits.

The establishment of a new nation and a new breed of people was much more straightforward and natural. Once having subdued the local natives, Cortes' men began to intimately fraternize with them, and that fraternization created a new being—the Mestizos. Mestizos were the result of the inbreeding of the native Aztec Indians and the Spaniards. Mexico City became the first Mestizo city in history and the current stated ancestral heritage of Mexico is reported as being fifty-five percent Mestizo, twenty-nine percent Indian, and fifteen percent European.

Now the Mexican-American story begins. Three major causes contributed to the migration of the Mexican to what is now the southwestern and far western portions of the United States. First, the Spanish search for booty, conversion, and expansion did not end in Mexico. While acquiring Mexico and most of Central America, they sent bands of priests, soldiers, and unidentifiable scoundrels north in order to further the

Spaniards' purposes. Little trouble was encountered in doing so because the people present in these lands were mostly small tribes of rather primitive and unaggressive Indians. As usual, these adventurers began settling the land by converting, plundering, and again inbreeding with the locals (Longstreet, 1977).

The second and third causes of migration originate in what might be called the second phase of Mexicanization. Like Americans, the Mestizo decided that independence from Spain was in order and proceeded to accomplish that task. But freedom was not easy. Years of war, oppression, and poverty followed the decision to free themselves from Spain and establish an independent nation. Thus, because of the warfare and poverty, thousands left their native land and headed for greener pastures.

What then is the modern Mexican-American ancestry? That's not an easy question. All the peoples of the United States have inbred over the years so that it is nearly impossible to trace one's ancestry in any true linear fashion and very unlikely that there is a "pure" strain of any ancestry—biological, religious, political, or otherwise—in this melting-pot nation of ours. Surely, the Mexican-American is no exception.

The Mexican-American is mostly of Mestizo ancestry. With that is combined the inbreeding of the Spanish and Mexican Indian with the American Indian and finally all of those inbreeding with the North Americans who eventually took over the west and southwestern United States. Without question their history has been of a people seeking new and better lives, some coming from Mexico to settle new lands, but most fleeing revolution and poverty. While conditions in Mexico are constantly improving, that migration and hopeful seeking has not yet ended.

The Mexican-American experience has been disappointing. The dreams of a better life have been realized by a relative few and they have for the most part been treated as second-class citizens. In the beginning they were treated and exploited as slaves. Later they were accepted as a necessary evil, but segregated into ghettos or barrios and no less exploited. They have always been looked at as a cheap source of labor and been regarded by the majority with all the cruelty of rampant prejudice and discrimination. Some changes have occurred, but more Mexican-Americans still face the same problems that have plagued them from the beginning.

MINORITIES—BLAH, BLAH, BLAH

When a person decides to analyze minority groups, the first thing that sets in, if you are not a member of such a group, is boredom. Boredom, because so much of the information reads alike. To paraphrase, if you have looked at one of them, you've looked at 'em all. And, this is true. *In a very real way this is true*; unless, of course, you are looking at the priviledged minorities like the rich and famous. But oppressed, dispossessed, poor minorities *are* the same in many ways. They all fit the cycle of poverty and they are all the victims of prejudice and discrimination. Thus the general descriptions and statistics are the same over and over again.

The authors want least of all to bore the reader. Therefore, we shall, here and now, quickly dispense with the description and statistics. Like every minority the Mexican-American is as follows:

1. The victim of prejudice and discrimination.

2. Alienated from his/her and the greater society.

3. Segregated and isolated.

4. Mostly poor.

What else is new? Not much. The facts of the matter are as follows (Carter, 1979; Hernandez, 1973):

1. Approximately five million Mexican-Americans are in the United States.

2. One-third live in poverty and are disproportionably represented in the low earning, manual labor occupations.

259

3. They obtain, on the average, 7.1 years of education.

4. They have a lower educational level than blacks or whites and a greater school drop-out rate than either.

5. They have the highest illiteracy rate of any group in the U.S.

6. By the 12th grade, 40% have dropped out of school.

7. Only 1% go to college.

8. Many schools are so segregated that their students are almost all Mexican-American.

9. Many are 2, 3, or even 5 years behind in school.

Sound familiar? Of course. All statistics on oppressed minorities sound like a broken record.

BUT—THERE ARE DIFFERENCES

Now that we have taken care of the statistics, let's go on with the focus of this article. That focus is understanding. The writers believe that one of the most important characteristics a counselor must have if he/she is to be successful is empathetic understanding of the client. If the counselor does not understand the unique qualities of his/her client, he/she cannot help that client. The major purpose of this chapter, then, is to give the reader a better idea of what it means to be a member of the Mexican-American minority.

What are some of the factors that make this minority different from others?

Language

Language, of course, is the most obvious problem for the Mexican-American. However, the problem is not the same for all. Some Mexican-Americans speak virtually no English, some speak no Spanish, and some speak every possible state between these extremes. All are, however, members of the same minority group and subject to the same experiences, especially those experiences of a prejudicial nature. The less English spoken, however, the worse the problem.

Little, if anything, is more frightening or will give a person more of a sense of helplessness than will being surrounded by people speaking a language one does not understand. Thousands of Mexican-Americans of all ages are in this predicament. Older individuals often can find protection by surrounding themselves with other Spanish speaking people, but children are sometimes thrust into the greater society without the tools to express even their most basic needs. Youngsters consequently withdraw, become quiet, and hope that they at least do not get in harm's way. Imagine what it is like to be a nine or ten year old child in a room with twenty or thirty other people and not be able to comprehend a word that is spoken. Of course, those around the child are confused and unable to communicate also, and behave in ways that are not conducive to growth such as rejecting, ignoring, or aggravating the exotic child. In any case, what results is a frightened, confused, isolated, and lonely little child. As time passes, such children generally will react in one of two ways. They may become more withdrawn and isolated; they may develop various defenses to protect themselves, as, for example, developing the "Uncle Tom" syndrome; or do the opposite and react with open aggression and hostility.

Migrant Status

Unlike most other minorities, a tremendously disproportionate number of Mexican-Americans are in the migrant labor force. What does this mean? In terms of physical health alone (Hernandez, 1973) the picture is not a pretty one:

1. The infant mortality rate for migrants is 12 percent higher than the national average.

2. The rate of death from influenza is 200 percent, from tuberculosis 260 percent, and from accidents 300 percent higher than the national average.

261

3. The life expectancy of the migrant worker is 49 years of age.

The psycho-social picture is no better. Migrant means moving—constant moving. Many Mexican-Americans remain in one place for only three or four months. They have no roots, no home, no place to belong. Each time they follow the crops they are thrown into a totally new situation with no psychological anchors to grasp. When they arrive at their destination, conditions are disgusting and they are totally exploited. Little is as depressing as the sight of migrant camps and the abuse to which the migrant is too often subjected. Worst of all, they are in a cycle which offers little hope of being broken. The process keeps the adults from being able to improve their skills or positions and the children are simply sunken deeper and deeper into a hopeless situation.

Viva Mexico

The Mexican-American is in a unique situation because they are so close to the country with which they are identified. This causes the larger society to misunderstand the real nature of the Mexican-American and confuse two groups of people which are in some respects very different. Mexican-Americans are not simply displaced Mexican nationals. The problems of Mexicans and the problems of Mexican-Americans are not the same. While many can and do take pride in their heritage it is as Americans and not as Mexican nationals.

Back to Africa movements have failed because blacks in this country are native Americans, not Africans. They do not go back to Africa because Africa is not their country. For the same reason many Mexican-Americans have little or no desire to see, hear, or talk about the "old" country. When Mexican nationals and Mexican-Americans encounter one another, often no sense of loyalty or brotherhood is felt as one might expect. In fact, they may well have little in common. Mexicans from Mexico have their problems and Mexicans who are American and a distinctly different group, have theirs. Furthermore, possibly on occasion one may detect a degree of hostitlity between the Mexican Nationals and the Mexican-Americans, as though the Nationals regarded the Mexican-Americans as being a bit beneath them and perhaps considered as "having deserted the ship." By the same token, those Mexicans who migrated to the U.S. did so because they were unhappy and were escaping a past they did not want following them. Therefore, they can be very uncomfortable when the past interjects itself into their present lives in the form of a Mexican national. The authors, although of Mexican-American heritage, have not particularly identified themselves with Mexico. They have visited there, but when they did the visits were clearly perceived as trips to a foreign country.

It is a bit naive, then, to assume that Mexican-Americans have a longing nostalgia for the old country. They may not long for it and they may do their best not to be identified with it.

Who Am I?

A circumstance the writers believe to be unique to the Mexican-American has to do with two characteristics. The first is about appearance. Mexican-Americans can range from appearing very much like the North American Indian in their physiognomy to having no facial characteristics of their Indian ancestral past, but looking like many Latin or European people. This appearance can be true of members of the same family. The consequences of this characteristic are strange indeed!

The more a person resembles an Indian, the more prejudice and discrimination he/she will encounter. Mexican-Americans who do not have these features experience much less discrimination than those who do and have found it much easier to gain access to and integration into the larger society. Those Mexican-Americans who most closely resemble the North American Indian suffer the same kind of nightmarish experiences as the American Indian and American black, while those who do not have these features may go through life relatively untouched by prejudice and discrimination. These conditions have to do with how easily one is identified with a minority and how much different that minority is from the majority. Blacks, as a total group, have suffered the most in this country because they have the most easily identifiable physical characteristic that is considered as making them

263

different from other Americans—the color of their skin. Mexican-Americans who have distinct Indian features know exactly the kind of prejudicial hell that the Blacks have experienced, because Mexican-Americans have experienced and continue to experience the same. The authors have often heard the expression, "Niggers and Spics! They are just alike. Dumb, dirty, lazy, and smelly." The referents were usually talking about Mexican-Americans who "look" Mexican. Hollywood has always known about and taken advantage of this situation. For years Mexicans have been playing Indians and Indians have been playing Mexicans. Yet, not one of either group has ever become a superstar except perhaps Anthony Quinn—but after all he only looks a tiny bit Indian.

The second strange aspect of being Mexican-American is related to the first. That is, the Mexican-American who does not have the Indian features of his brothers and sisters can, with only a little trickery, self and social denial, and maybe the help of some form of transportation, escape nearly all the hazards of prejudice and discrimination. For you see, Mexican is not necessarily Mexican all the time.

When one of the authors was a young boy, he had occasion to mail a package on which was printed the family name, Avila. The postal clerk read the name and brightly asked, "Is that your name?" The author answered that it was and the clerk then asked in a very friendly manner if the name was Spanish. The author in his, then, boyish naivete said, "No, it's Mexican." At that, something happened which the author did not understand until sometime later after he had seen it happen many times. The clerk's entire demeanor changed. He said, "Oh" and was no longer cheery and friendly, but cold and distant. The business was conducted with no further verbal exchanges. The author discovered that people of Mexican and Spanish descent were not the same, and that Spanish was somehow better than Mexican. He also discovered that by simply saying he was Spanish he could be treated much better and have many more doors open for him. (He didn't do this very often though, because when he said he was Mexican and there were no flinches or character changes, he knew he was meeting a potential friend. There were times, however, when it was necessary to do so in order to avoid the possible loss of something or someone important to him.)

Thus, "Spanish" people are welcome in many places across this land where Mexicans are not. And many Mexican-Americans have played this game throughout their lives to avoid discrimination. Some, just to be sure, have gone so far as to deny both Mexican and Spanish heritage, passing themselves off as Italian, Jewish, or any other nationality for which they thought they could be mistakenly identified.

One aspect of this game that would be comical if it were not so sad, is what the authors call the "Castilian Hussle." A belief among some Mexican Nationals as well as Mexican-Americans is that throughout the history of Mexico a strain of Mexicans dating from the time of Cortes has been able to keep their ancestors pure and untainted by the blood of the natives of the countries they counquered. These true believers refer to themselves as Castilians, and even if they were born in Mexico they will say, "Yes, I am from Mexico, but I am not Mexican, I am Castilian Spanish." And it works!, which probably tells us more about the people it works on, than those who play the game.

The authors' intent is not to make fun of anyone, but to emphasize the desperation that oppressed people can feel and the lengths to which they must go in order to escape injustice. But it is sad, because the kind of self-denial we have been discussing *must* leave terrible psychic scars upon those forced to engage in the process.

In any event, while the Mexican-American is like all other minorities, he or she is different, too.

WHAT'S ALL THAT CRAP ABOUT . . .

Intelligence

To the authors, one of the most insensitive, damaging, and inconceivable pastimes in which academicians engage is the attempt to compare the intelligence of minority groups with that of the majority, particularly if the minority group involved has experienced the consequences of extreme prejudice and discrimination. Individuals who persist in suggesting that the native intelligence of the majority can be compared with that of a minority simply do not have a basic understanding of intelligence measurements and their limitations.

Our most sophisticated intelligence measurements are not culture free and our so called culture free measurements are notoriously foul with regards to validity and reliability. *Intelligence tests do not measure basic capacity*. They measure a person's total life experience and cultural milieu. The closer one's life experience is related to the structure and content of an intelligence test the higher he/she will score; the less related the lower he/she will score. Intelligence tests in their present form, rather than measure basic potential, more accurately compare how closely one group's socialization process resembles another group's.

Individuals born into a lower socioeconomic class, shut out of the society, suffering mental and physical deprivations and having different cultural values are most certainly going to score lower on intelligence measurements constructed by members of groups not fitting this sociocultural model. No data tell of the effects name calling has on a child when he/she is called and for the first time understands the meaning of Nigger, Greaser, or Kike; nor does the data tell how long that effect will last. We submit that the effect is devastating and leaves a life-long scar. Furthermore, until better measurements are developed or a universal indicator of basic intelligence is found, any attempt to compare one group's intelligence with another's is futile, and studying the current research on this topic will tell the reader little about the ability of Mexican-Americans or any other minority group.

Self-Concept

The self-concept is one of the most important aspects of behavior. It must be at least mentioned when speaking of any human beings. Yet, little time will be spent on the topic because in relation to minorities so little is known about it. The research available on the self-concept of minorities is totally conflicting. Some of the data reveals no difference between the self-concept of minority and majority members; some of it says that majority members have a higher self-concept than minorities; and some says that minorities have a higher self-concept than majorities. It is confusing just to say it.

The self-concept is probably the most important factor in anyone's life and the ability of counselors to understand the self-concept of their clients may be their most important task. But a study of literature will not help the counselor much in trying to do so.

The conflicting data most likely arises from two factors. One is the nature of the groups being sampled and the other is the nature of the instrument used. Minorities cannot be treated as a total group in self-concept studies. If they are, the data is bound to be spurious. Study after study has demonstrated that social class is a much greater group differentiater than is minority status. In other words, members of the same social class are more alike and more different from other social classes than are different racial, religious, or national members when compared with one another. Therefore, when you compare a minority group with a majority group, especially when one has a much larger percentage of its members in lower socioeconomic classes, you are bound to get a more positive response from the group with the greater representation in the higher socioeconomic classes. And, when examining the converse, the situation where you might be studying a sample of minority members who are mostly in the higher socioeconomic classes, you may well discover that they have better self-concepts than a normally distributed population. They, because of their association with an oppressed minority, have had to have extraordinary ability and personal strength to get where they are.

Instruments being used may be totally inadequate for reflecting the true picture of a particular minority group, especially if class representation is biased. Self-concept instruments are based on middle-class majority values. Examining the self-concepts of groups not representing these values may completely distort the data that results.

Mexican-Americans in particular, have class and social values that not only differ from but also are in direct contradiction to the values of the middle-class majority. The Mexican-American has many conflicts with the institutions of the larger society, i.e., educational, legal, social, and so forth, but these conflicts do not mean that they do not have a great deal of self-respect and confidence in themselves. These positive feelings simply may not be related to the kinds of items one finds on the typical self-concept scale. The young Mexican-American male may not feel too competent with regard to reading, "ritin," "rithmetic," and social skills, but he may feel and experience a great deal of confidence and self-respect from being a member in one of the toughest gangs in a Los Angeles barrio. Let it be enough to say that if teachers or counselors approach the Mexican-American expecting a shy, self-depreciating, inadequately feeling individual with no self-respect, the professionals are in trouble; at best they will be put on, at worst they may be igniting a very explosive situation.

The authors suggest that Mexican-Americans and all minority groups probably have as good a self-concept and as much self-respect as any member of a majority which is why many minority groups are refusing to be oppressed any longer.

CASE EXAMPLES

Let's briefly examine some of the experiences typical of those the Mexican-American encounters in his/her growth and socialization process. The following are real life anecdotes common to the Mexican-American experience.

John: John's real name is Juan, but the school has changed it in order to accelerate the acculturation process. John's father has managed to escape the backbreaking work of the migrant laborer and find a menial, but less demanding job in the city. Unfortunately only a few other Mexican-American families reside in the area. John and the rest of his family can speak only enough English to satisfy their basic needs.

John is dutifully placed in the local school in the grade appropriate to his cohorts. After two or three days we find his teacher speaking to one of her co-workers:

"May, does anyone on the staff speak Spanish?"

"Not that I know of, why?"

"Well, I have this little Mexican boy in class and he doesn't understand a word I say. I'm at my wit's end. I can't find any teacher or student who speaks Spanish."

"What are you going to do?"

"I don't know."

"Well, if I think of anything, I'll let you know."

We run into the two colleagues several days later. May speaks first:

"How are things working out with that little Mexican kid, Julie?"

"Oh, I don't know. The principal is looking into some possibilities for help, but he says we don't really have a program for kids like that. He's a quiet kid, and mostly just sits. He does like to draw, so I let him do that a lot. If he doesn't cause any trouble I guess I will just let him be and maybe the problem will take care of itself. It is tough, though. The other kids won't play with him because they can't understand him either. They think he's weird. So do I."

Mike: Mike finally sorted it all out to his own satisfaction, but it wasn't easy. Decisions made by others and things happening over which he had no control complicated his life and confused him. He was the product of a mixed marriage, his mother being Mexican-American and his father a typical American mixture of ancestry. Their story is related because it is representative of the kinds of experiences minority group members have and the lengths to which they must sometimes go in order to try and fit in.

269

Mike's parents gave him an Anglo name because they believed he would have an easier time of it. They also refused to teach him Spanish. They were afraid he would develop an accent and they knew children with accents were treated badly in schools.

These two decisions, alone, caused him trouble throughout his life and the problems began immediately. His maternal grandparents and assorted aunts and uncles could not speak English. Therefore, the only way he was ever able to communicate with them was non-verbally or by having his mother sit beside him and translate the conversations. Thus, not once in his life had he ever spoken directly to his own grandparents or other relatives.

These things also made it difficult for him to relate to his peers. Living in a multicultural neighborhood, none of the other children was sure what he was or where he belonged, and neither was he. The Blacks knew he wasn't one of their's but the Mexicans and "whites" weren't sure whether he was one of their's or not. "What kinda Mexican can't speak Spanish?", and "What kinda American has a Mexican name and mother?"

As a child, Mike adjusted to this particular problem by being meaner and tougher than all the other kids so that he could go where he pleased. In the type of neighborhood in which he lived, that made him a leader, so sometimes he roamed with the Mexican kids and sometimes with the non-Mexican kids, but it was a hard way to go.

Confusion really set in as he would often hear his relatives on his father's side speak about those "Dirty Mexicans" and "Smelly Niggers." He knew he wasn't Black, but weren't he and his mother Mexican? He would often try to get one of his relatives to explain what they meant, if it meant that they didn't like him and his mother, but he wouldn't get much satisfaction. He would usually get a response like, "Aw, you and your Mom ain't like that. You're not greasers, you're different." This worked out well, however, for he came to the conclusion the whole world was a little crazy and grew up almost totally free of prejudice.

Mike's mother probably was right and his life may have been much more difficult had he been more easily identifiable as a Mexican-American. But he suffered many adjustment problems as he grew up because of the confusion over his identity and on many occasions wished he could speak his mother's native tongue. He tried in later years to learn Spanish, but was unable to do so. Since he had three college degrees, it didn't seem likely that this was due to a lack of intelligence. He concluded, therefore, that not only did he not learn Spanish as a child, but also at some level of awareness he must have developed a kind of mental block to its acquisition.

By his wits and some luck, Mike has made it well enough, but he has many scars left from making it as a minority group member, and the making it, itself, was a difficult process. There is no telling what he might have become or have contributed had he not been burdened by the evils of prejudice.

Gloria: Maria had just arrived at her friend's house in answer to a tearful phone call from Gloria in which the latter had said she and her boyfriend had broken up.

"What happened," asked Maria.

"It was his parents. He didn't even have the guts to tell me himself. His mother called and told me that she and her husband did not think that different races and religions mix and that they just thought it better if their son did not go around with a Mexican Catholic."

Maria sighs and says, "Oh shit."

"What is it, Maria, this thing about being Mexican? Why does it seem to make everything so hard?"

"I do not know."

"Does it last forever?"

"I think so, Gloria, I think it does."

Friends: Five boys were sitting in a restaurant having lunch. They looked like a group of typical anglo-Saxon, middle-class American teenagers. One, however, was not. He was a Mexican-American. His name was Henry.

Four members of the group, including Henry, had been friends for some time and the other three knew Henry was of Mexican descent. The fifth boy was a relatively new member of the group and the heritage of the others had not crossed his mind.

As they sat, a couple entered the restaurant. The man could have been of Indian or Mexican descent because he had very black, long, straight hair and the physiognomy spoken of earlier that is typical of American Indians and many Mexican-Americans. The lady had blonde hair and fair skin.

The boys all glanced up at the couple as people will do when someone enters a room. At that point the boy who was a newcomer to the group said softly, but so that all at the table clearly heard him:

"God damn! Will you look at that! Nothing pisses me off more."

The other four boys looked up at the fifth, and Henry asked, "What?"

"Seeing a beautiful white woman hunched all up against a greasy spic."

The other four boys froze. Henry's three friends had seen him tear into many another boy for much less. Fortunately, though young, Henry was maturing and beginning to learn the futility of trying to beat the prejudice out of people. He let it pass, but you can be assured that the other three friends of his soon clarified an issue for the fourth, and such an incident, in this group, did not happen again.

A CULTURAL HERITAGE

Aside from the dual-headed monster of prejudice and discrimination, two things seem to be the major complications of the problems in the Mexican-American experience. The first is a cultural heritage that often contradicts that of the majority. The second is the attitude of majority group members.

Some Mexican-American values are in direct conflict with those of the majority and place the minority group member at a disadvantage when trying to survive. First, the nature of the Mexican-American cultural heritage is socialistic. The family is of primary importance and takes precedent over any outside concerns, whether these concerns deal with school, work, or whatever. The family members develop a sense of cooperation rather than competition. Many Mexican-Americans, therefore, enter the competitive society of the majority favoring group rather than individual success. Second, the Mexican-American culture, like all Latin cultures, is highly authoritarian. The children are taught to give unquestioning obedience to the head of the family and to be strongly dependent on that authority for decision making. Thus, partly because of their training to be obedient, partly because they are taught to be polite, and partly as a defensive coping behavior, Mexican-Americans may be quiet and submissive. Third, many Mexican-Americans have a present orientation that does not stress preparation for the future nor place importance on the acquisition of material goods. Fourth, the Mexican-American may have a code of honor that emphasizes the "Macho" image, where one suffers frustration and disappointment in silence, is not put in a position where he/she may lose face, and where there is a tendency to adjust to problems rather than solve them. Finally, the status of women is clearly inferior.

Without question, in our present day American society, any child, brown, black, or white, who is not adamantly achievement and competitively oriented, is unquestioning of authority, submissive, uninterested in material things, more loyal to a group than to themselves and considers females to be inferior, *is in trouble*.

Situational Factors

Aside from the long-term factors of cultural heritage that conflict with the potential development of the Mexican-American, situational factors make integration difficult. These are behaviors that have grown out of the Mexican-American attempt to adjust to the majority society or failure to do so.

Many Mexican-American parents feel unable to give their children the necessary skills to cope with the larger community. They actually feel inferior to the anglo members of the society and avoid them, not from lack of concern, but because of this fear. Mothers and fathers will not question their employers and will not go to school or may not even answer the door when some perceived authority comes calling. It is not uncooperativeness but fear of making a fool of themselves or embarrassing their children that causes this behavior.

Related to this sense of inadequacy is the fact that parents will sometimes be hesitant or refrain altogether from helping their children with school work. They are concerned that they will not know how to help or might do more harm than good if they interfere with their child's studies.

Another consequence of situational factors is that parents, knowing their values conflict with the majority, refrain from trying to instill them in their children. They hope their children will somehow assimilate the values of the majority, making a better adjustment than they themselves did. This, of course, is no answer. What usually happens is the children reach adolescence without a clear set of values, being more confused and having more trouble coping.

Last, because of all the conflicts, the Mexican-American family is not stable with all the problems related to domestic disharmony—delinquency, hostility, academic difficulty and the like.

SOCIAL ATTITUDES AND ACTION

The other factor mainly responsible for the failure of our society to adequately integrate the Mexican-American is the attitude and actions of the larger society toward this minority.

The most tragic and inexcusable circumstance in the greater society is that where large numbers of Mexican-

274

Americans are found something very much like a caste system exists. This is similar to the situation of Blacks, but needs to be emphasized because many do not realize that the Mexican-American experience is often no less oppressive or restrictive than that of Blacks. As always, the system results in geographical isolation, job and pay discrimination, restriction of interpersonal interactions, and all of the other deprivations associated with racial or religious prejudice.

Our schools, institutions which should be most responsive to the integration of our minorities, are where some of the worst injustices are perpetrated. When studies have been made, the following kinds of attitudes have been found to exist among non-Mexican public school personnel. Many teachers and administrators believe Mexican-American characteristics are the following (Carter, 1970; Hernandez, 1973):

1. Inferior
2. Lazy
3. Unable to learn
4. Happy with their lot
5. Peculiar
6. Hopeless
7. Dangerous

Some of the school practices found to exist are the following (Carter, 1970; Hernandez, 1973):

1. Teachers ignoring students.
2. Schools making no allowance for the schedule of migrant workers.
3. Universities not preparing teachers to deal with any minority.
4. Schools assigning teachers, who do not speak Spanish, to predominantly Mexican-American classes or schools.
5. Banning of the Spanish language or reference to anything Mexican.
6. Prohibiting students from speaking Spanish.

RECOMMENDATIONS

The failure of our society to fully integrate the Mexican-American as a first-class citizen is long standing and inexcusable. This integration is not going to be accomplished by the publication of a single chapter in one book. Hopefully, though, from this reading the counselor will be better able to contribute to that integration in a more effective way. Toward that end we offer some recommendations. The reader may consider them to be no more than common sense. But, we humans are often guilty of not using common sense enough and are more likely to do so if we receive little reminders now and then of just what that commodity is.

Before we enumerate these recommendations we would like to point out what as counselors we are definitely *not* trying to do. Too often the Mexican-American is looked upon as a foreigner who has to be acculturated, that is, taught the characteristics and values of the larger society, usually at the expense of his/her own cultural heritage. Mexican-Americans are not foreigners. They are Americans who have historical roots different, but not inferior to, those of other Americans. Our purpose is not to make them like all other Americans, but to give them the skills and knowledge that enable them to succeed, as they share with us those positive things from their culture. Our task is to *integrate*, not acculturate the Mexican-American.

Acculturation is an insult. It says that one set of principles, values, beliefs, and behaviors is right while another is wrong. An attempt to acculturate almost always results in an approach where the majority member says, "What you are is bad and what you have is useless. Leave all that behind and let me show you the way."

The quickest way to failure is to begin our first interaction with other persons by telling them that what they are is bad, wrong, inept, or immoral. If we do so, not only are we doomed to failure, but also we are usually dead wrong! Most often our own house is not in such great order that we can offer it up as a perfect model at the expense of another life style.

276

In light of this purpose, recommendations of the authors and of Carter (1970) and Hernandez (1973) when working with Mexican-Americans or any minority are as follows:

1. Always accept your clients exactly as they are, accepting their values, beliefs, and behaviors, and go from there. Take the position that what they are is good and that your function is to add to what they are, not to subtract or distract from it. Project an attitude that says, "What you are is good. What I want to do is lend you some things of mine that I think will make life easier for you and give you a better potential for success."

   If you can't honestly and sincerely do this, we suggest you do not take on the counselee. You're wasting time, or worse.

2. Although you are working with a Mexican-American, that person is an individual. The purpose of this article has been to give the reader some insight into Mexican-Americans, not to suggest that they are all alike. They are not. They are like every other group, their members differ from each other in as many ways as they differ from another group. Ascertain those differences before you go blundering in and making a fool of yourself with some kind of generalization.

   A word about the term "Chicano" may be in order. It is currently the "In" word and many writers use it to designate the Mexican-American. Militant and numerous poor Mexican-Americans also are using it as a designation of pride or unity. It has not always been so. The exact origin of the term is not known, and it has no exact meaning. To many, especially older members of the minority, it represents a picture of the poor, uneducated, exploited field hand. To many Mexican-Americans it, historically has and still does have the same distasteful meaning as the word "nigger" or "spic." These individuals would consider it an insult to be addressed in that way and do not consider it an honorable term. That is why these authors have used the term Mexican-American throughout. To their knowledge no one is offended by that designation. It is discussed here in order to emphasize the importance of knowing the individual to whom you are talking.

3. Some professionals find group counseling very effective with the Mexican-American because of their orientation to group cohesiveness. Also, it is helpful that these groups be of homogeneous consistency at times for better self-understanding and heterogeneous at other times for better minority-majority group interaction and understanding.

4. The more successful counselors have been found to be those who initiate programs early in the year and work on them throughout the year. Such programs are of an invitational nature but counselors have found that starting early has a snowballing effect and accomplishes much more than waiting until specific problems arise. Some examples of such programs are as follows:

    a. Occupational exploration groups

    b. Sensitivity groups

    c. College orientation programs which include bringing to the group Mexican-Americans who are successfully pursuing college programs.

    d. Role model groups which invite successful Mexican-Americans, from all walks of life, to discuss their lives and work with the members.

    e. Cultural exploration groups.

5. Whenever possible, integrate the values and beliefs of the Mexican-American into your counseling with them, showing the use and place of such values and beliefs.

6. The teaching of skills is usually more useful than the teaching of values. They have most likely already been exposed to any value that you might hope to

introduce to them. What they need most are better, more effective skills.

7. In initiating a counseling program do not delay the beginning, get at it right now and make subsequent appointments soon and frequently.

8. When counseling is initiated, get to the problems. Do not delay with the accumulation of long case histories or explorations of the past.

9. Be flexible. This client is not likely to be susceptible to "pure line" counseling theory. Get a feel for the client, then select what you believe will be the best process approach to use, whether that be client-centered, behavioristic, rational, or combination.

10. Use standardized tests for individual guidance, not for comparative purposes.

11. Many counselors find more productivity in focusing on the accomplishment of one objective at a time rather than taking a shotgun approach. Sometimes this gives a particular client a better sense of success and more confidence in the counselor.

12. Be a leader in initiating programs in your school that recognize the special needs and problems of this group and in getting the school to utilize and accept the cultural heritage of the Mexican-American.

13. Don't judge your Mexican-American clients by your own value system. Find out as much as you can about their culture and make your judgments from that frame of reference.

The greater the community involvement the more successful a program will be. Every attempt should be made to utilize the total available Mexican-American population in what you and the school are doing. You will be most successful if you will.

14. The greater the Mexican-American community involvement, the more successful a program will be. Every attempt should be made to utilize the total available Mexican-American population in what you and the school are doing. You will be most successful if you will:

   a. Involve parents.

   b. Form community groups such as the following:

      1) Language improvement
      2) Community counseling
      3) Sensitivity
      4) Community orientation which orients community members to the agencies and people available to assist them and to the facilities available.

   c. Engage in public relations.

   d. Encourage the employment of Mexican-Americans in the schools.

   e. Utilize as many of the successful Mexican-Americans as you can find in your programs.

There you have it. No masterpiece, this, nor a document of world-shattering importance. But, a presentation the authors hope will aid the reader to become a better soldier in the army of professional helpers, and a better counselor, particularly when working with Mexican-Americans.

POST TEST

Directions: After reading the chaper, mark the following items either true or false.

T F 1. Mexican-Americans have a lower educational level and illiteracy rate than blacks.

T F 2. Mexican Nationals and Mexican-Americans feel that they have many problems in common.

T F   3. Many Mexican-Americans *long* to return to the "Old Country".

T F   4. There was a good deal of intimate fraternization between the Spanish and the natives of the lands they conquered in North America.

T F   5. The speaking of Spanish is often banned in our public schools.

T F   6. When counseling Mexican-Americans, it is best to spend a fairly large amount of time exploring each individual's personal history.

T F   7. Group counseling is effective with Mexican-Americans.

T F   8. One of the most important aspects of counseling Mexican-Americans is helping them learn new values.

T F   9. Standardized tests are useful when counseling Mexican-American for individual guidance, but not for comparisons with members of other ethnic groups.

Scoring Guide for Post Test

1. T	4. T	7. T
2. F	5. T	8. F
3. F	6. F	9. T

Bibliography

Carter, T.P. *Mexican-Americans in schools: A history of educational neglect.* New York: College Entrance Examination Board, 1970.

Encyclopedia Americana. Danbury, Connecticut: Americana Corporation, 1978.

Encyclopedia Britannica. Chicago: Hellen Hemingway Benton, 1974.

Hernandez, N.G. Variables affecting achievement of middle school Mexican-American students. *Review of Educational Research*, 1973, *43*, 1-39.

Longstreet, S. *All star cast: An anecdotal history of Los Angeles*. New York: Thomas Y. Crowell Company, 1977. pp 15-18.

Prescott, W.H. *The conquest of Mexico*. Garden City, New York: International Collectors Library American Headquarters, 1934.

12

An Epilogue

Preparation For

Helping Professionals

Working With

Special Populations

Larry C. Loesch, Ph.D.
Associate Professor
Department of Counselor Education
University of Florida
Gainesville, Florida

Larry C. Loesch, Ph.D.

Larry C. Loesch, Ph.D., is currently an Associate Professor and Graduate Coordinator in the Department of Counselor Education at the University of Florida, Gainesville, Florida. He received both his undergraduate and graduate degrees from Kent State University. He has been at the University of Florida since completion of his doctoral program in June of 1973. Dr. Loesch has had over forty articles published in professional journals, including more than a dozen specifically relating to the professional preparation of counselors. He also has made several presentations on this topic at meetings of professional organizations. Dr. Loesch also is actively involved in several counseling, educational, and psychological organizations. He is the current editor of **Measurement and Evaluation in Guidance**. *He and his wife, Barbara, have four daughters.*

AN EPILOGUE: PREPARATION FOR HELPING PROFESSIONALS WORKING WITH SPECIAL POPULATIONS

Larry C. Loesch

The purpose of this chapter is to discuss some of the basic facets of the professional preparation of persons who intend to assist persons from special populations. However, before this purpose can be addressed, its paradoxical nature must be considered. Special populations are *by definition* unique: they differ significantly in one or more regards from "typical" client groups. It follows that in order for helping activities to be effective with persons from special populations, those activities also must be unique. Therefore, to speak of the "basic facets," or commonalities, in the professional preparation for such helping activities is to raise an inherent contradiction. Fortunately, however, this situation is not without resolution.

If a certain perspective is maintained, it is in fact possible to discuss commonalities. This perspective holds that the *implementation* of a preparation method is unique with regard to special populations rather than the method itself. In other words, it is not unique training methods that are needed but rather unique applications of existing training methods. Thus, many of the preparation methods for assisting "typical" populations also are effective for training in helping special populations *if* the methods can be adapted successfully. The emphasis in training is therefore shifted from a focus on the nature of the activity to a focus on the method of implementation. Relatedly, the preparation method selection process may be shifted from evaluation of the relative merits among various methods to evaluation of the ease with which any chosen method may be implemented with regard to a given special population.

Distinctions within this perspective are subtle, yet they are essential if preparation for helping special populations is to be truly effective. The major benefit of these distinctions is that they allow for the use of proven techniques; ones with a high probability for success. This situation, however, should not be construed to mean that there are not, nor is there a need for, innovative preparation methods. On the contrary, innovative methods are an excellent complement to the implementation of established methods. The point is that, as with the preparation for helping *any* client group, a solid foundation must be built before the garnishments may be added (Dash, 1975).

Preparation methods offered in this chapter fall in the proven or established category because space does not permit allusion to all possible methods. In reading the following discussion it may be helpful to keep a particular special population in mind in order to consider the question, "How do the points or suggestions made apply to that special population?" Hopefully, this consideration will provide a more practical frame of reference.

Potential Counseling Functions

The professional preparation of helping professionals who intend to counsel, or otherwise work with, persons from special populations must necessarily take into account potential professional functions (McDavis & Parker, 1977). In other words, for what are these helping professionals being prepared?

A multitude of specific answers could be provided, but practical constraints again only allow for discussion of several major functions.

For current purposes, a convenient categorization of functions is that provided by the Association for Counselor Education and Supervision in their *Standards for the Preparation of Counselors and Other Personnel Services Specialists* (ACES, 1973). These standards identify six major counselor functions: individual and group counseling, vocational counseling, assessment, consultation, and research. In order to be as comprehensive as possible, two additional functions also will be considered: special types of counseling (e.g. marriage, family, life style, leisure, and so forth) and teaching.

1. **Individual Counseling**. Conceptualizations of "counseling" typically bring to mind the individual counseling process (Burke, 1978). The one-to-one interaction inherent in this process seems particularly pertinent to working with persons from special populations.

The helping professional's functioning in individual counseling is typically dictated by a preferred orientation, or degree of "directiveness", or both. Therein lies the crux of the issues of individual counseling with persons from special populations. That is, the question is not whether individual counseling is an appropriate function with persons from special populations, but which approach is potentially the most effective. Selection of the "right" counseling approach is a tenuous proposition at best; no proven guidelines are readily available.

2. **Group Counseling**. Like individual counseling, group counseling has been viewed as a typical or common helping professional function. It has the advantages of maximizing the helping professional's use of time and providing clients with simultaneous multiple interactions and perspectives. It has the disadvantages of reducing the amount of individual "client-counselor" interaction and a somewhat reduced degree of confidentiality. Theoretically, any concern which might be covered in individual counseling also might be covered within the group counseling context.

The helping professional's functioning in the group context also is dictated by preferences for various possible orientations and thus preferences are an issue here, too. In addition, the group context brings into consideration the natures of the interactions among the group members. Persons from some special populations are much more willing to interact under such circumstances than are other groups. Accordingly, the social interaction characteristics of a special population may be an important issue in the group counseling process (Kaneshige, 1973).

3. **Vocational Counseling**. The process of vocational counseling, as a distinct function within the helping professions, has enjoyed an immense growth in importance and popularity during the last decade or so. (Hohenshil, 1979)

The key issues in vocational counseling with persons from special populations center on the unique characteristics of those persons (Lewis, 1969; Locke, 1969). To what extent do these unique characteristics effect the nature of the vocational counseling offered? How do they effect the vocational development of these persons? What about their interactions with vocational opportunities? Questions such as these will be faced by any helping professional working with persons from special populations.

4. **Assessment**. More than any other function, assessment has been, and remains, at the center of controversy within the helping professions (Samuda, 1975). Assessment procedures range from unobtrusive measures to performance or behavioral criteria. Yet, regardless of the procedures employed, the end result is that some *evaluation* is made.

Bias is the term applied when the comparison process is deemed "unfair." Bias in assessment with persons from special populations has been chronic because these persons by definition are unique. Yet this does not necessarily mean that assessments should not be made with such persons. Rather, it suggests that assessments (and subsequent evaluations) should be made carefully.

288

5. **Consultation**. The function of the helping professional as a consultant is a relatively new and emerging one. Perhaps more than any other function, consultation activities allow helping professionals to impact very large numbers of persons (Dinkmeyer & Carlson, 1977). Thus through consultation activities a helping professional might aid a large portion of a special population much more effectively than through other, smaller scale activities.

The major concerns in the consultation function relate to the fact that the helping professional is "one step removed" from the people to be effected by the consultation activity (Moracco, 1977). The consultant helps one or more persons help still other persons in the special population. This distance between source and impact raises significant questions about which (consultation) tactics have the greatest potential for success. The unique characteristics of the special population, as well as those of the intermediary, further compound the situation.

6. **Research**. The research function in the helping professions is another one which has been a source of controversy, though certainly not to the extent of assessment. The *need* for research generally is acknowledged and widely espoused (Sweeney, 1979). However, only a minute proportion of helping professionals actually ever engage in research projects. Relatedly, only a small portion of the research is specifically concerned with applications or implications for special populations.

The major issue in research on working with persons from special populations has traditionally been the lack of significant numbers of persons from which to derive data to subsequently derive significant conclusions. That is, relatively large samples of subjects are difficult to obtain because large groups of persons from special populations often are not available in readily accessible geographic areas. More recently some special population groups have resisted participation in research endeavors because of concern about the validities of previous research done with, or applied to, them. These situations necessitate caution and sensitivity from helping professionals engaging in research activities with special population groups.

7. **Special types of counseling.** The rapid growth of the helping professions and the increasing recognition of their positive values in our society have allowed for the development of many new functions. Among the more recent innovations (at least in terms of relatively widespread practice) are such things as marriage and/or family counseling, bereavement counseling, life style counseling, leisure counseling, midlife and pre-retirement counseling, values clarification, stress management, and assertiveness. Yet while services such as these have expanded the helping professions in general, their implementation with persons from special populations has been somewhat slower (Pedersen, Lonner, & Draguns, 1976). It seems reasonable, however, that this latter implementation lag is only a temporary phenomenon.

8. **Teaching.** The teaching function is not one normally associated with the "counseling" connotation of the helping professions. Yet much of what helping professionals do is "teaching" in its most rudimentary form (Rustad, 1975). In concert with the reasoning throughout this chapter, the teaching methods used with persons from special populations must at least be uniquely adapted or implemented.

Evaluating Functions for Use

Eight functions described previously are all potentially useful for working with persons from special populations. The word potential must be emphasized, however, because each of these functions will not necessarily be helpful for all the special population groups. Indeed, some of the preceding chapters have provided specific examples of functions which would have little or no utilitarian value to helping professionals for work with some persons. Further, specific recommendations about specific functions for specific groups would be too numerous and lengthy to be of much practical help. Accordingly, a more fundamental approach is in order.

The appropriateness (and therefore potential for success) of any of these eight functions for a given special population may be easily evaluated by considering three basic questions, in the following order:

1. *Is it feasible to use the function with the person(s) in question?* If the function is "completely out of the question" for the person(s), the evaluation process obviously stops here. However, an affirmative response raises another question.

2. *Is the use of the function necessary?* Feasibility in and of itself is insufficient justification for the application of a function. A definable need must be established. Again, a negative response stops the evaluation process here, while an affirmative response raises another question.

3. *Is the use of the function worth the effort?* A particular function may be feasible, desirable, and necessary, yet its implementation "costs" may far exceed the potential benefits to be derived. To engage in a function under such conditions is to be highly inefficient. A negative response to this question implies either termination of the evaluation or re-evaluation of the answer to the second question. Perhaps an alternative approach is more appropriate. Of course an affirmative response suggests that the function should be implemented.

Effective preparation programs will provide helping professionals with the skills and knowledge necessary to provide sound answers to these questions. This then is a good time to consider the components of an effective preparation program.

Components of a Training Program

Preservice and inservice training programs for helping professionals intending to work with persons from special populations must of course encompass a wide variety of dimensions and experiences. In order to acknowledge the complex interrelations among these dimensions and

291

experiences, a training program may be more appropriately described in terms of its major, basic components. For our purposes, four such components will be addressed: knowledge acquisition, attitude awareness, experiential interaction, and skill development. Obviously these components are related integrally in actual practice but they are separated here for discussion clarity only.

1. **Knowledge Acquisition**. A strong cognitive base is an acknowledged foundation for any aspect of the helping professions (Calia, 1974). Indeed, for this particular type of preparation program, a significant portion of the trainees' time will be spent in attempting to answer the question, "What makes a special population *special*?"

One of the primary things a helping professional needs to know is the cultural and/or sociological characteristics of the special population (McDavis & Parker, 1977). What, if anything, is unique about them in terms of their appearance, dress, or other aspects of self presentation? Where do they live? What are the identifying characteristics, if any, of their lifestyles? What are their common, if any, personality traits? Do they have socioeconomic, political, or religious similarities? In general, the helping professional needs to learn how the special population is similar to, or different from, other groups in regard to identifiable cultural or sociological characteristics.

In a like manner, a helping professional needs to be informed about the normative behaviors, both verbal and nonverbal, within the special populations. Do they have unique speech patterns? Do they have a specific vocabulary? Do they use unique gestures, facial expressions, body movements, and so forth? In essence, the helping professional needs to know what is acceptable behavior within the special population and how such behavior differs from other groups.

A helping professional also must know which behaviors are idiosyncratic within the special population. That is, there may be some behaviors which are sometimes evident within the special population which are not modal within that group but also are not necessarily characteristic of other groups.

292

Knowledge of these and modal behaviors will afford the helping professional insight into "socially acceptable" behavioral interactions within the special population.

If helping professionals are to be able to interact effectively with persons from special populations, the professional also must be familiar with the socio-political functioning within that population. That is, they must know who the leaders are and what types of persons earn the greatest respect. More importantly, they must understand the reasons why those persons are influential.

With regard to direct contact helping functions (e.g., individual counseling), helping professionals must be knowledgeable of preferred modes of interaction (Pedersen, Holwill, & Shapiro, 1978). What helping techniques have been proven to be effective? Which have been ineffective? Which have been as yet untried?

Finally, the helping professional who works with persons from special populations needs a thorough knowledge of professional ethics as well as the "informal" ethics within the population. Do these sets of ethics ever come into conflict? In what ways, or areas, are they similar? This type of knowledge will, to a great extent, enable helping professionals to avoid situations which are both personally and professionally compromising or difficult.

A strong cognitive base is essential, yet it may be described as a "necessary but not sufficient" condition for effective helping. Accordingly, this foundation must be complemented by the second major component in the preparation process.

2. **Attitude Awareness**. Attitude awareness has been deemed especially important for working with persons from special populations (Gump, 1974). This includes personal attitude awareness as well as awareness of the special population person. This emphasis is typically based on the assumption of differences in attitudes between helping professionals and persons

from special populations. If such differences exist, they may interfere with the helping process. Of course this assumption may be invalidated to some extent if the helping professional is a member of the special population.

Given the need for professional preparation in terms of attitude awareness, the question then becomes of which attitudes should the helping professional be aware? For the purposes here, five types of attitudes will be considered within this preparation component.

The first type of attitude of which helping professionals should be aware is attitude about self (Banikiotes, 1975; Fuhrmann, 1978). A helping professional's self (attitude) awareness has been shown to be directly related to helping effectiveness. Those helping professionals who are able to assess and evaluate accurately their own attitudes generally are more effective in helping others (Gump, 1974).

Helping professionals' attitudes about special populations are a second important type. Helping professionals must be aware of their own biases, positive or negative, if they are to be able to work with persons from special populations effectively (Hulnick, 1977). This type of attitude awareness enables the helping professional to be "authentic," a characteristic generally understood to be necessary for competent interaction. Further, it enables professionals to compare their attitudes about the special population with their attitudes about themselves. This comparison then provides a framework from which to approach their helping activities.

A third type of attitude often overlooked, but which may be crucial to the helping process, is the special populations' attitude about helping professionals. Perceptions of the worth and value of the helping process (as typically conceived) vary greatly across special populations. Some groups readily enter into the helping process while others do so only if "forced." Preparation in the awareness of such attitudes is essential, particularly for the initial stages of the helping process.

A fourth type of attitude of which helping professionals should be aware is society's attitude about the special population. Particularly important in this regard are stereotypes. Which characteristics of the special population are typically stereotyped? What validity, if any, is there in the stereotype? How do such stereotypes relate to, or effect, people's behaviors? Which of society's attitudes about the special population are evolving or changing? What characteristics of the special population seem to be the basis of stereotypes? The answers to questions such as these allow the helping professional to have a perspective on the society in which the special population exists. This perspective should in turn enable the helping professional to understand some of the "realities" of people in the special population. Of course such understanding should facilitate the helping process.

The last type of attitude to be considered is the special population's attitude about themselves. What do they perceive as their positive and negative characteristics? What are their self-perceived strengths, weaknesses, assets, and liabilities? What is the nature of their collective self-concepts?

The establishment of a comprehensive cognitive base and the development of valid attitude awareness are absolutely essential for the effective preparation of helping professionals who intend to work with special populations. Yet, while they are essential, their worth will be diminished if they are not grounded in reality for the trainee. Thus they serve as the lead into the third preparation component.

3. **Experiential Interaction**. An effective preparation program will provide helping professionals with a diverse set of experiences with special populations (Woods, 1977). These experiences are important because they allow the helping professionals to validate their own knowledge base and attitude awareness. They also help the helping professional gain an appreciation for the lifestyles of the special population. On a different tact, they also have the subtle benefit of allowing the people from special populations to interact with potential helping professionals. Thus experiential activities play a significant role in the preparation process in that they benefit both the trainees and the helping professions as well.

The most obvious type of experiential activity helping professionals should have as part of a training program is interaction with the special population, under supervision (MacGuffie & Henderson, 1977). Beyond helping profession "laboratory" types of experiences, helping professionals also should be provided with opportunities for less formal interactions. Central among these should be experiences which help the helping professional become familiar with the lifestyles of the special populations. These experiences might include such things as visiting homes, social gathering places, or work locations typical of the special population. Helping professionals should note the environment, social and familial atmospheres, and behaviors of the special population. Observations such as these will enable helping professionals to solidify their conceptualizations of the lifestyles of the special population.

A related set of experiences should allow helping professionals to interact formally and informally with persons from special populations. Formal activities might include such things as participating in vocational activities or formal social meetings with persons from the special population. Informal activities might include such things as casual conversations, participation in leisure activities, or going to informal social events with persons from special populations. The intention of these types of experiences is to allow the helping professional to become aware of, and practice, ways of establishing rapport, in both formal and informal situations, with persons from special populations.

Another set of experiences which helping professionals should have is one which is typically overlooked. These are experiences with other groups of people who have reason to interact with persons from the special population. These experiences should be similar to those described previously, particularly in the areas of formal and informal interactions. These types of experiences will provide helping professionals with two additional "first hand" perspectives. The first concerns how the special population is perceived by members of the other group. The second concerns how persons from the special population are likely to be received by members of the other group. Again, such experiences will enable the helping professional to gain an appreciation and understanding of the life circumstances of the special population.

While experiences such as these generally will add significantly to the preparation of helping professionals, some caution should be noted. It is likely that in any preparation program only a relatively limited number of experiences with any given special population will be possible because of time and/or resource constraints. Accordingly, these experiences should be carefully selected and developed so that maximum benefit may be achieved. Relatedly, helping professionals should be cautioned against "overgeneralizing from very small samples." That is, they must realize that such experiences may have only limited representation value across the special population. Paramount is the need for helping professionals to evaluate realistically the nature of their experiences, or the experiences may do more harm than good.

Strong cognitive and experiential bases and attitude awareness will do much to aid helping professionals in their professional interactions with persons from special populations. Yet knowledge, perspective, and even social interaction skills are not enough. A professional must by definition have specific, identifiable skills. The provision of these skills constitutes the fourth preparation component.

4. **Skill Development**. A major portion of the professional literature in the helping professions has been devoted to the theoretical development, practical application, and subsequent evaluation of a variety of helping skills (Burke, 1978). These processes have led to the identification of a large number of such skills. However, they also have fostered considerable debate as to what constitutes *basic* helping skills. At best, the resolution of these debates seems to be that *the* basic skills are what any particular author believes them to be. The ones to be presented are no exception to this perspective.

In regard to helping persons from special populations, it seems imperative to adopt a perspective similar to the one recommended for helping functions. That is, it is not the skills

297

themselves that are so unique, but rather the ways they are used with particular individuals. Accordingly, each of the following types of skills should be considered in regard to their potential for use with persons from various special populations.

Active listening (or as they are sometimes referred to, facilitative responding) skills have been cited by numerous authors as being at the heart of helping. It would be wrong, however, to assume that active listening, from within the context of a nondirective approach, will be effective with all persons from special populations. Indeed, some research shows that in fact the opposite may be true. For persons from some special populations a highly directive approach may be necessary. Consequently, helping professionals intending to work with persons from special populations also should receive training in some of the directive helping approaches. Of course it follows that these helping professionals also should receive approach discrimination training so that they will be able to use the appropriate approach with any given special population.

Individual and group appraisal (i.e. measurement and evaluation) skills also are among the commonly cited basic helping skills. However, as mentioned previously, considerable debate has occurred as to the validities of appraisals made on persons from special populations. This debate suggests that helping professionals should receive two related but distinct types of preparation in appraisal. The first type is preparation for the more common methods of appraisal, typically referred to as "standardized" testing. This training is important because helping professionals will (a) sometimes use standardized testing procedures since such procedures will in fact be the most appropriate, and (b) need to know whether standardized testing procedures are the most appropriate or if some other procedures should be used. The second type of preparation is for the less common methods of appraisal. These methods would include such types as unobtrusive measures, behavioral observations, self reports, structured interviews, and so forth. For many special populations this latter type of appraisal may be the only possibility. However, failure to provide effective training in both types would seriously limit the helping professional's eventual professional effectiveness.

A third basic skill in which helping professionals should be trained is "vocabulary adjustment." Special populations, like any other societal group, have elements of speech which have interpretable meaning only in the context of the special population group. Helping professionals intending to work with persons from special populations must be aware of these dialectal patterns and subtleties if they are to interact with such persons effectively. This is not to suggest, however, that helping professionals must learn to use a "new" language. Rather, it means that they should gain an understanding and appreciation for differences in communication patterns and modes among people with different life circumstances. This "vocabulary adjustment" skill is one of the most important ones helping professionals must learn if they are to achieve acceptance with persons from special populations.

Nonverbal behavior interpretation is another skill which is essential to effective human interaction and communication (Seals & Prichard, 1973). As with verbal patterns and modes, nonverbal communication behaviors and their associated interpretations often differ dramatically across societal subgroups. Again, helping professionals must gain an understanding and appreciation of the differences in nonverbal behavior interpretations if they are eventually to be effective in helping persons from special populations.

The last of the so-called basic skills to be considered is confrontation. The process of confrontation within the helping process is indeed a difficult one for several reasons. First, it at least temporarily puts the helping professional and the person being helped in an adversary position. Second, it often raises feelings of defensiveness and withdrawal in the person being helped. Third, some helping professionals interpret confrontation as license to be aggressive and punitive. And fourth, because of these other reasons, confrontation is a common reason for premature termination of a helping relationship. Thus the use of confrontation is potentially "dangerous" in, or to, any helping relationship. This potential is increased when persons from special populations are involved because of the greater possibility for communication misinterpretation. However, confrontation is often the most powerful method of bringing about "psychological movement" within a helping relationship. Accordingly, helping professionals should have careful and thorough training in this powerful technique.

Effective training in these basic skills should allow helping professionals to be at least minimally competent in their helping efforts with persons from special populations. One should remember, however, that these are only *basic* skills. Other skills, including those specific to particular special populations, also should be included in the preparation process. Unfortunately, space does not permit discussion of these other skills, except save acknowledgment of their importance to a fully and completely trained helping professional.

Preparation Implementation

The professional preparation of a helping professional intending to work with persons from special populations must be a lifelong and extensive process if it is to be effective. Yet the process does not have to be a difficult one if careful attention is given to planning and implementation.

The first stage of the preparation process should provide a broad base of cognitive knowledge about special populations. Obviously a careful reading of this book is a first step toward establishing such a base. The following are some related activities which might be used to supplement this reading and lead toward the same goal.

1. Reread any two chapters of this book and develop a list of similarities and differences between the two special populations described.

2. Select any chapter (i.e., special population) and create an *annotated* bibliography of at least seven references provided for that chapter.

3. Select any particular point made by an author and write a paper, complete with references, "arguing" the opposite point of view. (For example, you might "argue" that intelligence tests are not unfair to

Mexican-American children because these children must exist and function within the "majority" society.)

4. Select any chapter of interest and then create five multiple-choice, factual questions not covered in either the pre- or post tests.

5. Identify ten sources of information (e.g., books, journal articles, and so forth) about a particular special population which are not cited in this book.

6. Assume that you have the opportunity to interview some persons from a special population of interest to you. Develop a set of at least ten questions which will enable you to obtain *factual* information from the persons you will interview.

7. Assume that you have been asked to describe a given special population to a class of fifth graders. Prepare a ten minute presentation you could use to fulfill this request.

8. Select any chapter of this book and attempt to recreate the outline the author(s) used to write it. Then identify other pertinent topics which might have been covered.

9. Identify a particular special population. Then write a paper, complete with references, defending the use of a particular helping orientation with persons from that special population.

10. Examine the reference lists from any two chapters of this book. Then identify the references from one chapter which might apply (approximately) equally to the other chapter; repeat for the second chapter.

Activities such as these should provide a strong cognitive base which should in turn serve as the foundation for subsequent activities.

The second stage of the preparation process should focus on attitude awareness. Activities such as the following may be helpful in bringing about such awareness.

1. Identify any particular special population. Then create a list of at least ten stereotypes you think people hold about that special population (exclude stereotypes presented in the pertinent chapter of this book).

2. Assume that you have the opportunity to interview some persons from a particular special population and that you would "like to know what they are really like." Create a list of questions that you would ask each person.

3. Assume that you are a "negotiator" between a group of persons from a special population and a group of persons from the "white, middle-class majority." Compose a *treaty* to settle the differences between these two groups.

4. Assume you have the power to enact legislation which would benefit a particular special population. List and explain the laws you would enact.

5. Assign each person in a group to be representative of a different special population. Then conduct a "mock United Nations" activity by having the representatives create a plan for the world wide "enrichment of the human condition."

6. Select any particular special population. Then ask students in the third, seventh, and twelfth grades to describe a person from that special population. Compare and contrast the responses.

7. Select any two special populations. Interview at least five persons from each special population as to their attitudes about the other special population.

8. Select any special population. Interview at least five persons from that special population as to their attitudes about the helping professions. Include a question about how they feel about being interviewed.

9. Create a "self attitude awareness" activity which would be effective for use with a given special population group.

Other activities intended to enhance attitude awareness may be found in the references of some of the chapters in this book.

Experiential activities constitute the next step in the helping professional preparation process. The following activities exemplify some possible experiential activities which are well-suited for training purposes.

1. Visit, individually or with others, a restaurant which caters primarily to persons from a particular special population.

2. Attend a religious ceremony (e.g., church service) which is intended primarily for members of a particular special population.

3. Interview an identified political leader of a particular special population. Incorporate questions about current issues and problems as well as future political actions for the special population.

4. Observe a group of children from a particular special population while at play. Note consistent behavioral patterns and interaction styles.

5. Interview at least five persons from each of three different special populations as to their favorite leisure activities. Compare and contrast their responses.

6. Interview a helping professional from a particular special population. Inquire as to the professional problems and issues that person most frequently encounters in professional activities.

The final stage in the preparation process is supervised practice in helping relationships with persons from special populations. The following activities might serve as initial activities in this regard.

1. Have one person role play the part of a helping professional and another the part of a person from a special population. Have a third person serve as an observer. Role play a helping session for approximately five minutes. Then stop and "critique" the activity. Change roles in the triad and repeat two more times.

2. Have one person role play the part of a helping professional and several other persons role play the parts of people from a given special population. Simulate a "group" helping session for approximately 20 minutes. Then "critique" the simulation. Change roles (i.e., of the helping professional) and repeat as time allows.

3. Critique, individually or with others, an audio or video tape of a session between a helping professional and a person from a particular special population.

4. Solicit volunteers from various special populations. Role play the part of a helping professional working with the person.

These culminating activities should allow helping professionals to "put into practice" all that they have learned from their previous learning experiences.

Successful completion of each of these preparation stages should result in a helping professional with adequate competencies to undertake unsupervised professional interactions. For many professionals this preservice or inservice training unfortunately terminates the preparation process. However, it shouldn't. Truly competent professionals continue the preparation process across their professional lifespans through additional training.

The additional training of helping professionals should be a continuation of all aspects of the preservice preparation program (George, 1974). Unfortunately, however, such training typically focuses only on the development of "new" skills at best, and on "relearning" of old skills at least. Certainly to expand continually a helping professional's repertoire of skills is a noble effort. But to develop these skills on a foundation of knowledge which is continually becoming outdated is to diminish greatly their potential utilitarian values. Thus additional training should provide for extension and improvement in all the preparation areas: cognitive knowledge, attitude awareness, experiential interaction, and skill development. To do less is to foster imbalanced professional growth.

Conclusion

The professional preparation of helping professionals intending to work with persons from special populations presents both unique problems and unique opportunities. It necessitates that helping professionals be prepared to work with persons from any population as well as those from special populations; a task which is by no means a simple one. On the other hand, there is something very special about being able to work with people who have needs, concerns, and problems that are different from those of the majority of society. In this light there is also something very special about preparing helping professionals with the necessary unique skills. Taken collectively, the merits of the rewards far outweigh the disadvantages of the effort involved.

Reference List

Association for Counselor Education and Supervision. *Standards for the preparation of counselors and other personnel services specialists.* Adopted October 1973. Retitled Spring 1979 as *Standards for entry preparation (Master's and specialists) of counselors and other personnel services specialsts.* Washington, D.C.

Banikiotes, P.G. Personal growth and professional training. *Counselor Education and Supervision*, 1975, *15*(2), 149-151.

Burke, J.B. A comment on skill training: Cautions and recommendations. *Counselor Education and Supervision*, 1978, *17*(3), 230-232.

Calia, V.F. Systematic human relations training: Appraisal and status. *Counselor Education and Supervision*, 1974, *14*(2), 85-94.

Dash, E.G. Counselor competency and the revised ACES standards. *Counselor Education and Supervision*, 1975, *14*(3), 221-227.

Dinkmeyer, D., & Carlson, J. Consulting: Training counselors to work with teachers, parents, and administrators. *Counselor Education and Supervision*, 1977, *16*(3), 172-177.

Fuhrmann, B.S. Self evaluation: An approach for training counselors. *Counselor Education and Supervision*, 1978, *17*(4), 315-317.

George, R.L. Inservice training for counselors: Teaching old dogs new tricks. *Counselor Education and Supervision*, 1974, *13*(4), 315-315.

Gump, L.R. Counselor self-awareness and counseling effectiveness. *Counselor Education and Supervision*, 1974, *13*(4), 263-266.

Hohenshil, T.H. Renewal in career guidance and counseling: Rationale and programs. *Counselor Education and Supervision*, 1979, *18*(3), 199-208.

Hulnick, H.R. Counselor: Know thyself. *Counselor Education and Supervision*, 1977, *17*(1), 69-72.

Kaneshige, E. Cultural factors in group counseling and interaction. *Personnel and Guidance Journal*, 1973, *51*, 407-412.

Lewis, S.O. (I) Racism encountered in counseling. *Counselor Education and Supervision*, 1969, *9*(1), 49-53.

Locke, D.W. (II) Racism encountered in counseling. *Counselor Education and Supervision*, 1969, *9*(1), 56-58.

MacGuffie, R.A., & Henderson, H. A practicum-internship model for counselor training. *Counselor Education and Supervision*, 1977, *16*(3), 233-236.

McDavis, R.J., & Parker, W. A course on counseling ethnic minorities: A model. *Counselor Education and Supervision*, 1977, *17*(2), 146-149.

Moracco, J.C. Counselor as consultant: Some implications for counselor education. *Counselor Education and Supervision*, 1977, *17*(1), 73-75.

Pedersen, P., Holwill, C.F., & Shapiro, J. A cross-cultural procedure for classes in counselor education. *Counselor Education and Supervision*, 1978, *17*(3), 233-236.

Pedersen, P., Lonner, W., & Draguns, J. (Eds.), *Counseling across cultures.* Honolulu: University of Hawaii, 1976.

Rustad, K. Promoting psychological growth in a high school classroom. *Counselor Education and Supervision*, 1975, *14*(4), 277-285.

Samuda, R.J. *Psychological testing of American minorities.* New York: Dodd, Mead & Company, 1975.

Seals, J.M., & Prichard, C.H. Nonverbal behavior as a dimension of counselor subroles. *Counselor Education and Supervision*, 1973, *13*(2), 150-153.

Sweeney, T.J., Trends that will influence counselor preparation in the 1980's. *Counselor Education and Supervision*, 1979, *18*(3), 181-189.

Woods, E. Counseling minority students: A program model. *Personnel and Guidance Journal*, 1977, *55*, 416-418.

INDEX

INDEX

McFadden, M 20, 38
McKinney, H 189, 194
McNeill, J 102
McPartland, J 185, 194
Meredith, C 185, 184
Meredith, G 185, 194
Marital counseling
  older persons 223
Mexican-Americans 253-281
  awareness index 255-256
  case examples 268-272
  counselor guidelines 277-279
  heritage 272-274
  history 256-259
  integration 273-274
  intelligence 265-266
  language barrier 260-261
  migrant status 261-262
  post test 280
  self-concept 266-268
  social attitudes 274-275
Michener, J 149
Migrant status
  Mexican-Americans 261-262
Miller, B 102
Miller, J 27, 38
Minorities 259-260
Modern Language Association
  93
Mood, A 185, 194
Mombello, R 93, 99, 102
Montero, D 194
Moracco, J 306
Moriarity, A 26, 38
Morin, S 85, 95, 96, 102, 103
Moser, A 75
Murphey, M 218-219, 227
Murphy, L 26, 38
Myers, I 69, 75
Myers, J 210, 227
Myths
  homosexuality 86-87

N

NGTF
  see National Gay Task Force
  97
Nagera, H 27, 38
National Committee for Amish
  Religious Freedom 50
National Council of Teachers of
  English 93
National Gay Task Force 93, 94,
  97, 102
National Institute for Mental
  Health 98, 102
National Plan of Action 134
New York City Gay Teachers
  Association 93
Normalization
  Among the disabled 239-242
Norton, J 63, 77, 78, 79, 94
Nursing home patients
  counseling 223
Nursing homes
  older persons 218

O

Oberstone, A 88, 102
Ochberg, F 183, 194
Ogawa, D 182, 194
Older Americans Act 213
Older persons 197-227
  ability to learn 207
  awareness index 199
  case examples 200-201
  counseling 209-213, 218-224
  counseling, bereavement 224
  counseling leisure activities
  223
  counseling needs 209-213
  counseling services 216-218
  counseling terminally ill 223

R

Racial segregation 157
Rational emotive counseling
170-171
Ravitch, D 8, 10, 12
Reality counseling 168-169
Religion
culturally different 41-75
Research
helping professions 289
Residential repair
older persons 217
Resistance
Indians, to change 117
Richards, A 31, 38
Riddle, D 85, 88, 102, 103
Riker, H 197, 198, 199
Robins, P 85
Rogers, R 167
Role models
careers, blacks 160
Rook, K 102
Roy, R 88, 102
Rubin, Z 102
Rustad, K 290, 306

S

Saghir, M 85, 103
Samuda, R 288, 306
Sawrey, J 26, 38
Scanzoni, J 38
Scanzoni, L 38
Schaie, K 227
Schlesinger, B 20, 39
Schools
Amish 64
disabled children 242
gays 86
lesbians 86
segregation 157
Schwartz, P 82, 101
Seals, J 306
Seaver, J 127
Segregation
racial 157

schools 157
Self-concept
Mexican-Americans 266-268
Self-reliance
Asian-Americans 186
Seneca Indians 109-113
Senility
older persons 207
Senior centers 216-217
Sensitivity
Asian-Americans 178-180
Serenity
older persons 208
Sex
same sex preference 77-103
Sex preference 77-103
case example 80-82
Sexual activity
older persons 208
Shapiro, J 306
Shertzer, B 169-170
Silverman, P 34, 39
Silverstein, C 91, 99, 103
Single parents
awareness index 15-16
case example 16-17
change of status 23-24
counseling 32-33
definition 17-18
loneliness 25-26
personal issues 20
personal needs 23-26
population 18-19
post test 36-37
problems in society 19-20
services 32-35
sexuality 24-25
social agencies 33
standard of living 21-22
therapy, psychosocial 32-33
Skill development counseling
297
Sloan, I 157, 173
Smart, L 39
Smart, M 39
Smith, E 68, 75
Smith, K 88, 102

Smyth, A 127
Social attitudes
  Mexican-Americans 274-275
Social workers 93
Society
  understanding homosexuality
    94-95
Sollenberger, R 187, 194
Special groups
  mainstreaming 7
Special populations 4-12
  counseling functions 286
  professional preparation 285-
    306
STAR
  see Street Transvestites
    Action Revolutionaries
Statistics
  women 135
Stereotyping
  homosexuality 87
Stone, S 166, 169-170
Street Transvestites Action
  Revolutionaries 96
Stress, personal
  Asian-Americans 185
Strickland, B 166, 174
Stuart, I 20, 27, 39
Stuffle, C 75
Sturgis, T 90, 101
Sudia, C 29, 38
Sue, D 175, 177, 176, 184, 185,
  187, 189, 191, 194, 195
Sue, DM 185, 187, 191, 195
Sue, DW 178, 184, 187, 189, 191,
  195
Sue, S 185, 187, 191, 194, 195
Sukoneck, H 88, 102
Support systems
  older persons 225
Sweeney, T 289, 306
Szasg, T 249, 251

T

Teaching
  helping professions 290

Telford, C 26, 38
Teng, L 195
Terminally ill
  counseling older persons 223
Tessman, L 20, 27, 31, 39
Testing
  Asian-Americans 184-185
  limitations, Amish 70-71
Therapy
  psychosocial, single parents
    32-33
Thorstad, D 96, 102
Title IX
  Educational Amendments Act
    144
Tourism
  Amish 65
Training
  peer counselors 224
Training programs
  counseling 291-301
Transexuals 77-103
Tribes
  differences, Indians 115
Tripp, C 85, 98, 103
Tsai, M 195

U

Understanding
  subgroups 6
Unproductiveness
  older persons 205-206
Users of book 10-12

V

Vacc, N 3, 229-233
Values
  Amish 51
  Asian-Americans 186, 189
Vida, G 98, 103
Volunteer work
  older persons 217

317

W

Wallerstein, J 27, 38, 39
Washington, B 157
Watanabe, C 185, 189, 195
Wealth
   personal vs tribal 118
Weinberg, G 95, 103
Weinfeld, F 185, 194
West, D 82, 103
Willis, I 31, 38
Wilson, E 34, 39
Wilson, E 39
Wittmer, J 4, 41, 43, 75
Wolfe, H 129, 130
Women
   awareness index 131-132
   battered 132
   case examples 132-133
   career needs 138
   child care needs 137
   counseling 129-149
   counselor's role 145-148
   definitions 133-135
   history of counseling 143-144
   needs 138

planning 140
post test 148-149
problems 135-138
statistics 135
status 134
Wong, K 182, 195
Woods, E 295, 306

Y

Yamamota, K 68, 75
Yee, A 195
Yee, M 184, 195
York, R 194
Young, A 87, 102
Young, D 88, 102

Z

Zunin, L 168, 173
Zettel, J 242, 243, 251